The Psychologist's Companion, 4th edition

The Psychologist's Companion, 4th edition, is intended to be a definitive guide to scientific writing for students and researchers. It covers a wealth of topics, including misconceptions about psychology papers, steps in writing library research papers, steps in writing experimental research papers, rules for writing psychology papers, commonly misused words, Internet resources, American Psychological Association guidelines for writing psychology papers, guidelines for data presentation, references for psychology papers, standards for evaluating psychology papers, guidelines for submitting papers to journals, how to win acceptances of papers by psychology journals, how to write grant and contract proposals, how to find book publishers, and how to write lectures and articles. The book contains a sample psychology paper as well as an appendix relevant to writing for British and European journals. The book is written in a lively and witty style that will make it easy reading for even the busiest student or professional.

Robert J. Sternberg is IBM Professor of Psychology and Education and Director of the Center for the Psychology of Abilities, Competencies, and Expertise at Yale University. He is also 2003 President of the American Psychological Association and Editor of the *APA Review of Books: Contemporary Psychology.* Professor Sternberg is the author of roughly 950 books, book chapters, and articles in the field of psychology.

The Psychologist's Companion

A Guide to Scientific Writing
for Students and Researchers

FOURTH EDITION

Robert J. Sternberg

Yale University

Chapter 5 was contributed by
Richard C. Sherman and Beth Dietz-Uhler
Miami University

Chapter 8 and Appendix B were contributed by
Chris Leach
University of Newcastle upon Tyne

CAMBRIDGE
UNIVERSITY PRESS

CAMBRIDGE UNIVERSITY PRESS
Cambridge, New York, Melbourne, Madrid, Cape Town, Singapore, São Paulo

Cambridge University Press
40 West 20th Street, New York, NY 10011–4211, USA

Published in the United States of America by Cambridge University Press, New York

www.cambridge.org
Information on this title: www.cambridge.org/9780521460736

First edition published 1977 by Barron's Educational Series, Inc., as
Writing the Psychology Paper
Second edition published 1988
Third edition published 1993
Fourth edition first published 2003

Printed in the United States of America

A catalog record for this book is avialable from the British Library.

Library of Congress Cataloging-in-Publication Data
Sternberg, Robert J.
　The psychologist's companion : a guide to scientific writing for students and
　researchers / Robert J. Sternberg ; chapter 5 was contributed by Richard C.
　Sherman and Beth Dietz-Uhler ; chapter 8 and appendix B were contributed
　by Chris Leach. – 4th ed.
　　p.　cm.
　Includes bibliographical references and index.
　ISBN 0-521-82123-1. – ISBN 0-521-52806-2 (pbk.)
　1. Report writing.　2. Psychological literature.　I. Dietz-Uhler, Beth.　II. Leach,
　Chris.　III. Title.
　BF76.8.S73　2003
　808′.06615–dc21　　　2003043595

ISBN-13 978-0-521-82123-0 hardback
ISBN-10 0-521-82123-1 hardback

ISBN-13 978-0-521-52806-1 paperback
ISBN-10 0-521-52806-2 paperback

Contents

Acknowledgments   *page* vii

Introduction   1

1 Eight Common Misconceptions about
   Psychology Papers   6

2 Steps in Writing the Library Research Paper   19

3 Steps in Writing the Experimental Research Paper   35

4 Rules for Writing the Psychology Paper   65

5 Using the Internet to Aid the Research Process   77

6 Commonly Misused Words   98

7 American Psychological Association Guidelines
   for Psychology Papers   119

8 Guidelines for Data Presentation   142

9 References for the Psychology Paper   165

10 Standards for Evaluating the Psychology Paper   198

11 Submitting a Paper to a Journal   216

12 How to Win Acceptances from Psychology
    Journals: Twenty-Nine Tips for Better Writing   221

13 Writing a Grant or Contract Proposal   232

14 How to Find a Book Publisher   244

15 Writing a Lecture   255
16 Article Writing 101   259

References   267
Appendix A: Sample Psychology Paper   271
Appendix B: Writing for British and European Journals   285
Index   287

Acknowledgments

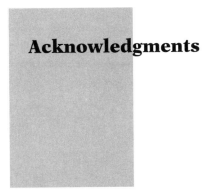

The American Psychological Association graciously permitted me to summarize the *APA Publication Manual,* Fifth Edition, in Chapter 7. I am grateful to Alex Isgut for his help in preparing this manuscript.

Introduction

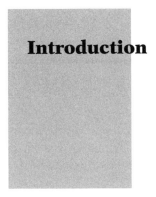

Most students of psychology receive little or no formal training in how to write psychology papers. Nor do they learn how to write grant and contract proposals, book proposals, or talks and lectures. Many people believe that students receive sufficient training in writing through informal channels and thus will acquire the necessary skills on their own. The conventional psychology curriculum provides evidence that this belief is widespread. Whereas almost all psychology departments offer courses in how to design experiments and analyze experimental results, or in how to write proposals or lectures, very few departments offer courses in how to report experiments. Although some departments may include these topics as parts of other courses, even this modest amount of training appears to be rare.

Do students learn the writing techniques for psychology on their own? My experience reading psychology papers suggests that they do not. Moreover, this experience is shared by other psychology professors, and by professors in other disciplines as well. Indeed, many professors themselves have never learned to write as well as they would have liked.

The purpose of this book is to provide the basic information that students and professionals alike need to write in psychology. This information is contained in 16 chapters. Although the intent is that you read the chapters in the order in which they are presented, they are for the most part self-contained and hence can be read in almost any sequence.

Chapter 1 presents and discusses eight common misconceptions that students hold about psychology papers. I have found that many of these misconceptions are reinforced rather than extinguished by conventional academic training. Most students come to believe, for example, that journal articles are and should be autobiographical – that the logical development of ideas in a psychology paper reflects their historical development in the psychologist's head. Accepting this notion as a presupposition, the students often believe that authors of journal articles can plan their research and predict their findings well in advance, often down to the last detail. Readers will know better after finishing Chapter 1.

Chapters 2 and 3 present the sequence of steps that psychologists follow in writing papers. Chapter 2 deals with library research papers, Chapter 3 with experimental research papers. The sequence of steps begins with the search for ideas and ends with the publication of a finished paper. Many students have only a fuzzy idea of the sequence of steps and of how this sequence is presented to the reader of a psychology paper. Consider two examples. First, would the procedure by which subjects are assigned to treatment groups be described more appropriately in the *Procedure* section or in the *Design* section of a psychology paper? Second, do journal editors encourage or discourage extensive use of tables and figures in articles to clarify the presentation of experimental data? The answer to the first question is "Design"; the answer to the second question is "discourage."

Chapter 4 presents rules for writing psychology papers. The rules are ones that many students and even professionals fail to follow. One of the reasons they fail to follow these rules is that they forget what the rules are. The chances are good that you remember learning something about avoiding "dangling constructions," but that either you don't look for dangling constructions in your writing or you don't even remember exactly what a dangling construction is. Chapter 4 will remind you about dangling constructions and other pitfalls in writing papers.

Students and professionals alike are increasingly using the Internet to do their research. Chapter 5 discusses how to use the Internet effectively. It also discusses how to be critical of information obtained over the Internet, so that one does not simply accept whatever a given site may say.

Chapter 6 contains a list of commonly misused words and describes the proper use of each of these words. The meanings of these words, like the rules of writing, are quickly learned but quickly forgotten early in one's career as a student. For example, probably fewer than 10% of the papers (that, which) are published in psychological journals consistently use the relative pronouns *that* and *which* correctly. (While, Although) these papers are certainly publishable, their readability would be enhanced by the proper use of English. Which word belongs in each place where two choices are given within parentheses? In the first sentence, the proper word is *that;* in the second sentence, the proper word is *Although.*

Chapter 7 summarizes the American Psychological Association guidelines for writing psychology papers. Regardless of how well you write, you must learn a number of different rules that are specific to the writing of psychology papers. Different disciplines follow different guidelines for writing, and one is expected to learn to write according to the guidelines of the appropriate discipline. A common mistake occurs when students follow Modern Language Association (MLA) guidelines, which are the ones most students learn in high school. Although these guidelines are appropriate for writing in the humanities, they are not appropriate for writing in psychology. Test yourself. Does one abbreviate "centimeters" as *cm* or as *cm.?* Does one abbreviate "feet" as *ft* or as *ft.?* Does one test *10* subjects or *ten* subjects? Does one test *8* subjects or *eight* subjects? The rules of the American Psychological Association lead to answers of *cm, ft, 10,* and *eight.* The rules of the Modern Language Association lead to answers of *cm., ft., ten,* and *eight.* Learning to write a psychology paper involves learning certain rules that are unique to writing psychology papers.

Chapter 8 provides guidelines for data presentation. It gives rules for presenting data in the form of tables or graphs as well as guidance on the advantages and drawbacks of different types of presentations. Following these guidelines will aid both your understanding of your data and your ability to communicate them effectively to others.

Chapter 9, fully updated for this edition of *The Psychologist's Companion,* contains a list and description of many of the references that psychologists use when writing psychology papers. The list includes both general references and journals. Familiarity with these references can save enormous amounts of time. Suppose, for example, that you are writing a paper in which your main thesis is that the work of Julius

Schnitzelbonk has been undervalued in the psychological literature. To what source could you turn for a virtually complete listing of citations to the work of Schnitzelbonk – or that of anyone else, for that matter? The answer is the *Social Science Citation Index*. This work and other valuable references are described in Chapter 9.

Chapter 10 deals with the criteria psychologists use to evaluate a particular paper's contribution to knowledge. What characteristics distinguish truly exceptional psychology papers from good ones, and good ones from poor ones? Why do some papers continue to have an impact upon the field long after other papers have been forgotten? Chapter 10 answers these questions.

Chapter 11 contains practical suggestions for submitting a psychology paper to a professional journal. What considerations enter into the choice of a journal? What happens to a paper once it is submitted? What are the possible courses of action a journal editor can take? You will find out when you read Chapter 11.

Chapter 12 describes techniques you can use in order to enhance your chances of acceptance by a journal. Many writers of articles have only foggy notions of what editors expect. As the editor of a psychology journal, I have been impressed by the number of rejected papers that might have been saved had the authors known what editors' expectations are. This chapter describes these expectations, and more.

Chapters 13 through 15 are oriented more toward professional users of this book than toward student users. Chapter 13 contains techniques people can use in order to increase the chances of their getting funding through a grant or contract. Ultimately, the most important determinant of funding is the set of ideas in the proposal. But many proposals are rejected on grounds that have little or nothing to do with ideas. Competition for grants and contracts is extremely stiff. Therefore, every edge can help. This chapter helps grant writers maximize their chances of winning funding, giving them the edge that may make a difference to the outcome.

Chapter 14 describes the steps a person takes in seeking a book publisher. How do you write a book proposal, and what do you do with the proposal once you are done? Despite the importance for scholars of writing books as well as articles, people tend to know even less about how to find a publisher for a book than they do about how to get an article published. This chapter describes from beginning to end the process of finding a book publisher.

Chapter 15 discusses the writing of effective lectures. Many psychologists end up, sooner or later, teaching. For some, it may be in the form of courses for undergraduate and graduate students. For others, it may be in the form of public lectures. And for still others, it may be in the form of occasional seminars. All of us who have gone through school know how important good lectures are to learning. This chapter will help the reader write and deliver such lectures.

Chapter 16 is a primer on effective writing of articles for psychological journals. It contains tips both on what you should do and what you should *not* do.

Appendix A contains a sample paper typed according to APA guidelines. The paper is presented as it was typed, rather than as it would appear in a journal. The paper illustrates many of the principles described in Chapter 7. Appendix B contains guidelines for writing for British and European journals.

As you learn more and more about psychology, you will discover that writing for an audience of psychologists requires a unique set of skills. For most students and psychologists alike, merely reading and writing psychology papers is an insufficient way of acquiring these skills. This book is intended for and dedicated to all of you who want to improve your writing.

Chapter One

Eight Common Misconceptions about Psychology Papers

Misconception 1. *Writing the psychology paper is the most routine, least creative aspect of the scientific enterprise, requiring much time but little imagination.*

Many students lose interest in their research projects as soon as the time comes to write about them. Their interest is in planning for and making new discoveries, not in communicating their discoveries to others. A widely believed fallacy underlies their attitudes. The fallacy is that the discovery process ends when the communication process begins. Although the major purpose of writing a paper is to communicate your thoughts to others, another important purpose is to help you form and organize your thoughts.

Reporting your findings in writing requires you to commit yourself to those findings and to your interpretation of them, and opens you to criticism (as well as praise) from others. It is perhaps for this reason as much as any other that many students are reluctant to report their research. But the finality of a written report also serves as a powerful incentive to do your best thinking, and to continue thinking as you write your paper. It requires you to tie up loose ends that you might otherwise have left untied. As a result, reporting your findings presents just as much of a challenge as planning the research and analyses that led to those findings.

I have often thought I knew what I wanted to say, only to find that when the time came to say it, I was unable to. The reason for this, I believe, is that in thinking about a topic, we often allow ourselves conceptual gaps that we hardly know exist. When we attempt to communicate our thoughts, however, these gaps become obvious. Organizing and then writing down our thoughts enables us to discover what gaps have yet to be filled.

Misconception 2. *The important thing is what you say, not how you say it.*

As a college student, I was mystified to find that students who wrote well consistently received better grades on their compositions than did students who wrote poorly. Even in my own compositions, I found that the grades I received seemed less to reflect what I had to say than how I said it. At the time, I was unable to decide whether this pattern in grading resulted from the professors' warped value systems, or from their inability to penetrate the facade of written prose. Whereas their criteria for grading papers might be appropriate for an English course, these criteria seemed inappropriate for courses in subjects like psychology.

As a college professor, I have at last discovered the secret of the mysterious grading practices. The discovery came about in two stages, each one part of the initiation rites new college teachers must go through. The first stage occurred when I found myself having a large number of students' papers to read and very little time in which to read them. I was then sincerely grateful to students who wrote well because I could read their papers quickly and understand what they were saying. I did not have the time to puzzle through every cryptic remark in the poorly written papers, however, and I resented the authors' presenting their ideas in a way that did not enable me to understand or evaluate them properly. I also found myself with no desire to reward the authors for this state of affairs. If their ideas were good, they should have taken the time to explain them clearly.

The second stage of discovery occurred when I found myself with just a few seminar papers to read, and plenty of time in which to read them. Now, I thought, I can be fair both to students who write well and to those who do not. I was quickly disabused of this notion. I discovered that whereas it is usually easy to distinguish well-presented good ideas from well-presented bad ideas, it is often impossible to distinguish poorly presented good ideas from poorly presented bad ideas. The problem is that the professor's comprehension of what the student says is solely through the student's way of saying it. Professors can't read minds better than anyone else. If an idea is presented in a sloppy, disorganized fashion, how is one to know whether this fashion of presentation reflects the quality of the idea or merely the quality of its presentation?

The question is not easily answered. In one case, I had talked to a student beforehand about what he was going to say, and I expected an outstanding paper on the basis of these conversations. During our conversations, certain details had not been clarified, but I expected these details to be clarified in the paper. Instead, the same ideas that had been inadequately explained in the conversations were inadequately explained in the paper as well. Either the student was unable to clarify these ideas for himself, or he was unable to clarify them for others. The outcome for the reader is the same: confusion and disappointment.

A comparable situation exists for researchers. One quickly notices that the best and most well-known psychologists are also among the best writers. Although there are exceptions, they are infrequent: Poorer writers have fewer readers. One reason for this fact is that poorly written articles are usually rejected by journal editors. Although journal editors are willing to make minor editorial changes in the articles they receive, they are usually unwilling to publish or rewrite poorly written articles. Even if a poorly written article is accepted and published, however, psychologists who receive a journal with 5 to 20 articles in it do not want to spend their limited time reading such an article. It is therefore important that you learn now how to present your ideas in a readable fashion.

Misconception 3. *Longer papers are better papers, and more papers are better yet.*

Until my first year of teaching, I believed that longer papers were better papers. Teachers had for years told me and my classmates that they didn't evaluate papers on the basis of length, but I viewed their remarks as a benign ruse designed to discourage length for its own sake. I changed my viewpoint when I started reading students' papers. Evaluating papers on both quality and quantity of ideas, I found little relation between either of these two criteria and the length of students' papers. Sometimes students wrote longer papers because they had more to say; other times they wrote longer papers because it took them several pages to say what could have been said in several sentences. There is nothing wrong with length per se so long as length is not used as a substitute for tight organization and clear writing.

Rather than writing longer papers, some people have taken the other route of writing more papers. Why say in one paper what can be said in two for twice the credit? This kind of mentality meets the needs of people who count publications, but not of those who read publications. An integrated series of related experiments will have more impact if published as a single, tightly knit package than if published as a string of hastily written articles, none of them of much interest in itself.

Misconception 4. *The main purpose of a psychology paper is the presentation of facts, whether newly established (as in reports of experiments) or well established (as in literature reviews).*

A common misconception among the general public is that the goal of science is the accumulation of facts. This misconception is fostered by popular scientific writing that emphasizes scientific findings, which may be easy to describe, at the expense of explanations of these findings, which may be both diverse and difficult to describe. Diverse explanations, however, are the hallmark of science.

Students in introductory psychology courses are prone to this misconception, and it carries over into their writing. I could cite numerous examples of this carry-over, but one in particular comes to mind. I received some years ago a beautifully written paper reviewing the literature on the testing of infant intelligence. This was one case, however, in which flowing prose was insufficient to obtain a high grade. The paper was flawed in two respects. First, the author made no effort to interrelate the various attempts to measure infant intelligence. Each attempt was described as though it had been made in isolation, even though the various attempts to measure infant intelligence have drawn upon each other. Second, the evaluative part of the paper consisted of a single sentence in which the author stated that it is still too early to draw final conclusions regarding the relative success of the various infant intelligence tests. This sentence is literally true: It is too early to draw *final* conclusions. But it will be too early to draw final conclusions as long as new data about the tests continue to be collected. Because data will continue to be collected for the foreseeable future, and because the tests date back to the early part of the 20th century, it now seems appropriate to draw at least tentative conclusions. In writing a psychology paper, you must commit yourself to a point of view, even if you may change your mind later on. If the evidence on an issue is scanty, by all means say so. But draw at least tentative conclusions so that the reader knows how you evaluate what evidence is available.

Your paper should be guided by your ideas and your point of view. Facts are presented in service of ideas: to help elucidate, support, or rewrite these ideas. They provide a test against which the validity of ideas can be measured. You should therefore select the facts that help clarify or test your point of view and omit facts that are irrelevant. In being selective, however, you must not select only those facts that support your position. Scientists demand that scientific reporting be scrupulously honest. Without such honesty, scientific communication would collapse. Cite the relevant facts, therefore, regardless of whose point of view they support.

Misconception 5. *The distinction between scientific writing, on the one hand, and advertising or propaganda, on the other, is that the purpose of scientific writing is to inform whereas the purpose of advertising or propaganda is to persuade.*

Successful advertising or propaganda need only persuade. Successful scientific writing must both inform and persuade. Students often believe that a successful piece of scientific writing need only inform the reader of the scientists' data and their interpretation of the data. The reader is then left to decide whether the theory provides a plausible account of these (and possibly other) data. This conception of scientific writing is incorrect.

When a scientist writes a paper, he or she has a product to sell. The product is his set of ideas about why certain phenomena exist. Occasionally, it is the only product on the market, and he need only convince the consumer to buy any product at all. Whether or not the scientist is successful will depend in part upon how persuasive he is, and in part upon how much the product is needed. No advertising campaign is likely to sell flowers that are guaranteed not to germinate, nor an explanation of why people don't normally stand on their heads rather than their feet. In most cases, however, there is an already established demand for the product. Because competing salespersons are trying to corner the market, the scientist must persuade the consumer not just to buy any product, but to buy his product.

One of the most common mistakes students make is to sell the wrong product: They misjudge the contribution of their work. I recently received a paper that was full of good, original ideas. The presentation of these ideas, and of other people's as well, was unusually lucid. The only major problem with the paper was that the discussion of the original ideas was condensed into one paragraph buried inconspicuously in the middle of the paper, whereas the discussion of the other people's ideas spanned about 10 pages, starting on page 1. The contribution of this paper should have been in its new perspective on an old problem. But the author had deemphasized this potentially significant contribution in favor of a relatively unimportant one: providing a well-written but unexciting review of other people's perspectives. The hurried reader will usually take the author's emphasis at face value. In this case, the reader might conclude that the paper did not have much of an original contribution to make.

At the opposite extreme, it is possible to dwell so heavily on the contribution of your paper that the contribution is actually muted. I learned this lesson the hard way. A colleague and I wrote a paper intended (a) to compare different measures of a psychological construct called subjective organization, and (b) to demonstrate that one of these measures is superior to all the rest (Sternberg & Tulving, 1977). We compared the measures on a number of different criteria. One measure proved to be superior to the rest on every one of these criteria. Despite my colleague's warnings, I explicitly called attention to this fact several times in the paper. Leaving nothing to chance, I pointed out the inescapable conclusion that one measure is better than all the rest, and therefore should be the measure of choice.

We submitted the paper for publication, and several months later received two scathing reviews. We were attacked for making what both reviewers believed to be exorbitant claims. According to the reviewers, we had by no means developed an open-and-shut case in favor of the measure we claimed was best. I thought that the arguments made by the reviewers were weak and in some cases plainly incorrect. I was so annoyed with the whole affair that I let the paper sit on my shelf for about a year. Rereading the paper and the reviews a year later, I still believed the reviewers were on the wrong track. My colleague and I decided to tone down our claims for our preferred measure, however, while retaining the same basic line of argument. We resubmitted the paper, and this time received a very favorable review. We achieved much more effective results by understating our case than we had by overstating it, an outcome my colleague (but not I) had anticipated from the start. My subsequent experiences have confirmed repeatedly that in psychology papers, a soft selling technique is more successful than a hard selling technique. By using the latter, you invite a reaction against you as salesperson that is likely to hurt the sale of your product. I can recall numerous occasions on which I refused to buy a product because I detested a pushy salesperson. In writing the first draft of the paper on measures of subjective organization, I unwittingly occupied the role of the pushy salesperson, and I received what should have been a predictable response.

Misconception 6. A good way to gain acceptance of your theory is by refuting someone else's theory.

A surprisingly common ploy in scientific papers, even some published in prestigious journals, is to resort to explanation by default. Whereas students may not know better, professionals should. The investigator describes two (or more) theories of the well-known XYZ phenomenon. She then presents devastating evidence against all theories except one. She concludes on the basis of this evidence that this one theory is correct.

This indirect method of proof is compelling only when the two (or more) alternatives are (a) mutually exclusive and (b) exhaustive. Mutually exclusive alternatives are ones in which one outcome precludes the other(s). If a coin lands heads, for example, it cannot at the same time land tails. Exhaustive alternatives are ones that include all possible outcomes. A flip of a coin can result in heads or tails, but nothing else.

The ploy described above has been used in some (but by no means all) research studying sources of differences between groups in intelligence test scores. A study would be presented in which obtained differences in test scores could not be attributable to environmental factors. The author would conclude on this basis that the differences must be due to hereditary factors. These alternatives, however, are neither mutually exclusive nor exhaustive. First, it is possible – indeed, probable – that both heredity and environment influence intelligence test scores. Second, a further source of influence upon intelligence test scores is the interaction between heredity and environment – the effect produced by their joint influence. As an example, certain genes for intelligence may manifest themselves only under favorable environmental conditions.

One other disadvantage of the indirect method of proof bears mention. Criticism of other people's theories often gains one more opponents than it does converts to one's own theory. This was another lesson I learned the hard way. I once wrote a paper that had two major goals: (a) to show that my theory of a phenomenon was correct; (b) to show that someone else's theory of the phenomenon was incorrect. I presented what I believed was strong evidence in favor of my theory and in opposition to the other person's theory. I submitted the paper to a journal, and it was rejected. The main reviewer of the paper, predictably enough, was the other theorist. It is a common practice to send papers attacking Theory X to Theorist X, with the editor then using her judgment as to whether the review is a fair one. The reviewer criticized not the positive aspect of my paper, but its negative aspect. He argued that our theories actually dealt with somewhat different aspects of the phenomenon under investigation, so that there was no need to attack his theory in the process of supporting my own.

In retrospect, I think the reviewer probably had some valid points; I also think he overreacted. In papers I've reviewed that attack my work, I've probably overreacted as well. Scientists have a reputation among the general public for being objective seekers and impartial evaluators of the truth. I think this reputation is generally deserved, but only when it comes to each other's work. When it comes to their own work, scientists lose their objectivity. When a scientist is attacked, he or she behaves in much the same manner as anyone else under attack. When someone lunges at you with a fist flying toward your face, you don't stop to reflect upon the various considerations that may have led your opponent to attack you. You counterattack. Because scientists are personally so involved in their work, they often treat an attack on their work as a personal attack, even if there is no rational basis for treating it as such. The result can be a personal confrontation in which scientific issues are placed on the back burner.

In conclusion, it is wise to stress the positive contribution of your paper. This does not mean that you should forgo criticizing other theories. Such criticism may be essential to your point. If it is, keep in mind my earlier admonition that understatement is a more effective means of persuasion than is overstatement. Avoid statements that can be interpreted as contentious but lacking in substance. And if you publish your paper, don't expect the investigator you criticize to congratulate you on your cogent refutation of her work.

Misconception 7. *Negative results that fail to support the researcher's hypothesis are every bit as valuable as positive results that do support the researcher's hypothesis.*

Because science is a fair game, the scientist wins some and loses some. Students often believe that the only honest course of action is for the scientist to report his losses as well as his wins. To do otherwise would seem to present a false picture of both the scientist and the state of nature.

After reading a diverse sampling of journal articles, the student is bound to arrive at one of two conclusions – either scientists have uncannily sound intuitions about the way experiments will turn out or they maintain closets full of unsuccessful and unreported experiments. Although scientists usually have at least fairly sound intuitions about how experiments will turn out, the state of the journals is more a reflection of well-stocked closets than of unerring intuitions.

Scientists' failures to report failures are attributable not to their dishonesty, but to the frequent uninterpretability of negative results. Suppose, for example, that an investigator predicts that giving children rewards after learning will increase their learning. The investigator conducts an experiment with two groups. In one group, children receive rewards after learning; in the other group, they do not receive rewards. The investigator finds no difference in learning between groups. What can she conclude? Unfortunately, not much. Whereas a significant difference between groups would have provided good evidence that rewards can facilitate learning, absence of a significant difference could be explained in a number of ways, most of them uninteresting. Consider three such uninteresting explanations:

1. The reward used in the study did not prove a powerful enough incentive. If the reward, for example, was a peanut, then children's cravings

for a single peanut might not have been strong enough to increase their efforts to learn.

2. The sample of children might not have been large enough. It is a well-known rule of statistics that if any treatment effect exists at all, then it can be discovered if one's sample is large enough. A small effect may be detectable only with a relatively large sample. If there were only three children in each group, then the investigator might have failed to detect the effect of the reward.

3. The measure of learning might have been inadequate. Suppose, for example, that the task was to learn the set of multiplication facts for one-digit numbers, and that the measure of learning was a single multiplication fact. This measure probably would have been inadequate to detect learning in either group, and hence a difference in learning between groups.

Under two sets of circumstances, negative results can be of interest:

1. An investigator repeatedly fails to replicate someone else's results. Suppose someone reports that subjects who stand on their heads for 30 seconds prior to taking a test of visual-motor coordination perform better on the test than do control subjects who do not stand on their heads. Another investigator, suspicious of this result, tries to replicate it with two groups of subjects, and fails. Realizing that his failure to replicate the result may be due to sampling fluctuations, the investigator tests two more groups of subjects, and again finds no significant difference between groups. At this point, he feels ready to report the result. Whereas one failure to replicate a result is not informative, repeated failures to replicate can be informative. The number of failures needed depends in large part upon the strength of prior evidence in support of the result in question. Two failures are probably more than adequate for the "headstand hypothesis," whereas a great many failures would be needed to overthrow a more well-established result, such as that under normal circumstances learning increases with practice.

2. A significant result vanishes when a methodological weakness is corrected. Suppose that the experimenter who wrote the "headstand" paper knew which subjects had stood on their heads, and which had not. This aspect of the methodology suggests a possible bias in the experimenter's scoring of the coordination test (especially if the experimenter is Public Relations Director of the American Association for

the Advancement of Acrobatics). A worthwhile methodological refinement would be to conduct the experiment under circumstances in which the experimenter does not know which subjects stood on their heads and which did not. A negative result would be of interest in this case, because it would suggest that the significant difference between groups in the first experiment was due to experimenter bias.

Misconception 8. *The logical development of ideas in a psychology paper reflects the historical development of ideas in the psychologist's head.*

If one were to take journal articles at face value, one would conclude that scientific results come in neat, attractively wrapped packages. One need only go through a uniform series of well-defined steps in order to ensure delivery of such packages:

1. The scientist starts with some clever ideas about a phenomenon, which she explains in the introduction to the paper. These ideas are carefully formulated before the scientist has collected any data, and the data merely serve to confirm (or in rare cases disconfirm) their validity.
2. The scientist tests these ideas by carefully choosing variables that can be manipulated in a controlled experiment. The scientist's deep understanding of the phenomenon under observation and of scientific method enables her to choose the correct variables and experimental manipulation on her very first attempt, which she describes in the *Method* section of the paper.
3. The scientist performs the experiment, presenting in the *Results* section of her paper the outcomes of data analyses scrupulously planned in advance.
4. The scientist finally reflects upon the broader implications of the results, presenting her reflections in the *Discussion* section of the paper.

I doubt that 1% of the papers published in scientific journals developed in a way even remotely resembling the outline sketched above. Yet the large majority of published papers are written as though they had developed in this way, or in some way closely resembling it. Let us reconsider the series of steps:

1. Before carrying out an experiment, one usually has only a vague and tentative idea of what the outcome will be, if only because there are so many possible outcomes that one can scarcely even enumerate them all. One's ideas develop along with the experiment.

2. One sometimes finds oneself performing the right experimental manipulation on the wrong variables, or the wrong experimental manipulation on the right variables. In order to avoid wasting large amounts of time and money, scientists frequently conduct small-scale pilot experiments that test the feasibility of the experiment as designed. Adjustments in method can then be made in preparation for the full-scale experiment, or the experiment can be scrapped altogether.

3. Major data analyses are usually planned in advance. Indeed, it is necessary to do this planning in order to assure that the design of the experiment permits one to analyze the data in the most advantageous way. Minor data analyses are frequently decided upon after the data have been collected. Often the results of a planned data analysis will suggest a subsequent unplanned one. Only fools fail to go where the data lead them. One of the most valuable skills scientists can have is a knack for getting the most out of their data. A given set of data can be analyzed in an infinite number of ways, some of them more revealing than others. The scientist must select a small number of ways that are likely to yield maximum payoff.

4. Ideas for the *Discussion* section of a paper usually start forming at the same time the experiment does, not merely after it has been completed. The reason for this fact is simple. Unless the experiment has at least some potentially broad and interesting implications, or unless it can lead to some sensible next step in research, it is probably not worth doing.

Why does the picture of research presented by journal articles correspond so poorly to the actual state of affairs? There are at least three reasons:

1. Journals operate under severe space limitations. A large percentage of articles submitted to the journals must be rejected for lack of space. In some journals, more than 90% of submitted articles are rejected. Those articles that are accepted must be as concise as possible. An "autobiographical" form of presentation, describing all one's false starts and initial misjudgments, consumes a great deal of space. This space is more profitably devoted to other articles.

2. An autobiographical account of an experiment tends to be of more interest to oneself than to one's colleagues. An associate recounted to me the way in which he learned this lesson. He submitted a 20-page theoretical article to one of the most prestigious psychological journals. He spent the first 19 pages of the article describing how he had come to his

conclusions after a lengthy series of false starts; he presented his final conclusions on the 20th page. The article was rejected, not because the final conclusions were wrong, but because the editor believed that there was only one publishable page in the article – the last. The editor was interested in the psychologist's conclusions, but not in the lengthy soul searching the psychologist had done to arrive at them.

3. The object of description in a scientific report is a phenomenon and its explanation, not the reporter of the phenomenon and explanation. The focus of the report must reflect this fact. A graduate student and I once completed an experiment investigating the development of reasoning skills in children at the second-, fourth-, and sixth-grade levels. Children were presented with reasoning problems, which they were then asked to solve. Because the experiment involved a considerable investment in time and money, we decided to pretest our reasoning problems on some colleagues' children. Our original plan had been to use number of problems correctly solved as the dependent measure. We discovered, however, that even the youngest children made almost no errors on the problems once they fully understood the task. We therefore changed our dependent measure when we did the full-scale experiment, using response time to solve problems correctly instead of numbers of problems correctly solved. Had someone else planned this experiment, she might have realized immediately that the problems were too easy to use number correct as the dependent measure; or she might have stumbled longer than we did until the discovery that the problems were too easy. A description of this trial-and-error process is slightly informative about the development of the investigator's intuitions, but it is uninformative about the object of the investigation, in our case, the development of reasoning in children. The scientifically informative statement is that the problems were of a level of difficulty that made response time an appropriate dependent measure.

There is often a fine line between the omission of autobiographical information and the omission of critical details. If a hypothesis is post hoc, then one is obliged to indicate this fact.

In sum, the steps one follows in planning and carrying out research do not neatly correspond to the successive sections of the psychology paper. In the next two chapters, we will consider the steps in carrying out library and experimental research and how to describe them in the psychology paper.

Chapter Two

Steps in Writing the Library Research Paper

Most undergraduate research papers, and many graduate and professional research papers as well, are based upon library research. Library research can proceed smoothly if you follow a sequence of simple steps.

DECIDING UPON A TOPIC FOR A PAPER

Your first task is to decide upon a topic for a paper. This is, in a sense, the most important task because the paper can be no better than the topic. I have found five mistakes that repeatedly turn up in students' choices of topics.

The Topic Doesn't Interest the Student

Many students put off thinking about their choice of topic until the latest possible date. They then find themselves pressed to select a topic, and hastily decide upon something that is of only marginal interest to them. Procrastination in thinking about a topic is a mistake because interesting topics don't often pop into your head overnight. So allow yourself plenty of time to think of a topic. Then, if you are unhappy with the first few ideas that come to mind, you can try out others before you resign yourself to a topic that doesn't interest you. Unless you are at least somewhat interested in the topic you pick, you will find the exercise of doing library research a deadly bore, and your paper will probably show it. Having once written and having now read a large number of student papers, I am convinced that a major determinant of quality is the degree of interest the student sustains in the topic about which he writes.

The Topic Is Too Easy or Too Safe for the Student

The purpose of student papers is for the student to learn something about some topic. It is therefore to the student's advantage to select a topic with which he is relatively (although not necessarily totally) unfamiliar. Students sometimes seek to optimize safety (or grades) rather than learning, however, choosing a topic with which they are quite familiar. I saw an example of such a choice one year in my Theories of Intelligence course. A student showed in class that she was quite familiar with the literature on creativity in children, perhaps because she had previously written a paper on it. Her remarks in class also showed, however, that she had little background in other areas covered by the course. I was therefore disappointed when she proposed to write a paper on creativity in children. Although she could probably learn something from writing such a paper, it was clear that she had more to gain by selecting a topic from one of the many areas in which she had little background.

The Topic Is Too Difficult for the Student

The opposite problem from that discussed above is the selection of a topic that is too difficult for the student. In my Theories of Intelligence course I also had a student write a paper on the heritability of intelligence. The student was obviously interested in the topic and wanted to do a good job, but he found that most of the literature went over his head. Understanding the literature on inherited traits requires a knowledge of certain advanced statistical concepts that most undergraduates have not yet encountered. Consequently, it is not possible for them to write a really sophisticated paper on this topic unless they are prepared to learn the necessary statistics. This task is both difficult and time-consuming. In general, you should make certain that the topic you choose does not require understanding of concepts that your background does not permit you to grasp.

There Is Inadequate Literature on the Topic

For various reasons, some of the potentially most interesting topics in psychology have been little investigated. In some cases, people simply haven't thought much about the topics; in other cases, they have thought about the topics but found that the topics did not lend themselves to experimental (or other types of) analysis. These topics are not suitable for literature reviews. Before committing yourself to a topic, make sure that there is adequate literature on it. As a student, I was interested in how people understand proverbs. The topic seemed to deal with a psychologically important function (one that is tested in several intelligence tests), and seemed to have considerable real-world relevance. I found almost no relevant experimental literature, however. Although there was more literature on related topics, such as metaphor, it was obvious that my tentative choice of a paper topic would have to be changed.

The Topic Is Too Broad

The most common mistake that students make in the selection of a topic is to select one that is too broad. This problem is understandable because, before writing the paper, students have only a vague idea of how much literature has been published on a given topic. Textbooks usually only scratch the surface, and it is not until one delves into primary sources that one discovers the extent of the relevant literature.

Once you tentatively decide upon a topic, it is a good idea to start compiling a list of references, and to scan some of these references quickly, before starting note-taking in preparation for writing the paper. By following this procedure, you avoid the pitfall of too broad (or too narrow) a topic. By narrowing your topic before you start note-taking, you save yourself the time wasted on taking notes that later will prove of no use in writing the paper.

If you have settled upon a topic that proves to be too broad, you should consider ways in which you can narrow the topic without abandoning it altogether. Consider as an example the topic *Problem Solving*. A search of the available references quickly reveals that this topic is too broad. This topic (and others) might be narrowed in any of several ways:

1. *Restriction by age.* The review is limited to problem solving in adults or children or infants.
2. *Restriction by species.* Only problem solving in humans or in rats is considered.

3. *Restriction by clinical type.* The review deals with problem solving by nonhandicapped people or by people with a mental handicap.
4. *Restriction by psychological perspective.* The review is of the behavioristic, information-processing, or psychometric approach to problem solving; or the review compares these perspectives, dealing only with issues that are relevant to the comparison.
5. *Restriction by content.* The review deals only with the solution of verbal, or mathematical, or spatial problems.

There are obviously many ways in which you can limit the scope of your topic, and the best way will depend upon the topic, the available literature on the topic, and your interests. Be sure to state in the opening paragraphs of your paper what restrictions you have imposed. A good title will also help the reader understand how you have limited your topic.

SEARCHING THE LITERATURE

I have found it useful to maintain two sets of note cards when conducting a literature review. These two sets are author cards and topic cards.

Author Cards

Format of author cards: Use small (3″ × 5″) index cards for author cards. Or, if you prefer to use a computer, you can create virtual cards on the computer that function like author cards. You should record on these cards all the information you will later need in order to compile the references for your paper. Each source should be documented. The form of documentation differs somewhat depending upon the nature of the source:

1. *Journal articles.* Your documentation for journal articles should include (a) the author's last name, and first and middle initials, (b) the year of publication, (c) the title of the article, (d) the name of the journal, (e) the volume number, and (f) the page numbers of the article. A sample author card would look like this:

> Janis, I. L., & King, B. T. (1954). The influence of role-playing on opinion change. *Journal of Abnormal and Social Psychology,* *49,* 211–218.

2. *Books.* Your documentation for books should include (a) the author's last name, and first and middle initials, (b) the year of publication, (c) the title of the book, (d) the city in which the book was published, and (e) the name of the publisher. If the city of publication is not well known, include the state as well. Include the country if the city is not in the United States and is not well known. For publishers in Canada or Australia, include the name of the province (e.g., Saskatchewan) in which the publication took place. For example,

> Festinger, L. (1957). *A theory of cognitive dissonance.* Evanston, Illinois: Row, Peterson.

In this case, the author does not use a middle initial.

3. *Edited books.* Your documentation for articles in edited books should include (a) the author's last name, and first and middle initials, (b) the year of publication, (c) the title of the article, (d) the editor of the book, (e) the title of the book, (f) the pages of the book in which the article appears, (g) the city in which the book was published, and (h) the name of the publisher. For example,

> Webb, E. J., & Salancik, J. R. (1970). Supplementing the self-report in attitude research. In G. F. Summers (Ed.), *Attitude measurement* (pp. 317–327). Chicago: Rand McNally.

Advantages of Author Cards. Although this system of documentation may appear cumbersome when you do your research, it will have several advantages later on:

1. *You will have a complete set of references.* There is no possibility of forgetting any sources you need, because you recorded all your sources at the one time when you can't forget them – the time you used them.
2. *You will have complete documentation for each reference.* Students sometimes keep a complete list of references but fail to keep complete documentation on each reference. They must then relocate the references later on – if they can find them – to complete the documentation.
3. *Your References section of the paper will be all but done.* When you are ready to type this section, simply reorder the author cards alphabetically and type the information from the card.

Topic Cards

Format of Topic Cards. Large cards (5″ × 7″) are preferred for topic cards. Or, if you prefer to use a computer, create virtual topic cards on your machine. You should record on each card (a) the name of the topic at the top, (b) information about that topic, (c) the source of each item of information, and (d) comments.

Only one topic goes on each card. Each time you encounter a new topic on which you want to take notes, make a new topic card. You will save time later on if you avoid multiple topic cards that express the same topic in different ways. For example, the topics *Rorschach Test* and *Inkblots Test* can be combined (unless more than one inkblots test is used).

Your notes on each topic should be complete enough so that you will not have to return to your sources later. Avoid extraneous words that convey no useful information. In taking notes on arguments, make sure you capture the gist of the arguments so that later you can reconstruct the author's point of view.

For each statement you compile, record the source by writing down the author's last name and the date of publication. If you make a direct quotation or paraphrase, be sure to indicate this fact in your notes, citing appropriate page numbers.

When you make comments on a source or the information supplied in it, indicate clearly on the topic card that the comment is yours and not the author's. The best time to make comments on what you read is often when you read it, because at that time the material and its context are freshest in your mind. These comments will be valuable to you later on, because you will be expected in your paper to evaluate information as well as to summarize it. In reading through psychological literature, you should be constantly evaluating five characteristics of the author's arguments:

1. *Validity of arguments.* On what basis does the author make each argument? Are the arguments properly substantiated? How? Almost any psychologist who has reviewed papers for a journal (or read student papers) becomes very sensitive to the question of proper validation. A surprisingly common ploy is for an author to present a theory, which may well be plausible, design an experiment or marshal evidence to test some other theory, which also may be plausible, and then conclude that the original theory is correct. In reading an article or book, therefore, assure yourself not only that a test of a theory is a strong one, but also that it assesses the proper theory.

2. *Internal consistency of arguments.* Are the arguments consistent, or do

they contradict each other? Are the arguments consistent with the author's general point of view? Whereas in validity you are concerned primarily with the relation between arguments and facts, in internal consistency you are concerned primarily with the relation between arguments and other arguments. Authors are often unaware of internal inconsistencies in their own data. As a result, readers sometimes spot contradictions that authors have lived with for many years, blithely unaware of their existence.

3. *Presuppositions of arguments.* What does the author presuppose in making each argument; especially, what presuppositions does the author make that he does not communicate to the reader or may not even be aware of? Are the presuppositions realistic? Do the presuppositions strengthen or weaken the impact of the argument? Consider, for example, the statement: "The Bozo theory of cognitive development is incorrect because it is based upon the assumption that cognitive development is continuous." What presuppositions does the statement make? First, it presupposes that the Bozo theory assumes continuity in cognitive development. Second, it presupposes the theory making this assumption is incorrect. Third, it presupposes (incorrectly, as it turns out) that there is such a theory as the Bozo theory of cognitive development.

4. *Implications of arguments.* What are the implications of each argument; especially, what implications does the author overlook? Do the implications strengthen or weaken the impact of the argument? Are these implications consistent with others reached from other arguments? Consider, for example, the statement: "I violently object to violent objections." What is the obvious implication of the statement?

5. *Importance of arguments.* Is a particular argument an important one, and therefore one you will want to describe in detail in your paper? Or is it unimportant, and hence not worthy of mention, or worthy of mention only in passing? A common flaw in student papers is to emphasize all arguments equally, regardless of their importance. This flaw inevitably reduces the impact of the paper as a whole.

By keeping in mind these five criteria for evaluating the literature you read, and by writing down your evaluative comments immediately subsequent to the relevant argument, you will supply yourself with much of the substance you will later need to write your paper. Later on, of course, you can always expand upon or change your evaluation. But you will have your evaluative notes from the topic cards to work with, rather than having to start from scratch.

Advantages of Topic Cards. By compiling your notes on topic cards, you will gain several advantages:

1. *When you are ready to write your paper, you will have available to you all the information you need to write it.* You won't have to do any more library work at the last minute when you may no longer have time to do it.
2. *You will have available to you the source of each argument or piece of information.* You won't have to try to remember who said what.
3. *You will find it easier to organize your paper than you might have otherwise.* The reason for this greater ease is that the topic cards form the input to the next step, preparing an outline.

PREPARING AN OUTLINE

Use of Topic Cards

After you have finished note-taking, you are ready to prepare an outline. The topics on the topic cards form the basis of this outline, because they readily can be used as headings and subheadings. Write down all the topics on one or more pieces of paper. Then, cut out strips of paper, one for each topic. Or, if you are using a computer, you can use an outlining feature that is available in most word-processing programs. Your job now is to rearrange the topics on the strips of paper to form a logical order of presentation. The various topics need not and should not be at the same level of specificity. Some of the topics form major headings, others form minor headings, and others are nested under these minor headings. You may have to add introductory and concluding sections to the outline, as well as any intermediate headings that are needed for smooth transitions. The lowest level of subordination for each heading should represent a single sentence of the final paper.

Types of Outlines

Once you have ordered the headings of your outline, you must decide upon one of three ways in which you can complete the outline

(Harris & Blake, 1976). We will discuss the three kinds of outlines with reference to a miniature example in which we will compare two personality tests, the Thematic Apperception Test (TAT) and the Minnesota Multiphasic Personality Inventory (MMPI).

The Keyword Outline. In this kind of outline, you restrict yourself to keywords at each level of description. For example,

I. Introduction
II. Content
   A. TAT: pictorial
   B. MMPI: verbal
III. Administration
   A. TAT: oral
   B. MMPI: written
IV. Scoring
   A. TAT: subjective
   B. MMPI: objective
V. Conclusion

The Topic Outline. In this kind of outline, you use phrases and clauses at each level of description. For example,

I. Comparison between the TAT and MMPI
II. Type of content
   A. TAT: pictures of people in various settings, some realistic and others not
   B. MMPI: statements describing behaviors or beliefs that the examinee marks as true or false as descriptions of himself
III. Mode of administration
   A. TAT: pictures sequentially presented by examiner to subject, who supplies a narrative of events leading to, during, and following from the pictured scene
   B. MMPI: booklet containing entire set of statements given to subject, who proceeds through the booklet at his own pace
IV. Method of scoring
   A. TAT: scored subjectively, often using Murray's taxonomy of needs and press
   B. MMPI: scored objectively by means of a separate key for each diagnostic scale
V. Differences: content, administration, scoring

The Sentence Outline. In this kind of outline, you use complete sentences at each level of description. For example,

I. This outline compares the TAT and MMPI with respect to content, administration, and scoring.
II. The tests differ in type of content.
    A. The TAT consists of a series of pictures of people in various settings, some realistic and others not.
    B. The MMPI, on the other hand, consists of a series of statements describing behaviors or beliefs that the examinee marks as either true or false as descriptions of herself.
III. The tests also differ in mode of administration.
    A. In the TAT, pictures are sequentially presented by the examiner to the subject, who supplies a narrative of events leading to, during, and following from the pictured scene.
    B. In the MMPI, a booklet containing the entire set of statements is given to the subject, who proceeds through the booklet at her own pace.
IV. Finally, the tests are scored by different methods.
    A. The TAT is scored subjectively, often using Murray's taxonomy of needs and press.
    B. The MMPI is scored objectively by means of a separate key for each diagnostic scale.
V. In conclusion, the tests differ substantially in content, administration, and scoring.

Choosing a Type of Outline. You should use the type of outline that most facilitates your writing. People vary according to which type of outline they find most facilitating. Some people find a keyword outline most helpful because it organizes their thoughts while leaving them maximum flexibility in actually writing the paper; others find a keyword outline too sparse in content to be of much use. Some people like a sentence outline because it essentially writes their paper for them; others find a sentence outline time-consuming to write and of no greater use in organizing their thoughts than a topical outline. By experimenting with all three types of outlines, you will learn from your own experience which is most suitable for you.

Organization of Outlines. Outlines can be organized in many ways, and many decisions regarding organization are unique to each particular situation. Five principles of organization, however, are common to all outlines and the papers that evolve from them:

1. *The organization should include a beginning, a middle, and an end, in which you say what you're going to say, say it, and say what you've said.* When the reader begins a paper, he needs some general statements that tell him what the paper is about and how it is organized; without this orientation, he may become lost almost as soon as he starts the paper. When the reader completes the main part of the paper, he needs a summary of the main ideas, and whatever final comments you want to supply; without this review, the reader may not realize what you consider to be your main points.

    Suppose that the keyword outline presented earlier had consisted only of a "middle":

    I. Content
       A. TAT: pictorial
       B. MMPI: verbal
    II. Administration
       A. TAT: oral
       B. MMPI: written
    III. Scoring
       A. TAT: subjective
       B. MMPI: objective

    The reader of a paper based upon this outline would encounter immediately a comparison between the content of the TAT and the MMPI, without any idea of what the paper intends to accomplish and how it intends to accomplish it. The reader would finish the paper without any idea of what the author believed to be her main points and of what conclusions the author wanted to draw. Although the main body of the paper is well organized, the reader is left with no sense of direction or purpose in the paper.

2. *Once you decide upon a principle of organization, stick with it.* Beginning writers often change their way of organizing papers midstream, usually without first informing the reader that the change is about to take place. The change confuses the reader. If you must change your organization principle, be sure to let the reader know. But avoid the change if possible. Consider the plight of the reader faced with a paper based upon the keyword outline at the left on the next page. The original keyword outline is reproduced at the right:

I. Introduction	**I.** Introduction
II. Content	**II.** Content
A. TAT: pictorial	**A.** TAT: pictorial
B. MMPI: verbal	**B.** MMPI: verbal
III. TAT	**III.** Administration
A. Administration: oral	**A.** TAT: oral
B. Scoring: subjective	**B.** MMPI: written
IV. MMPI	**IV.** Scoring
A. Administration: written	**A.** TAT: subjective
B. Scoring: objective	**B.** MMPI: objective
V. Conclusion	**V.** Conclusion

Notice that the outline at the left switches its principles of organization, beginning with topic III. Topic II is organized by theme, whereas topics III and IV are organized by test. The outline at the left makes obvious what the careless writer hopes will remain hidden – that the paper is confusing and the author is confused.

3. *Organize your writing thematically.* Thematic organization enhances the clarity of a paper. The keyword outline as originally presented was organized thematically. The three themes were content, administration, and scoring. The reader would complete a paper based upon this outline with a clear idea of how the TAT and MMPI differ in these three respects. Compare this original outline, presented at the right, to the new outline presented at the left. This new outline is organized by test:

I. Introduction	**I.** Introduction
II. TAT	**II.** Content
A. Content: pictorial	**A.** TAT: pictorial
B. Administration: oral	**B.** MMPI: verbal
C. Scoring: subjective	**III.** Administration
III. MMPI	**A.** TAT: oral
A. Content: verbal	**B.** MMPI: written
B. Administration: written	**IV.** Scoring
C. Scoring: objective	**A.** TAT: subjective
IV. Conclusion	**B.** MMPI: objective
	V. Conclusion

The organization by test in the outline at the left is not confusing, but it is inferior to the thematic organization at the right. In the thematic organization, the reader can compare the two tests on each theme as he reads through the main part of the paper, gradually developing a perspective on how the tests differ. In the organization by test, the reader is unable to begin comparing the tests until he is halfway through the main part of the paper. By this time, the reader may have forgotten the characteristics of the first test, because he had no motivation to remember them. In reading the section of the paper on the MMPI, he probably will have to refer back to the section on the TAT in order to draw a comparison. If the reader is unwilling to spend the time or effort doing what the writer should have done, he may never understand the comparison altogether.

The same principle would apply if, say, one wished to compare the viewpoints of Sigmund Freud and Konrad Lorenz on aggression toward oneself, aggression toward others, and aggression toward objects. The preferred way to organize the paper would be by the successive themes of aggression toward self, others, and objects, not by the successive authors, Freud and Lorenz.

There are two exceptions to this principle. The first arises when there are no well-developed themes in the literature you plan to review. Each theorist, for example, may deal with a different set of issues. The second exception arises when your focus is genuinely upon the objects of comparison rather than upon the themes along which they are compared. In a book presenting theories of personality, for example, the author's emphasis might be upon the individual perspective of each theorist, rather than upon the themes dealt with in their theories.

4. *Organize your outline hierarchically.* Beginning writers tend to overuse coordination of ideas and to underuse subordination of ideas. If a paper contains a large number of "main" ideas, the reader will have some difficulty understanding the ideas and more difficulty remembering them. When you find yourself with a large number of "main" ideas, try to subordinate some of them. You will then communicate the same number of ideas at the same time that you increase the effectiveness with which you communicate them.

Suppose that the keyword outline for the tests had taken this form:

    I. Introduction
    II. TAT content: pictorial
   III. MMPI content: verbal
   IV. TAT administration: oral
    V. MMPI administration: written
   VI. TAT scoring: subjective
  VII. MMPI scoring: objective
 VIII. Conclusion

Notice that this outline is much harder to follow than the original keyword outline because all ideas are presented at the same level, with no subordination. The outline therefore is much less effective in comparing the two personality tests.

5. *Organize for your audience.* In arranging your outline, it is essential that you keep your audience in mind. The level of description for each topic in the outline should be appropriate for the target audience; level of description that is adequate for one audience may be inadequate for another. Consider, for example, the original keyword outline presented earlier. The introductory heading has no subheadings subordinated under it. Because the lowest level of subordination under each heading represents one sentence, this introduction will be just one sentence in length. A brief introduction of this kind may be adequate for a professional seeking a one-paragraph description of salient differences between the TAT and the MMPI, but it probably will be inadequate for a layperson unfamiliar with personality tests. Such a person requires more orientation to the topic of the exposition. An expanded introduction is therefore appropriate:

I. Introduction: personality tests

    A. Purpose

    B. General characteristics

    C. Divergences

        1. Personality tests in general

        2. TAT and MMPI in particular

The general reader will now be able to follow the remainder of the exposition.

Advantages of Outlines. Students often wonder whether outlines are worth the time and trouble. Using outlines has three advantages that more than offset the extra work they require:

1. *Outlines help you organize your writing.* In writing the actual paper, organization will be just one of many concerns you have. Because there are so many different things to keep track of in writing the paper, and because your capacity to keep track of many things at once is limited, organization will receive only limited attention. Because organization of a paper is so important, however, it pays to insert a step prior to writing the paper in which you can devote your full attention to organizing the paper.

2. *Outlines prevent omission of relevant topics.* In doing your research or

in compiling your topic cards, you may have inadvertently omitted a topic that you intended or should have thought to include in your paper. Omissions are much easier for the author to spot in an outline than in a paper. They are also much easier to correct before writing of the paper has begun.

3. *Outlines prevent inclusion of irrelevant topics.* Authors sometimes find that a topic that had seemed relevant to the paper in the early stages of research no longer seems relevant when the research is being organized. Irrelevant material shows itself in an obvious way during preparation of an outline, because the material seems to have no place in the outline. By discovering irrelevancies during preparation of the outline, the author can discard them so that later they do not distract her in writing the paper.

WRITING THE PAPER

This section of the chapter is briefer than the previous ones because most of the principles that apply to writing library research papers apply to experimental papers as well, and these principles are discussed in later chapters. In writing the library research paper you should keep in mind particularly the five criteria for evaluating authors' arguments that were described earlier. Readers of your paper will evaluate your paper by the same (or similar) criteria to those you used to evaluate the papers and books you read:

1. *Validity.* Are your arguments consistent with the literature you reviewed? Have you explained inconsistencies? Have you properly substantiated each of your arguments?
2. *Internal consistency.* Are your arguments consistent with each other? Are they consistent with your general point of view?
3. *Presuppositions.* Have you made clear to the reader what you presuppose? Are your presuppositions reasonable ones that the reader is likely to accept? Has the impact of your presuppositions upon your conclusions been discussed?
4. *Implications.* Have you discussed the implications of your arguments? Are these implications realistic? Do these implications strengthen or weaken your arguments?
5. *Importance.* Have you emphasized your important arguments and

conclusions, and subordinated the less important ones? Have you explained why you view certain arguments and conclusions as important and others as less so?

By using these five criteria to evaluate your literature review, you will improve its quality. Later, we will consider in more detail criteria for evaluating the quality of all psychology papers.

Chapter Three

Steps in Writing the
Experimental Research Paper

When a research psychologist talks about "writing a paper," he is talking about a lengthy and complicated chain of events that includes a great deal more than just reporting research results. In this chapter I outline these events from start to finish.

PLANNING EXPERIMENTAL RESEARCH

Getting an Idea

For most psychology students, getting an idea for an experiment is the hardest part of research. There are no steps one can take that will guarantee generation of a good idea. The following suggestions may prove helpful, however.

Whom to Consult. In many colleges and universities, the faculty is among the most underutilized of resources. In my first semester of teaching at Yale, I set aside three hours each week for "office hours." I encouraged – sometimes I practically begged – students to come see me during these hours for advice on papers, projects, and the like. I left my door wide open to encourage students to enter. For the most part, though, I sat staring at the walls, or at the people scurrying by (but not in) the door. I also encouraged students to make individual appointments if they were unable to see me during my prearranged hours, but for the most part, students also failed to take me up on this offer. More recently, business has picked up, although much more so among graduate than among undergraduate students.

I and many of my colleagues are perplexed by the timidity of students in seeking faculty advice. Recently, the psychology department faculty at Yale spent the better part of an hour trying to figure out why students are so timid in approaching faculty. Sometimes students try once, are unsuccessful in reaching the faculty member, and give up. Sometimes they don't try at all. Faculty members (as well as postdoctoral students and graduate students) can be a student's most helpful first avenue of approach in writing a paper. Students should be more assertive in seeking their advice.

What to Read. Ideas often come out of one's reading. Some kinds of reading are more likely to lead to good ideas than are others.

1. *Pursue a small number of topics in depth.* Most undergraduate psychology courses, and many graduate ones, are not well suited to the stimulation of creative ideas for experiments. This unsuitability is because they cover a large amount of material superficially, rather than a small amount in depth. In order to come up with a good idea for an experiment, it helps to have a deep understanding of the issues involved in some relatively small area of psychological research. The superficial understanding acquired in survey courses is usually inadequate. Find some topic in or related to your coursework that interests you. Then use your course lectures and reading material as guides to the published literature. Pursue the references that your teacher and textbook cite, and pursue the references most frequently cited in these references. By digging into the literature on a topic, you will acquire a deeper understanding of the issues that are the focus of psychological research.

2. *Acquaint yourself with research at the frontiers of knowledge.* As an undergraduate, I once followed the advice of the preceding paragraph, only to find myself acquiring a deep understanding of an issue that had ceased to interest psychologists twenty years before. In pursuing a topic, consider whether it is of current interest. Because of the long time lag between the writing and publication of a book, most textbooks are somewhat out of date by the time they are published. Within five to ten years, they usually become hopelessly out of date. As a result, students relying on these textbooks may find themselves generating ideas that someone else thought of several years before. In order to become acquainted with literature on the frontiers of knowledge, scan recent journal articles and make use of the references described in Chap-

ter 9 of this book. Ask your professor or advanced graduate students for leads to the most recently published work on particular topics.

3. *Start with general readings and proceed to more specific ones.* Because of space limitations, authors of journal articles are often unable to present in detail the previous research that motivated their particular experiments. If you are unacquainted with this previous research, you may find yourself unable to understand the rationale of the experiments. It is therefore wise to start your reading with a review of the relevant literature, if you can find one, or with a theoretical article that compares the major theoretical positions. Reports of individual experiments will make more sense to you if you are first acquainted with the research context in which they were done.

How to Read. How you read is as important as what you read. Suppose, for example, that you read an article testing the theory that repeated exposure to persuasive communications results in attitude change toward the viewpoint advocated by those communications, regardless of one's initial attitudes. You might pursue further research taking you in any one of four directions:

1. *Extend the theory.* After reading the article, you may be persuaded that the theory is sound and could be extended. You might want to show that repeated exposure to communications advocating a viewpoint, but in a nonpersuasive manner, also results in attitude change toward the position taken by the communications.

2. *Generate an analogous theory.* If you find the theory and data compelling, you may want to think up an analogous theory. Perhaps repeated exposure to a particular kind of music increases liking for that music. Or perhaps repeated exposure to any kind of communication increases positive affect toward that kind of communication.

3. *Limit the theory.* Perhaps you believe that the conclusion derived from the data is too broad. If the subjects in the experiment were all children, for example, you may wish to show that the theory is applicable only to children. Or if the communications used in the experiment were all health-related ones, you may want to show that the theory is applicable only to arguments related to bodily care.

4. *Challenge the evidence testing the theory.* In reading the article, you may spot a methodological, statistical, or logical flaw in the author's argument. In this case, you may want to test the theory in a way that corrects

the flaw. For example, suppose that the author of the paper tested his hypothesis merely by showing that after two hours of listening to a set of three persuasive communications, most subjects agreed with the viewpoint advocated by those communications. If the author has not shown, however, that at least some of his subjects disagreed with the viewpoints of the communications prior to the test, then the conclusion does not follow from the data.

Drawing Upon Personal Experience. Your own experience can be a valuable source of ideas. You may have found, for example, that you are more likely to conform to group norms if you are only marginally accepted by a peer group than if you are fully accepted by it. Or you may have found that you remember more material if you form vivid images of the words to be remembered than if you merely try to remember the words. Hypotheses such as these should be followed up by a literature review investigating what research has already been done. Even if your particular idea has been investigated, you may then think of another, related idea that has not yet been tested.

Selecting Independent Variables

After you have come up with an idea, you need a way to test it. In order to test the idea, you need one or more independent variables. Independent variables are those variables that are manipulated by the experimenter. In the persuasibility experiment described above, possible independent variables include (a) amount of exposure to persuasive communications, (b) content of persuasive communications, and (c) level of agreement between subjects' initial attitudes and the position advocated by the persuasive communications. Once you have chosen your independent variable(s), you must decide how many and what level of the independent variable(s) to use. For example, you might include in a persuasibility experiment (a) three levels of exposure to the persuasive communications – no exposure, 10 min of exposure, and 1 hr of exposure – and (b) two communications – one message dealing with capital punishment and one message dealing with compulsory use of seat belts in cars.

In most experiments, there are a large number of potentially interesting independent variables, but it is possible to choose only a small fraction of these. In most experimental designs, each time you add an independent variable to your experiment, you increase the size of your experiment multiplicatively. You must therefore choose your independent variables with care. In the persuasibility experiment, the type font in which the persuasive communications are presented is not likely to affect the outcome of the experiment, and hence would be a poor choice of an independent variable. The medium of communication, oral or written, might affect the outcome of the experiment, and hence would be a possible choice. The amount of exposure to the persuasive communications is almost certain to affect the outcome of the experiment, and hence is a very good choice.

In selecting independent variables, there is usually a tradeoff between experimental control and ecological validity. Experimental control refers to the ease with which the experimenter can manipulate and later monitor the effects of the independent variables. Ecological validity refers to the generalizability of the obtained results to real-world situations. Total loss of experimental control can lead to uninterpretable results. Disregard of ecological validity can lead to trivial results. Researchers differ widely in the importance they assign to each of these items: Everyone must strike some sort of balance between the two.

Selecting Dependent Variables

In addition to choosing one or more independent variables, you must select one or more dependent variables. The dependent variable is the variable affected by (dependent upon) the independent variables. It serves as the outcome to be measured. Whereas it is common to choose more than one independent variable in a single experiment, it is relatively uncommon to choose more than one dependent variable. When multiple dependent variables are used, they are usually studied separately, without much attempt to interrelate the outcomes. The major reason for psychologists' reluctance to deal with multiple outcomes is the greater difficulty involved in statistical analysis, not the inability of multiple outcomes to provide more meaningful data than single outcomes.

In most experiments, there are at least several possible dependent variables of interest to choose from, so the choice must be made carefully. In the persuasibility experiment, two possible dependent variables are (a) response to an opinion questionnaire administered at the end of the experimental session, and (b) willingness 1 month later to join a citizens' lobbying group devoted to the cause advocated by the communication. Note that the first dependent variable measures immediate overt opinion changes within the context of the experiment, whereas the latter dependent variable measures delayed covert opinion change outside the context of the experiment. Ideally, an experiment will include both kinds of measures. If only one is to be chosen, the experimenter must evaluate an important tradeoff that frequently confronts psychological researchers. The first measured outcome is much more likely than the second to be influenced by the experimental manipulation, but it is also of much less practical importance. Even if the opinion questionnaire administered at the end of the experiment shows a significant effect of the experimental treatment, one has no assurance that the effect will last for any long period of time, or even for any time beyond the conclusion of the experimental session. The second measured outcome is of considerable practical interest, but in relying upon it, the experimenter may be throwing away any chance of an observable experimental effect. The experimenter must therefore decide upon a dependent variable that gives a reasonable chance of obtaining an outcome that is both statistically and practically significant.

Deciding Upon Between-Subjects and Within-Subjects Variables

Each independent variable can be studied either between subjects or within subjects. A between-subjects independent variable is one in which a given subject receives only one level of the experimental treatment. A within-subjects independent variable is one in which a given subject receives all levels of the experimental treatment.

Return again to the persuasibility experiment. If both independent variables were between-subjects, then each subject would receive (a) either no exposure, 10 min of exposure, or 1 hr of exposure to (b) either the communication on capital punishment or that on compulsory use of seat belts. Because there are three levels of the first independent variable and two levels of the second, there are 3×2 levels in all, or six different experimental groups, each composed of different subjects. If both independent variables were within subjects, each subject would receive both persuasive communications, and would be tested before receiving the communications, 10 min after receiving the communications, and 1 hr after receiving the communications for her current opinion on each.

In some cases, it is easy to decide whether to test a particular variable between subjects or within subjects. In other cases, however, the decision is a difficult one for the experimenter to make, and a potentially consequential one. The experimenter must evaluate a delicate tradeoff. On the one hand, earlier within-subjects treatments may spoil the subject for later treatments. In other words, the subjects receiving one experimental treatment may have unforeseen consequences for their responses to subsequent treatments. On the other hand, within-subjects designs guarantee matching of subjects across treatment conditions, because the subjects are the same. This matching can be particularly important when there are relatively small numbers of subjects.

Consider again the design of the persuasibility experiment. Suppose we administer the three opinion questionnaires – before treatment, 10 min after treatment, and 1 hr after treatment – to the same subjects. We run the risk that the mere answering of an earlier questionnaire will influence subjects' responses to later questionnaires. This influence can contaminate the results and render equivocal any interpretation of them. Suppose that instead we administer the three opinion questionnaires to three different groups of subjects. We then have no way of knowing that our groups are matched in important ways. They may differ in initial level of agreement with the persuasive communication; or they may differ in persuasibility (so that some are more susceptible by nature than others to persuasion attempts); or they may differ in the speed at which they assimilate new information, and hence in the speed at which their attitudes are affected by new information. The list can go on ad infinitum. Although random sampling of subjects provides some protection against poor matching of groups, the adequacy of this protection depends upon the size of the sample. Unless groups are quite large, protection may be inadequate. With six different groups in the full design of the persuasibility experiment, it is unlikely that very large groups can be obtained in a reasonably economical way.

A compromise can be worked out whereby all subjects receive the opinion survey before treatment, but only some receive it after 10 min of treatment, whereas others receive it after 1 hr. This compromise, however, does not solve the basic dilemma, because the subjects' receipt of the pretest can still affect their performance on the subsequent test. In deciding whether to test a particular variable between subjects or within subjects, the experimenter must decide which kind of risk she is more willing to take.

Deciding How Data Will Be Analyzed

Major decisions about data analysis should be made prior to the collection of data. There are two reasons why these decisions should be made in advance. First, statistical tests must be interpreted more cautiously if decided upon post hoc. As it is sometimes said, everyone has 20/20 hindsight. Second, if major decisions about data analysis are not made in advance, the experimenter runs the risk of finding later that the experimental design does not permit him to analyze the data the way he wants to, or to analyze the data at all. Decisions about specific kinds of data analysis require statistical background that is beyond the scope of this book.

Selecting Subjects

Three major decisions must be made in selection of subjects. First, from what population will subjects be selected? Second, how will subjects be selected from this population? Third, how many subjects will be selected?

The population from which subjects are selected is the population to which the experimental results will be generalizable. Hence, if one is interested in making generalizations to the general population of the United States, then one must select a sample that is representative of the general population of the United States. If one is interested in a population of gifted children, then one must select a sample representative of gifted children. The question of generalizability of results is often quietly placed in the background of an experimental report, if it is discussed at all, because most experiments are conducted on samples that are not representative of the population of interest. Many of the experiments conducted today use college students as subjects, although the experimenters' intent is to generalize the result to the population of adult Americans (or even to adults all over the world).

One faces a tradeoff in deciding upon a population from which to draw subjects. On the one hand, researchers usually want to generalize their results to as broad a population as possible. On the other hand, subjects are much easier to obtain from some populations than from others. College and university students are often readily available, whereas other groups of adults are much harder to corral into the laboratory.

Subjects can be selected in any number of ways from the population. The two most common models of selection are the random and the stratified sample. In a random sampling procedure, the experimenter selects individuals from the population at random. In a stratified sampling procedure, the experimenter selects individuals in a way that assures that major subdivisions of the population are represented in some proportion, usually the population proportion. In practice, it is almost never possible to obtain a purely random or stratified sample, because the entire population is not available to the experimenter. The subjects who are available usually form a biased sample of the population from which they are drawn. Even if one's population is college students, for example, the sample of college students at any one university is inevitably going to be biased.

Decisions about numbers of subjects are usually made on the basis of two considerations. First, how many subjects can be tested feasibly, given the constraints of time, money, and subject availability? Second, how many subjects are needed to show statistical significance for an effect of a certain magnitude? This latter consideration involves statistical concepts beyond the scope of this book. The basic idea, though, is that in order for a small treatment effect to be statistically significant, a large sample is needed. The greater the magnitude of the treatment effect, the smaller the sample size needed to show statistical significance.

Choosing Experimental Materials

Four considerations must be taken into account in choosing materials for an experiment:

1. Do the materials represent a reasonable sample of the universe of materials to which one wants to generalize?
2. Are there enough materials to obtain generalizable measurements?
3. Are the materials suitable for the subjects to whom they will be administered?
4. Are the materials suitable for testing the hypothesis?

Students and psychologists alike tend to pay too little attention to the generalizability of experimental materials. General conclusions about a broad universe of materials are often drawn on the basis of an experiment or several experiments using just one kind of material. Suppose, for example, that an investigator is interested in how people solve syllogisms. A subject is presented with two premises, called the major premise and the minor premise, and a conclusion. The subject's task is to say whether the conclusion follows logically from the premises. A simple syllogism would take the form:

1. All B are C.   (Major Premise)
   All A are B.   (Minor Premise)
   All A are C.   (Conclusion)

As an investigator, you might vary structural properties of the syllogism. For example, you might substitute for the major premise statements like *Some B are C, No B are C,* or *Some B are not C.*

Your theory of how people solve syllogisms, however, could not be complete unless you took into account content as well as structure. Suppose, for example, that we leave the structure of the syllogism unchanged, varying only its content. Compare the difficulty of the following two syllogisms with each other and with the syllogism above:

2. All birds are animals.
   All canaries are birds.
   All canaries are animals.
3. All birds are canaries.
   All animals are birds.
   All animals are canaries.

You will probably find, as others have found before you, that the content of the syllogism greatly affects its difficulty. Most people find syllogisms like (2) easier to comprehend than syllogisms like (3) because the premises of the former syllogism conform to real-world experience, whereas the premises of the latter syllogism violate it. A complete theory of syllogistic reasoning would have to take into account these effects of content, something no theory yet does. The general point, of course, is that no theory can be accepted with confidence unless it has been shown to explain data for a wide variety of experimental materials.

It is important to have not only a relatively broad sampling of materials, but a relatively large sampling as well. The syllogism experiment would be unimpressive if it had three different kinds of content, but only one syllogism of each kind. In order to obtain reliable measurements, it is usually necessary to have at least several replications of each kind of item.

The investigator must take care that her experimental materials are suitable for the target subject population. Syllogisms such as the ones above would be suitable for an adult subject population, but not for a population of first-grade children. If these children failed to solve syllogisms like the ones above, the investigator would be unable to determine whether the failure was due to inability to reason syllogistically or due to inability to comprehend the materials. The investigator might use concrete play materials instead of verbal ones. For example, she might show the children plastic replicas of animals and then demonstrate to them that all the elephants are gray and all the animals with trunks are elephants. The children would then have to indicate whether all the animals with trunks are gray. Special care would have to be taken to ensure that the children understood the nature of the task.

The materials one uses must be appropriate to the hypothesis under investigation. Suppose, for example, that an investigator wants to test the hypothesis that syllogisms with counterfactual conclusions are more difficult to solve than syllogisms with factual conclusions. The following two sets of syllogisms would provide poor tests of this hypothesis:

FACTUAL CONCLUSIONS	COUNTERFACTUAL CONCLUSIONS
1. All integers are rational.	1. All rational numbers are natural numbers.
All natural numbers are <u>integers.</u>	All integers are rational <u>numbers.</u>
All natural numbers are integers.	All integers are natural numbers.
2. All sunny days are enjoyable days.	2. All sunny days are unenjoyable days.
<u>All bright days are sunny days.</u>	<u>All cloudy days are sunny days.</u>
All bright days are enjoyable days.	All cloudy days are unenjoyable days.

The first syllogism is inappropriate because most subjects (except, perhaps, in a population of mathematicians) would not realize which syllogism has a factual conclusion and which has a counterfactual conclusion. The second syllogism is inappropriate because the conclusions (as well as the premises) are matters of opinion; although some people might agree with the first conclusion and disagree with the second conclusion, these agreements and disagreements are not over matters of fact.

Choosing a Means of Presenting Experimental Materials

Experimental materials usually can be presented in many forms. The form of presentation generally is determined largely by convenience, because little is known about the effects of form of presentation upon performance. Investigators usually assume the effects of form of presentation upon performance will be trivial. Suppose, for example, that an investigator is interested in the effect of concreteness upon free recall of a list of words. His hypothesis is that more concrete words, like *banana,* will be better recalled than more abstract words, like *freedom.* In order to test this hypothesis, the investigator compares recall of two lists of words, one concrete and the other abstract.

The list of words might be presented either visually or auditorily. If the words are presented visually, they might be presented via flash cards, slides, or a computer terminal. If the words are presented auditorily, they might be presented via word of mouth or tape recorder. Modality of presentation (visual or auditory) and vehicle of presentation (e.g., slides or tape recorder) within modality might affect level of recall, but it is assumed that this effect will be constant across treatment conditions. Thus, if on the average two fewer concrete words are recalled when auditory rather than visual presentation is used, it is assumed that on the average two fewer abstract words will be recalled as well. The investigator is not likely to use both auditory and visual presentation in order to show generality of the hypothesis to both modalities. In some experiments – for example, experiments on vision or audition – modality of presentation will be a critical variable. In most experiments, however, it is considered relatively unimportant. Investigators turn their attention to variables more likely to influence their results. In preparing experimental materials, you may *not* reproduce copyrighted material, such as tests or reading passages, without permission. Doing so subjects you to the possibility of legal action against you.

Writing Directions

Once you have decided upon the experimental task and materials, you have to write directions telling subjects what is expected of them. It is essential that the directions be clear and complete, because unclear or incomplete instructions can result in subjects doing a task different from that you intend. The directions may be presented auditorily or visually. I usually have the experimenter present the directions aloud while the subject reads them silently. Subjects thereby are exposed to the directions in two modalities.

In the free-recall experiment, the following directions might be used:

Directions for Free-Recall Task

In this task, the experimenter will read aloud a list of words. You should listen carefully to these words. After the experimenter has completed reading the list, he will pause, and then say the word *Recall*. At this point, you should recall as many words as you can from the list in any order you wish. Write your answers on the sheet in front of you. If you are not sure of an item – guess. Your recall will be scored for the number of words correctly recalled.

If you have any questions, please ask them now.

Deciding Upon a Means of Scoring Data

Because scoring can be time-consuming, the layout of subjects' response sheets or booklets should be planned carefully in advance. An easy-to-score layout can save many hours of work later on. If the subjects' responses are simple – letters, numbers, words – their answers usually can be recorded in successive columns of each page. An easily readable format such as this one will facilitate scoring, possibly enabling you to devise a stencil key that can be placed either next to or over each column. Stencil keys are frequently used in scoring objective tests and can be used to equal advantage in scoring of experimental data.

If the data will be entered for subsequent computer analysis, it is wise to show your answer sheet layout to the data-entry person. If the layout is easily readable, the person (who may be you) may be able to enter the data directly from the answer sheets, bypassing the time-consuming step of coding the data.

Writing a Consent Form

Several years ago, the National Institutes of Health (NIH) started re-quiring experimenters supported by NIH funds to have all participants sign statements of informed consent prior to participation in experi-ments. In the case of children, parents were required to sign. More re-cently, the National Science Foundation (NSF) has also started requir-ing this step for the protection of human subjects. Experimenters are also required to have their experiments approved by a human subjects committee at their college or university prior to conducting the experi-ments. In view of the widespread concern today with the protection of subjects, it is probably wise to use consent forms even for informal class projects. A sample consent form (in this case, for an experiment on decision making in groups) is shown in this chapter section.

The consent form must be modified to meet the needs of each partic-ular experiment. The forms must always include, however, (a) a state-ment of informed consent, (b) sufficient information about the ex-periment so that the participant's consent is truly informed, and (c) the participant's signature and the date.

The general purpose of the experiment is explained in item 1. I pre-fer to leave this explanation vague. First, a detailed explanation might affect the experimental outcome. If, for example, subjects were told that the experiment was designed to investigate interpersonal relations among group members, the subjects might be more cautious in the ways they related to other group members. Second, because subjects are given a detailed debriefing at the end of the experiment, a lengthy description of the experiment at the beginning is redundant.

Subjects must be warned if there are any known expected discom-forts. In an experiment requiring a subject to wear lenses that distort his vision, for example, the subject may experience brief discomfort after the lenses are removed. If you have no experience on the basis of which to draw a conclusion, or very little experience, then you are obliged to say so.

I include item 4 because (a) subjects are sometimes uneasy about participating in psychology experiments, expecting to be tricked, and (b) I never use disguised procedures. If you sometimes use disguised

DECLARATION OF INFORMED CONSENT

I give my informed consent to participate in this study of how people make decisions in groups. I consent to publication of study results so long as the information is anonymous and disguised so that no identification can be made. I further understand that although a record will be kept of my having participated in the experiment, all experimental data collected from my participation will be identified by number only.

1. I have been informed that my participation in this experiment will involve my joining a group faced with a decision to make.
2. I have been informed that the general purpose of this experiment is to study processes used by groups in making different kinds of decisions.
3. I have been informed that there are no known expected discomforts or risks involved in my participation in this experiment. This judgment is based upon a relatively large body of research with people solving problems of a similar nature.
4. I have been informed that there are no "disguised" procedures in this experiment. All procedures can be taken at face value.
5. I have been informed that the investigator will gladly answer any questions regarding the procedures of this study when the experimental session is completed.
6. I have been informed that I am free to withdraw from the experiment at any time without penalty of any kind.

Concerns about any aspects of this study may be referred to the Chairman, Committee on the Protection of Human Subjects, Imaginary University, Room 107, Memorial Hall.

_____   _____
(Experimenter)   (Experimental Participant)

                                        _____
                                                          (Date)

procedures and sometimes do not, however, you may be reluctant to use such an item, because its absence might be interpreted as implying the existence of disguised procedures.

Emphasis upon the technical details of obtaining informed consent can obscure the reason for obtaining it. The important question the experimenter must face is whether her experiment places the subject at risk. If so, then the experimenter must examine the risk/benefit ratio: Do the benefits of the research outweigh its risks? Students should consult faculty advisers for additional perspectives on whether subjects' rights are being protected, in particular, their rights to personal privacy and confidentiality. Often, the research will have to be reviewed further by a departmental or university committee in order to assure that subjects receive adequate personal protection.

Writing a Debriefing Sheet

After the experiment is over, subjects often want to know the purpose of the experiment and the various experimental procedures. Experimenters have a moral obligation, and in some universities, a legal obligation, to debrief subjects about the experiment. The debriefing should be informative and nontechnical. It should inform the subjects of what the experiment is supposed to test, how the experiment tests it, and what the anticipated outcomes are. Debriefing may be oral or written, although I prefer written debriefing because subjects as well as experimenters then have a record of having participated in the experiment. The following is a sample debriefing, in this case for the experiment on decision making in groups.

Before debriefing your subjects, it is wise to have your subjects debrief you. After the experiment is over, you should ask your subjects to tell you (preferably in writing) how they went about doing the experimental task. Subjects' comments can provide you with insights that you otherwise would not have obtained.

Testing Pilot Subjects

Before starting final data collection, you should consider testing pilot subjects. Pilot testing enables you to spot flaws in the experiment before you actually conduct it. You may find that your directions are unclear, that you have not allowed enough time for your subjects to complete the task, or that the task is too difficult for your subjects. The list of possible flaws is endless. Pilot testing is like an insurance policy. By making a small investment in advance, you can save yourself potentially enormous costs later on. The more careful the pilot testing (the larger the insurance premium), the less likely you are to end up

EXPERIMENTAL DEBRIEFING
DECISION MAKING IN GROUPS

The purpose of this experiment was to further our understanding of decision making in groups. The hypothesis tested by the experiment was that groups will make faster decisions if they are explicitly warned in advance that interpersonal frictions, rivalries, and animosities can impede the group decision-making process, and that therefore group members should take special care not to let these impediments hinder them at the decision-making task.

Four groups participated in the experiment. In two groups, subjects were asked to decide whether the United States should sell nuclear material for "peaceful purposes" to countries that have the capacity to manufacture atomic bombs. In two other groups, subjects were asked to decide in a rational way which two group members would receive a $2 bonus at the end of the experiment. They were informed that the other members would receive no bonus and that the decision could not be made using a random selection procedure (such as drawing lots). In one "nuclear material" group and in one "$2 bonus" group, subjects were warned in advance not to let interpersonal frictions, rivalries, and animosities impede their decision-making process. The other two groups received no warning of any kind.

It is expected that the forewarned group will reach a decision faster than the unwarned groups, regardless of whether they are making a decision about "nuclear material" or about the "$2 bonus." The purpose of using two different kinds of decisions was to show the generality of the instructional effect. The experiment is also being repeated four times with different groups of subjects in order to show that the instructional effect is a reliable one. The four repetitions of the experiment will be combined for data analysis.

If you have any questions, please feel free to ask them of the experimenter. If you would like a summary of the results when the research is completed, please leave your name and address with the experimenter.

Thank you for participating.

(Experimenter)

with disastrous results (the greater the insurance coverage). I have found that there is almost always some potential problem that is uncovered during pilot testing.

EXECUTING EXPERIMENTAL RESEARCH

If you have planned your experiment carefully, execution of the experiment should be straightforward. You should make sure, as much as possible, that extraneous variables are kept constant from session to session. Thus, things like lighting, ventilation, and seating arrangement should not be varied. Outside noise should be minimized. If the experiment involves a number of separate parts, you may want to keep a list so that you do not forget any of them. Experimenters, like subjects, sometimes get distracted; and once data are lost, they are difficult or impossible to replace.

Use the experimental sessions as an informal opportunity to gain insights into how subjects perform the experimental tasks. Subjects occasionally make comments about what they are doing or how they are doing it. Also be on the lookout for nonroutine problems – a subject who stayed up the night before writing a paper and can barely keep his eyes open, a subject who is not paying attention to the experimental task, a flickering lightbulb, an erratic stopwatch. You should write down notes on any unusual problems, and try to correct them. The subject who stayed up all night should be rescheduled; the subject who is not paying attention should be told politely to pay attention; the lightbulb should be replaced; the stopwatch should be fixed or replaced. You will collect much better data if you are aware of problems and correct them immediately.

In theory, the experimenter should be blind to assignment of subjects to treatments, so that any prior expectations about treatment effects will be unable to influence the experimental results. In practice, the experimenter often knows which subjects have been assigned to which treatments. In reading the word lists for the free-recall experiment, for example, the experimenter will probably recognize whether the words are abstract or concrete. If the experimenter observes the groups in the decision-making experiment, he will know whether or not he has previously warned them about impediments to group decision making. A voluminous literature exists on experimenter effects upon research results, and there is no question that the experimenter can influence the outcome in subtle ways. The experimenter might read the list of abstract words just a little more quickly or less clearly than the list of concrete words, or he might differentially reinforce the decision-making groups with facial expressions. You have a responsibility as experimenter to give your hypotheses the fairest possible test. Subtle and not so subtle experimenter effects undermine the interpretability and credibility of your results. It is therefore essential that you take care not to influence the outcome of your experiment through incidental and (presumably) unintended actions.

ANALYZING DATA FROM EXPERIMENTAL RESEARCH

After the experiment is completed, you are ready to analyze your data. Techniques for analyzing data are beyond the scope of this book, although some simple exploratory techniques are presented in Chapter 8. Two unusually lucid textbooks covering elementary statistical techniques are Minium (1978) and Runyon and Haber (1991). Hays (1973) is more advanced, presenting much of the theory underlying the statistical techniques. A standard reference for analysis-of-variance designs is Winer (1991), and some of these designs are also presented in Hays's book. For description and explanation of multivariate statistical techniques, I recommend Cooley and Lohnes (1971), Tatsuoka (1971), or Morrison (1976). The books named in this section are listed in order of difficulty. Only the first two books and possibly the third are suitable for most undergraduates. The last three books are suitable only for advanced graduate students. For an introduction to recent developments in statistics that are helpful for psychologists, see Lovie (1986) and the other statistical references in Chapter 8.

REPORTING EXPERIMENTAL RESEARCH

Once you have analyzed your data and thought about your results, you are ready to report them. I suggest that you write an outline prior to

writing the paper, just as you would if you were writing a library research paper. A standard format for the outline looks like this:

Title
Author's Name and Byline Abstract
I. Introduction
II. Method
    A. Materials
    B. Apparatus
    C. Subjects
    D. Design
    E. Procedure
III. Results
IV. Discussion
References
Author Notes
Footnotes
Appendix

Title

The title should inform the reader simply and concisely what the
paper is about. It is important that the title be self-explanatory. Readers will come across the title in other papers that refer to your paper
and in *Psychological Abstracts,* and they may have to decide on the
basis of the title alone whether they want to read your paper. The title
should include keywords, for example, the theoretical issue to which
the paper is addressed, the dependent variable(s), and the independent variable(s). Keywords are important because the title will be stored
in information-retrieval networks that rely on such words to determine the relevance of your study to someone else's research interests.
For the same reason, it is important to avoid irrelevant and misleading words, because such words may spuriously lead an investigator
uninterested in your topic to your paper. The title should not exceed
12 to 15 words in length.

Author's Name and Institutional Affiliation

Write your name as you wish it to be recognized professionally.
Thus, you might choose John Jones, John J. Jones, John James Jones,
J. Jones, J. J. Jones, or J. James Jones. A first name, middle initial, and

last name is the most commonly used form of presentation. Omit titles, such as B.A., M.A., Ph.D., Lover of Mankind, etc. Underneath your name, write your institutional affiliation: Podunk College, Fink University, etc. If you have changed your affiliation since you did the research, list the old affiliation under your name and the new affiliation in a footnote. A dual affiliation is listed under your name only if both institutions contributed financially to the study. If you are unaffiliated with any institution, list your city and state.

Abstract

The abstract summarizes your paper. Its length should be 100–120 words for a report of an empirical study, and 75–100 words for a theoretical article or literature review. The abstract, like the title, should be self-explanatory and self-contained, because it is also used for indexing by information-retrieval networks. The abstract should include (a) the major hypotheses, (b) a summary of the method, including a description of the materials, apparatus, subjects, design, and procedure, (c) a synopsis of the main results, and (d) the conclusions drawn from the results. Do not include in the abstract any information that is not included in the body of the paper. Because you will not know until you are done with the outline what information you will include, you are well advised to defer writing the abstract until after you have otherwise completed the outline, or even the paper itself.

Remember that most people will read your abstract only if your title interests them, and will read your article only if your abstract interests them. It is therefore essential that the abstract interest your reader. You can interest the reader by showing that the problem is an important one, that your hypotheses about the problem are insightful ones, and that you will test these hypotheses in a convincing way.

Introduction

The introduction orients the reader to the research. In the paper, it does not receive a heading, because its function is obvious. It should answer four basic questions:

1. What previous research led up to your research?
2. What does your research add to this previous research?
3. Why is the addition made by your research important or interesting?
4. How is the addition made?

The introduction usually opens with a brief review of the literature most pertinent to your research. A lengthy literature review is inappropriate, except, sometimes, for theses and course assignments. If a voluminous literature exists on the topic, cite a literature review to which the reader can refer for further information if it is wanted. Assume in your review, however, that the reader is familiar with the general area of research. The reader's main interest is in what you have to contribute. She is interested in the previous literature only as it relates directly to your contribution.

Once you have told the reader what is already known, you must relate what still needs to be known, that is, what you intend to find out. Tell the reader not only what you intend to contribute, but also what the nature of the contribution is. Does your research resolve an issue that has been unresolved in the past? Or does it deal with an issue that others have not thought about? Or does it attempt to correct an artifact in previous investigations? This information will give the reader a good idea of what you view as the purpose of your study.

Next, you should show the reader that the contribution is a potentially interesting or important one. Why have people paid attention to this particular issue? Or why is the new issue one to which people should pay attention? Or does an artifact in previous experimental research really undermine conclusions that previous investigators have drawn? Remember that a major purpose of the introduction is to interest the reader in your paper and that your explanation of why your study is potentially important can motivate the reader either to continue the article or to toss it aside.

Finally, you should tell the reader how you intend to make your contribution. Sketch your experimental design, leaving a detailed description for the *Design* section later in the paper. Show how your design relates to the theoretical issues you address. It is important to convince your reader at this point that your experiment actually does test the hypothesis you want to investigate.

Method

The *Method* section tells the reader how the experiment was conducted. You should include just enough information so that the reader could replicate your study. If you include less information, other investigators will be unable to verify your results. If you include more information, you risk boring and possibly losing the reader in needless detail. When you are uncertain as to whether a piece of information is essential, it is better to err in the direction of including too much rather than too little.

The section describing method is usually divided into a number of subsections. Although use of these subsections is optional, it usually simplifies and clarifies the presentation for the reader. The subsections most often used are *Materials, Apparatus, Participants, Design,* and *Procedure,* although not necessarily in that order. The term *subjects* is best applied only to nonhuman organisms involved in a study. It also can be used when referring to human individuals in the abstract or adults unable to give informed consent (e.g., adults with severe dementia). Use the order that best conveys the methods used in your particular experiment.

Materials. You should describe in this subsection the stimulus material used in the experiment. Sufficient detail should be given so that the reader could generate the same or equivalent stimuli. If the stimuli are unconventional, you might reproduce examples in a table or figure.

Apparatus. The apparatus used in the experiment should be described in this subsection. Present a general description of the apparatus, including any details that might affect the outcome of the experiment. If the apparatus is a standard piece of manufactured equipment, the name and model number will substitute for most details, because the reader can then learn the details from the manufacturer. If the apparatus is unusual, you might want to photograph it and present it as a figure. This entire subsection can be omitted if no apparatus is used.

Participants. You should describe in this subsection (a) the total number of participants, (b) the number of participants receiving each treatment, (c) the population from which the participants were drawn, (d) how participants were selected, and (e) the circumstances under which the participants participated (e.g., for pay, for course credit, as a favor to the experimenter). In describing the participation population, include any details that might affect the outcome of the experiment – sex, ethnic or socially defined racial groups, age, education, etc. The nature of the experiment will determine what other attributes of the participants might be relevant. The term *subject* can be used for nonhuman organisms or when referring to humans in the abstract, as opposed to particular individuals.

Design. This subsection should include a description of (a) the independent variable(s), (b) the dependent variable(s), (c) the various experimental and control groups and how they were constituted, and (d) the way in which subjects were assigned to groups. Be sure to indicate which variables were between-subjects and which within-subjects. This section is sometimes omitted, with the relevant information divided among the other sections. I prefer to include the section, because it provides the reader with a compact overview of how the experiment was put together.

Procedure. This subsection should describe what happened to the subjects in the experimental sessions from the time they walked in to the time they walked out. A chronological account is usually best. Paraphrase directions to subjects, unless they were unconventional, in which case you might want to present them verbatim. Because you assume that your readers have a general knowledge of the relevant literature, you can also assume that they are familiar with standard testing procedures. Therefore, describe such procedures more generally, always being sure to include any details that plausibly might affect the outcome of the experiment.

Results

This section should include (a) descriptive statistics, which summarize the data in a readily comprehensible form, and (b) inferential statistics, which test the likelihood that the obtained results were not due to chance. Techniques you used for data analysis should be reported with sufficient clarity that someone else could replicate them based on your description. If you plan to present a large number of results, divide this section into subsections. The particular subsections used will depend upon the nature of the experiment. It is expected that authors will provide effect sizes as well as significance values. The field is divided regarding the value of conventional significance testing, but it neverthneless is the most commonly used basis for reporting results.

As in the previous sections, you should make an effort to report the right amount of information, neither underreporting nor overreporting your results. And as in the previous sections, it is usually better to report a result if you are uncertain whether to include it. The criteria you should follow are to report (a) all data that are directly relevant to your hypotheses and (b) other data that may be peripheral to your hypotheses but that are of particular interest in their own right. Do not present data for individual subjects unless (a) you used an $N = 1$ (single-subject) design, (b) the individual data show trends that are masked in the group data, or (c) your hypotheses are relevant to each individual's data rather than to the group data.

The order in which results are reported is of critical importance. Authors often report first those results that are of most interest or relevance to the hypotheses being tested. Less interesting or relevant results are reported later. You may wish to report first a general conclusion or interpretation, followed by some descriptive statistics that support your assertion, followed only at the end by the inferential statistics that buttress the conclusion. This style of presentation often makes for more interesting reading than does a melange of facts and statistics, followed by an obscurely placed conclusion that the bored reader may never even reach, having given up on your article pages before.

It is often convenient to summarize your data in the form of one or more tables or figures. In planning tables and figures, keep in mind that (a) you should not repeat in the text information that is contained in tables and figures, and (b) tables and figures should be largely self-explanatory, although you should certainly discuss them in the text. Two more considerations are relevant, but only if you plan to submit a paper to a journal: (a) large numbers of tables and figures are discouraged (because they are expensive to reproduce in journals), and (b) one or two sentences can often summarize data that initially seem to require a table or figure.

In deciding between presentation of data in a table versus a figure, you face a tradeoff. On the one hand, figures tend to give the reader a better global sense of the data; on the other hand, tables convey information to the reader more precisely. In general, tables are preferred, but your own judgment of what best conveys your message should be the arbiter of how the data are presented.

In reporting tests of statistical significance (this paragraph may be skipped by those unfamiliar with such tests), include (a) the name of the test, (b) the value of the test statistic, (c) the degrees of freedom (if relevant), and (d) the significance level of the test. Readers should also be informed whether or not the test is directional, and what the direction of the effect was. Assume that your reader has a knowledge of basic statistics, but describe briefly the assumptions and theory underlying unconventional tests, giving if possible a reference to which the reader can refer.

Discussion

This section should include (a) an explanation of how well your data fit your original hypotheses, (b) a statement of your conclusions, and (c) a discussion of theoretical and, if relevant, practical implications of the results. It is appropriate to include in the discussion a consideration of why the findings are important, why the topic itself and the problem under it are important, why you chose the level of analysis you did, and how, if at all, the findings can be applied.

You should open the discussion with a general statement of how well the data fit your hypotheses. If the data fit your hypotheses, your task is straightforward. If the data do not fit your hypotheses, then you can approach the data from either of two angles. One angle is an acceptance of the data as uninterpretable; the other angle is an interpretation of the data as fitting hypotheses different from those you originally suggested. In either case, you should be as clear in describing lack of fit as you are in describing fit.

If your data are uninterpretable or only partially interpretable, say so. Convoluted explanations of unexpected data are easily recognized as rationalizations of failures. If you have good reason to believe that some aspect of your experiment was responsible for the uninterpretable results, say so briefly and let matters stand there. Do not, however, waste space listing possible reasons for the uninterpretable results: Such lists can go on forever and are boring to read.

If your data are unexpected but interpretable, it is permissible to interpret them in light of new, reformulated hypotheses. You must make clear, however, that your explanation is post hoc and speculative. There is a fine line between reformulation of hypotheses and empty rationalization, so you must convince your reader that your post hoc explanation provides a compelling account of the data.

After you have discussed the fit of your data to the original hypotheses, and any new hypotheses you might have, a concise statement of your conclusions should be presented. Because the conclusions are the major message of your paper, you should phrase them with great care, thereby assuring that the reader will interpret them as you intended.

Finally, you should discuss theoretical and possibly practical implications of the results. If you have drawn conclusions different from your original hypotheses, you might suggest ways in which these conclusions could be verified in future research. Do not merely say, however, that future research will be needed to clarify the issues, without giving the reader any inkling of what form this research might take. Every reader knows that more research can be done on any topic. What the reader wants to learn from you is what direction this research should take.

An Alternative: Results and Discussion

The *Results* and *Discussion* sections are sometimes combined into one section called *Results and Discussion,* especially when each section is relatively short. I recommend this combination even when the individual sections are not short. The problem with a *Results* section standing by itself is that it is difficult to follow and makes for dry reading. The reader is confronted with masses of statistics without being told what the statistics mean or why they are important. Meaningful discussion is deferred until later.

Reconsider our discussion in the previous chapter of thematic versus nonthematic organization. In the present context, one's choices are these:

NONTHEMATIC ORGANIZATION	THEMATIC ORGANIZATION
III. Results	**III.** Results and Discussion
A. Presentation of Result A	**A.** Result A
B. Presentation of Result B	**1.** Presentation
C. Presentation of Result C	**2.** Discussion
IV. Discussion	**B.** Result B
A. Discussion of Result A	**1.** Presentation
B. Discussion of Result B	**2.** Discussion
C. Discussion of Result C	**C.** Result C
	1. Presentation
	2. Discussion

In the format on the left, the reader will almost certainly have to refer back to the results from the discussion, unless the results are represented in the *Discussion* section, an undesirable redundancy. The reader is unlikely to remember all the results from the *Results* section if they have been presented in an unmotivated fashion with no interpretation to make them meaningful.

In the format on the right, there is no need for backward page turning. The results are discussed as they are presented, so that the reader can understand why they are important when they are presented. He does not have to wait until later to discover why the author bothered to present those particular results and not others. Consequently, he can form a more integrated and coherent representation of the author's results-discussion package.

If the thematic organization on the right is easier to follow than the nonthematic organization on the left, why has the organization on the left been the more widely used? I suspect it is because of a tacit fear that in a joint presentation of results and discussion, the discussion will somehow contaminate the results: Combining the sections will result in a blurring of the distinction between objective and subjective information. This argument, although understandable, is weak. Even a slightly skilled writer can interweave data and discussion of the data in a way that makes clear the distinction between the two. A writer can, of course, be dishonest and try to pass off his opinions as facts. But such a writer can distort his data regardless of the way in which the paper is organized.

Regardless of which organization one chooses, related results may be presented and discussed in clusters to increase the meaningfulness of the presentation. For example, Results A and B might be clustered together in the following ways:

NONTHEMATIC ORGANIZATION	THEMATIC ORGANIZATION
III. Results	**III.** Results and Discussion
A. Presentation of Result Cluster (A,B)	**A.** Result Cluster (A,B)
1. Presentation	
B. Presentation of Result C	**2.** Discussion
IV. Discussion	**B.** Result C
A. Discussion of Result Cluster (A,B)	**1.** Presentation
	2. Discussion
B. Discussion of Result C	

References

The references provide a complete list of the sources you cite in your paper. The format of the references is the same as for the author cards (see Chapter 2), and is discussed further in Chapters 7 and 9. Be sure your references are accurate. Incorrect citations are a disservice to readers and show sloppy scholarship.

Appendix

An appendix is rarely used in psychological papers, although it is valuable in certain cases. It is appropriate for (a) computer programs designed explicitly for your research, unavailable elsewhere, and possibly valuable to others, (b) unpublished tests, (c) mathematical proofs that are relevant to your paper but would distract the reader if included in the text, and (d) lists of stimulus materials, if the materials are unusual or particularly important to your conclusions (*Publication Manual of the American Psychological Association*, Fifth Edition, 2001). The appendix should be included only if it is especially enlightening or helpful in enabling others to replicate your study. Sometimes multiple appendices are used. In general, you should have no more than one table per appendix. Single tables in an appendix need not be numbered. Multiple tables per appendix must be (e.g., A1, A2, A3, etc.).

Order of Sections

Once you are ready to write your paper in final form, you should order the sections in the following way:

1. Title page (including your name and affiliation)
2. Abstract
3. Text
4. References
5. Author identification notes
6. Footnotes
7. Tables (one table per page)
8. Figure captions
9. Figures (one figure per page)

This ordering is to facilitate editing and printing. It is not the order in which the various parts will appear. Pages should be numbered consecutively using arabic numerals, beginning with the title page and ending with the figure captions. Figures should be numbered on the back with their respective figure numbers. Place page numbers in the upper right corner of each page. Immediately above the page number, write the first few words of your title, or the whole title if the title is short. This way, the pages can be returned to a manuscript in case they are temporarily misplaced.

The ordering above applies to papers written for submission to journals. For course papers, the following exceptions should be noted. First, footnotes usually should be placed at the bottom of the page on which they are cited. Second, tables and figures should be placed near where they are cited in the text rather than at the end. Third, figure captions should be placed immediately below the appropriate figures rather than in a separate section.

Once you have finished ordering and numbering your pages, the paper is complete. You are ready to hand it in or send it off.

Chapter Four

Rules for Writing
the Psychology Paper

Rule 1. *Your meeting should interest, inform, and persuade your reader.* Psychological writing should not be dull or stuffy. You must interest your reader in your paper; otherwise, the reader will find something else to do. Even teachers reading course papers will often read boring papers more quickly and less carefully than they will read interesting papers. Although you can lose your reader at any time, the major decision points for the reader are the title, abstract, and introduction.

The optimal title is one that concisely informs the reader of what the article is about. Such a title will minimize the number of people who start the article only to find that the topic doesn't interest them, and maximize the number of people who start the article because the topic does interest them. The abstract should summarize the article and at the same time convey to the reader why the topic, hypotheses, and results are of theoretical or practical interest. The introduction should further motivate the reader by pointing out why the research is a necessary next step in putting together the pieces of an as yet unsolved puzzle. The reader should finish the introduction believing that you have (a) put together one or more pieces of the puzzle, and (b) pointed the way for further pieces to be put together. The second accomplishment is as important as the first. No one likes to come to the end of an article only to find that the research has hit a dead end.

The best way to inform your readers is to tell them what they are likely to want to know – no more and no less. Experienced writers acquire a knack for knowing what to include and what not to include. Ask yourself which points are central to your main arguments and which are peripheral details possibly of interest to you but not to your reader.

The major means of persuasion is tight logic. Tight logic is more convincing to readers of psychological papers than are rhetorical devices. Remember that you must sell your ideas but not oversell them and that you must be persuasive without being condescending. In attacking alternative positions, stick to substance, avoiding ad hominem or irrelevant attacks. (People who disagree with this advice don't know what they're talking about!)

Rule 2. Write for your reader. Writing for your reader means keeping in mind four things. First, take into account the extent of her technical vocabulary. Terms that are familiar to professional psychologists may be unfamiliar to members of a general audience. Even within the field of psychology, specialists in different fields have different technical vocabularies. Whenever you can replace a complicated word with a simple word, do it. If you must use technical words, define them. It is most annoying to find a technical term used repeatedly without first having been defined. Second, maintain a level of formality in your writing that is appropriate for your audience. A book addressed to students (like this book) can be more informal than a book addressed to professional psychologists. Remember, though, that more formal writing need not and should not be stilted. Formality is not a substitute for readability. Third, include only those details that are appropriate for your audience. Readers of a popular journal such as *Psychology Today* will probably be less interested in methodological and statistical details than will readers of the scholarly journal *Psychological Review.* Fourth, avoid abbreviations. They can be annoying, and often interfere with the reader's comprehension of the text. (QED!)

Rule 3. Write clearly. You know an unclear sentence when you read it. Why, then, don't authors know unclear sentences when they write them? A major reason is their personal involvement in their own work. If an author omits or poorly describes certain details, he can subconsciously insert or clarify them. Because the reader does not share the author's cognitive structure, she cannot do the same. A large amount of unclear writing would never pass beyond the author's eyes if every author were willing to reread his papers in the role of a naive reader. A major reason for lack of clarity in writing is an author's unwillingness to go back over what has been written and rewrite it. One reason for this unwillingness is a delusion that the reader won't notice an unclear sentence. The writer hopes that the imperfections in his writing will pass by the reader unnoticed. Unfortunately, the typical outcome is the opposite of what the writer hopes for. The reader stumbles over the unclear sentence, and then rereads it, trying to make sense of it. Instead of the sentence blending into the background, it sticks out like a sore thumb. If there are enough unclear sentences, what started out as a temporary confusion may be come a permanent one. Hence, do not succumb to the delusion that you will get away with poor writing. Assume that your reader is as likely to detect an unclear sentence as you are to write one. (For the ideation of unclarity is the worst form of self-indulgence, and an ideological facsimile!)

Rule 4. Eliminate unnecessary redundancy. Elimination of redundancy from a paper is a difficult task, because one is never certain of how much redundancy should be eliminated. On the one hand, redundancy can reinforce your points. Readers may comprehend the second time a point that had eluded them the first time. On the other hand, redundancy can obscure your points. When a paper is highly redundant and the reader becomes aware of its redundancy, she may start reading the paper more quickly and less carefully, assuming that much of what she reads she will have read before and will read again. The reader assumes that if she doesn't quite understand a point the first time, she will have another chance when the author repeats the point in a slightly different way. The reader may then fail to understand the point because it is not in fact presented again, or because its second presentation is no more enlightening than was the first.

Because redundancy is a double-edged sword, you are better off attaining emphasis through other means. There are three alternative means you can use. First, you can discuss in more detail the points you wish to emphasize. Instead of repeating the points several times at different places in the paper, you give them additional space the first time you make them. Second, you can make important points at strategic places in the paper. People tend to remember best what they read at the beginning or the end of a paper. Third, you can state explicitly that one or more points are of special importance, and thus merit more careful attention. It may be obvious to you which points are your important ones, but it may not be obvious to your reader. Simply telling the reader which points are important can help guide her attention in an optimal way.

Writers usually find it much easier to spot redundancy in others' writing than in their own, because they have difficulty distinguishing what they have thought about from what they have written about. They may repeat a point for a second or third time, unaware that they have made the point before. Even in rereading their work, they may have trouble distinguishing their thoughts from their writing. It is therefore a good idea to have someone else read your paper, deliberately seeking out repetitious material. (Because other people usually will not have thought about your topic in the same way you have, they are more likely to recognize redundancy, repetition, reiteration, rehashing, restating, and duplication!)

Rule 5. Avoid digressions. Papers are usually difficult enough to follow without the added encumbrance of digressions. Digressions lead the reader away from the main points of your paper. Once the reader's attention is diverted from the main points, there is always a risk that his attention will never find its way back to the main point. Occasionally, a digression may be needed to clarify a point. Minor digressions of this kind can be incorporated into footnotes. Major digressions can be incorporated into an appendix. But keep the digressions out of the basic text, where they will distract the reader unnecessarily. (It's off the subject, but all this reminds me about a joke I heard. Two guys walk into a bar, and the first one says. . . .)

Rule 6. Don't overexplain. Students learning how to write psychology papers often explain too much. This problem is especially apparent in their *Method* sections. A student doing a simple free-recall experiment can end up explaining (a) why she used visual rather than auditory presentation of words, (b) why she used nouns instead of other parts of speech, (c) why she used 18-word lists rather than lists of some other length, (d) why she presented words at a rate of one word per second rather than some other rate, etc. Assume that readers of your paper (if they are professionals) are familiar with standard procedures, and will be interested only in explanations of nonstandard ones. Exclusive use of people's names, for example, would be nonstandard in a free-recall experiment.

The same warning is relevant to the presentation and discussion of results. If your experiment has only a few results, then you need not select among them. If your experiment has many results, or if you have analyzed the same data in many different ways, select the important results or analyses and concentrate on those. Your selection procedure must be honest: It would be unethical and unscientific to report and discuss only those results that support your hypotheses. The importance of a result should not be determined by its fit to your preconceived notions. (All of this will become clearer when I write my 1,000-page tome on how to avoid overexplanation!)

Rule 7. Avoid overstatement. Scientific writing should be conservative in its claims. By overstating your case, you undermine your credibility and put your reader on guard. Once on guard, the reader may cease to accept at face value anything you say. Consider, for example, the psychological phenomenon of writing a letter of recommendation for an undergraduate applying to graduate school, or for a graduate student applying for a job. On the one hand, you want to do what you can to assure that a good student obtains the best possible placement. On the other hand, you know that if your claims sound extravagant, you run the risk of damaging your case. Hoping that the major strengths will sell the candidate, writers of letters frequently look for minor weaknesses in their candidates so that their letters will appear impartial. Persons writing and reading letters know that some letter writers have reputations for writing inflated letters and, as a result, their letters are taken less seriously than the letters of others with higher credibility. The same reputations can be acquired by writers of psychology papers. Someone who is known to overstate his case will find others taking his claims less seriously than they would have taken the identical claims coming from someone else. (Anyone caught overstating his case ought certainly to be hanged on the spot!)

Rule 8. Avoid unnecessary qualifiers. Qualifiers serve a useful purpose when they honestly limit the scope of a statement. If, for example, only some subjects showed the effect of a certain treatment, then the effect of the treatment should be qualified as limited only to those subjects. Qualifiers serve no purpose, however, if they do not honestly limit scope. A *somewhat* noticeable tremor is not distinguishably different from a noticeable tremor: a *rather* loud pulse is not distinguishably different from a loud pulse. The use of *somewhat* and *rather* in the above contexts draws life from the prose without giving anything in return. In using qualifiers such as *somewhat, rather, mostly, largely, for the most part*, check that they make an honest addition to the sentence. If they don't, throw them out.

Sometimes authors use qualifiers to hedge their bets. Because psychology is an inductive science, proceeding from the specific to the general, psychologists can never draw conclusions with certainty. Psychologists may therefore express their uncertainty by qualifying their conclusions. For example, suppose that in a series of experiments, a psychologist finds that recall of a list of words always increases with practice. She concludes that "at least under some circumstances, certain subjects tend to recall more words after more free-recall trials." The qualifications are correct: There are indeed circumstances under which recall will not improve with practice; there are some subjects who will not show increasing recall over trials (e.g., dead ones); and because a given subject's recall may occasionally decrease from one trial to the next (if only by chance), one is safe in referring to a *tendency* toward increasing recall. The author's successive qualifications, however, have left her statement moribund and have not told the reader anything he doesn't already know. Had the author simply stated that "the results indicate that free recall increases over trials," she would have made the point without bogging the reader down in excess verbiage. (For the most part, it is usually true that, in most cases, absolutely unnecessary qualifiers can often impede communication!)

Rule 9. Use the precise word. In the course of writing your paper, you will probably find yourself occasionally stumbling over words, unable to choose a word that expresses the precise meaning you want to convey. Do not settle for an approximate word when a precise word is available. While writing, have available both a dictionary and a thesaurus, so that you can search for the optimal word. Settle for a suboptimal one only if you are unable to find the optimal one after diligent searching. (It is to your advance to alleviate use of ill-chosen words!)

Rule 10. Prefer simpler to more complicated words. The main purpose of writing is communication, and simpler words usually communicate more effectively than do complicated ones. The reaction of a reader coming across a complicated word he doesn't know is not awe for the writer's vocabulary but annoyance that communication has broken down. The reaction of a reader coming across a complicated word that he knows doesn't fit the context in which it is being used is often one of even greater annoyance. Every year, I have at least one student who seems to write papers not to communicate thoughts but to communicate the extent of his vocabulary. More often than not, this communication is unsuccessful: The student misuses complicated words. The most important decision regarding words is always to use the one that best expresses your meaning. (If you find that two words express your meaning equally well, use the simpler one, not the more reticular one!)

Rule 11. Use concrete words and examples. Much psychological writing is of necessity abstract. Whenever you have a choice, though, between an abstract and a concrete word, choose the concrete one. People will understand you better. When taking your reader through an abstract argument, use examples. If the argument is a long one, don't wait until the end to supply the example. The reader may have gotten lost in your argument a long time before, so that in reading your example she will have to go back through the argument anyway. Your argument will be clearer if you interweave your example(s) with the argument, alternating between the abstract and the concrete. The reader will then be able to understand your argument as she reads it, rather than when (or if) she rereads it. (Indeed, this paragraph would have been clearer if it had provided an example of what it was talking about!)

Rule 12. Prefer simpler to more complicated sentences. Sentence structure is largely a matter of style, and you should write in a style comfortable to you. Some major writers, like Hemingway, preferred short sentences; others, like Faulkner, preferred long sentences. The advantages of short sentences, from a journalistic point of view, are that they are (a) easier to understand and (b) less likely to contain errors of grammar or diction. When you find yourself becoming bogged down in a complicated construction, try to restate in two or more sentences what you had planned to state in one. You will probably find that you are able to say better what you wanted to say. (Having thought about this, you will realize as you read this sentence at the end of the paragraph why complexity in an already long sentence creates bewilderment!)

Rule 13. Use the active voice. Use of the impersonal third person in psychological articles encourages overuse of the passive voice. Psychology papers are replete with expressions like *It was found, It can be concluded, The tests were administered, The subjects were told, The session was completed,* etc. Expressions stated in the passive voice are harder to read and make for duller reading than expressions stated in the active voice. Whenever you use a passive construction, try to restate it as an active one. (Although it will be found that this cannot always be done by you, it will be appreciated by your reader, whose understanding of your prose will be enhanced!)

Rule 14. *Prefer affirmative to negative constructions.* Psychologists have established that negative constructions are harder to understand than affirmative ones (Clark & Chase, 1972). Your writing will therefore be easier to understand if you use affirmative rather than negative constructions wherever possible. In some cases, you will have a choice between an implicit and an explicit negation. For example, you might say either that "Writers should avoid negative constructions" or that "Writers should not use negative constructions." Similarly, you might say either "Six children were absent from school the day the testing took place" or "Six children were not present in school the day the testing took place." Implicit negations like the first example in each pair are easier to understand than explicit negations (Clark, 1974), and hence are preferred. (Wherever possible, do not fail to avoid explicit negations!)

Rule 15. *Avoid dangling constructions.* Dangling constructions make sentences ambiguous, including this one. The preceding sentence is ambiguous because it is not clear whether *one* refers to dangling constructions or to sentences. The source of the ambiguity is the phrase *including this one,* which dangles at the end of the sentence. Suppose a *Method* section informs you, "the subjects were falsely debriefed by the confederates after they finished their task." You cannot be certain whether *they* and *their* refer to the subjects or to the confederates. This sentence could be improved by eliminating the dangling construction. Depending upon who finished the task, the author might write either (a) "after they finished their task, the confederates falsely debriefed the subjects" or (b) "after they finished their task, the subjects were falsely debriefed by the confederates." Consider another example from a *Discussion* section: "The result would have been more easily interpretable if all the subjects had answered all the questions affirmatively, not just the first five." In this sentence, it is not clear whether just the first five subjects answered all the questions affirmatively or whether all the subjects answered just the first five questions affirmatively. The sentence should be rewritten in one of two ways, depending upon the author's intent: (a) "The result would have been more easily interpretable if all the subjects, not just the first five, had answered all the questions affirmatively" or (b) "The results would have been more easily interpretable if all the subjects had answered all the questions, not just the first five, affirmatively."

Rule 16. *Avoid participles without referents.* Suppose you read in a paper that "the rat was found dead while cleaning the cage." You probably would be correct to assume that an experimenter or a technician, not the dead rat, cleaned the cage. The sentence is ambiguous, however, because it lacks a referent for the participle. Less extreme examples of participles without referents abound in students' writing. Consider the following sentence from a *Method* section: "While monitoring the subject's heartbeat, adrenalin was injected into the subject's left arm." The sentence is unacceptable because it does not state who monitored the subject's heartbeat. Obviously, it wasn't the adrenalin that did the monitoring. But who did? The sentence should be revised to read, "While monitoring the subject's heartbeat, the experimenter injected adrenalin into the subject's left arm." In general, if you use active constructions when you use participles, you will eliminate participles without referents.

Rule 17. *Avoid pronouns without antecedents.* Students learn this rule early in their schooling, and yet they continue to violate it, usually in subtle ways. For example, many students will not recognize the following statement from a *Method* section as ungrammatical: "After the subject's task was completed, he was free to leave." To whom does *he* refer? Obviously not to *task*, but there is no other noun in the sentence, and the antecedent of a pronoun must be a noun. The author could reword the statement to say, "After the subject's task was completed, the subject was free to leave," or better, "After the subject completed the task, he was free to leave."

A possessive pronoun needs an antecedent as much as does any other pronoun. Consider, for example, a slight variant of an earlier sentence: "While monitoring the subject's heartbeat, the experimenter injected adrenalin into his left arm." The grammatical antecedent for *his* is *experimenter*, although it is obvious that the author intended otherwise. The author should rephrase the sentence: "While monitoring the subject's heartbeat, the experimenter injected adrenalin into the subject's left arm."

Rule 18. *Avoid use of the indefinite* this. A common problem in student writing is use of the word *this* without a definite antecedent. You will find this even in otherwise well-written prose, as, for example, in this sentence. The first use of *this* is indicative of sloppy prose. Note that there are two possible antecedents of *this, problem* and *use of the word* this *without a definite antecedent.* The ambiguity is eliminated by changing *this* from a pronoun to an adjective: "You will find this problem even in otherwise well-written prose."

Rule 19. *Avoid split infinitives.* Split infinitives seem to evoke two reactions. Some people use them regularly and barely notice when they read them. Other people never use them and wince every time they see or hear them. Usually, split infinitives make sentences less graceful without adding any clarity. To carefully weigh the evidence is the same as to weigh the evidence carefully, but the latter way of expressing the idea is more readable than the former. If the adverb with which you want to split the infinitive seems to fit nowhere else, consider rewriting the sentence in a different way. (Try to always follow this advice!)

Rule 20. *Use summary statements.* Psychologists frequently divide long papers into sections and subsections. It is often helpful to include one or two brief summary statements at the end of each section or at the end of a long argument. Such statements increase comprehensibility at very little cost in additional space. Summaries help the reader (a) quickly absorb the main point of each section as she completes it, and (b) keep track of where she is. A long summary in the middle of a paper is unnecessary and inadvisable, because it is redundant with the abstract and possibly the conclusions. (To summarize, a summary at this point in the chapter is unnecessary!)

Rule 21. *Use transitions.* Have you ever noticed that some people write clear sentences, and yet their writing nevertheless appears disjointed? A common cause of disjointed and choppy writing is missing transitions between ideas. Missing transitions are sometimes caused by careless thinking: The writer goes from step A to step C without thinking of the necessary intervening step B. More often, though, missing transitions are caused by quick thinking: The writer thinks faster than he writes. As the writer is writing sentence A, the writer is already thinking about sentence B. By the time the writer finishes writing sentence A, he has started thinking about sentence C, and so proceeds to write sentence C, forgetting to insert the necessary transitional sentence B. No matter how clearly sentences A and C are stated, the reader will pause in reading sentence C, wondering whether she missed something in sentence A, or even in some sentence further back. Missing transitions can be inserted if you reread your paper, checking carefully whether each sentence follows logically from the sentence immediately preceding it. (The price of rice also increased in China during this past year!)

Rule 22. *Place yourself in the background.* There was a time when it was considered bad form for the writer to place herself anywhere near the foreground of a paper. Writers avoided first-person references at all costs. When strictures against first-person references started to ease, single writers often started referring to themselves as *we,* even if they were sole author of papers. Today, references to oneself as *we* are discouraged. If you are the sole author of a paper and use the expression *we,* you should use it only to refer to yourself and your readers, not just to yourself. If you mean *I,* say *I.* Overuse of the first-person singular, however, tends to distract the reader, calling attention to you rather than to what you are saying. Stay in the background, therefore, surfacing only when you have good reason to draw attention to yourself, for example, in emphasizing that an idea is your own speculation, rather than a conclusion closely following from a set of data. (We cannot emphasize this point more strongly!)

Rule 23. *Cite sources as well as findings.* When you cite a finding, cite its source. There are four reasons why you should supply this information. First, the reader can check whether you have cited the source accurately. He may doubt the finding and want to verify that you properly cited it. Second, the reader can check whether the source is credible. If you merely cite a finding, the reader has no way of checking the quality of the evidence in support of that finding. Third, the reader can learn about a reference that he may have been unaware of and that he then wants to read. Fourth, you show your reader that you are familiar with the literature on your topic, thereby increasing your own credibility as a source of information. (In fact, research has shown that citing sources of research findings does improve credibility!)

Rule 24. *Proofread your paper.* I would estimate that fewer than one-half the papers I receive have been proofread by their authors.

Fewer than one-quarter are proofread carefully. I think that students often fail to proofread their work because they are afraid they won't like what they read. But other readers of your paper will like it even less if they have to put up with errors that the author easily could have corrected. I cannot emphasize enough the importance of proofreading. The time it takes to proofread a paper is a small fraction of the time it takes to write the paper. And there is probably no other thing you can do in so little time that will as much improve others' evaluations of your work.

The best method of proofreading is to have someone read the text to you from the original, while you check the final typed copy line-by-line. In following the typed text, read only for errors in spelling, punctuation, capitalization, and the like. Do not read for meaning. You should read the paper an additional time to make sure that you have said what you wanted to say, the way you wanted to say it. (Typografikal erors are uneccesary!)

Rule 25. Request a critical reading of your paper by an adviser or colleague. Because people are so involved in their own work, they find it much easier to criticize the work of others than to criticize their own work. It is therefore to your advantage to seek the advice of others on any paper you write. When asking someone to read your paper, ask her to read it *critically*, indeed, ruthlessly. It is a common experience for authors to receive compliments from their colleagues on their papers and then to find them torn to shreds by journal reviewers. One reason for the discrepancy is that colleagues you ask to read your paper may not willingly sacrifice the time or risk the loss of friendship that might be involved in a very critical reading of your work. Encourage your readers to be critical, therefore, perhaps offering your own critical paper-reading services in return.

Rule 26. Avoid sexist language. Do not use the pronoun *he* when you mean *he* or *she*. Excessive use of *he or she* is awkward and can be irritating as well. Use of plurals and rephrasing of sentences can often help eliminate both sexist language and excessive use of *he or she*.

Rule 27. Don't bother to say your results are "interesting" or "important." Let the results speak for themselves.

Rule 28. Don't end your article by saying, "More research is needed." This statement has become a cliché. There is almost always room for further research.

Chapter Five

Using the Internet to Aid the Research Process

BETH DIETZ-UHLER AND RICHARD C. SHERMAN

The Internet can be a powerful research tool. Its potential use-fulness arises from three important characteristics that we will discuss in this chapter. First, it allows easy and quick access to information about a wide range of psychological topics. This access can be very helpful in exploring potential research ideas as well as for gathering background information for writing papers. Second, the Internet can be used to collect data from people in online research projects, for example in online surveys. Data from many people can be collected in a short amount of time with this technique, and the respondents' background characteristics may be much more diverse than participants in typical psychological studies. Third, the Internet enables researchers to communicate with each other quickly and inexpensively, allowing them to share research findings and discuss ideas more easily and effectively than ever before.

There are also pitfalls in using the Internet for research that can mitigate its advantages. For example, although information may be accessed easily and quickly, much of it may be either irrelevant or invalid. Effective use of the Internet requires knowing how to search for information efficiently and how to evaluate the quality of the information that is found. Other potential pitfalls are involved in using the Internet to gather data. For example, people may respond differently to an online survey than to one presented in a more traditional format. Some may try to participate more than once. People not in the desired target population may participate. In short, the researcher must

77

overcome both logistical and inferential problems in order to obtain results that are reliable and valid. Taking advantage of the Internet's potential as a research tool requires avoiding its pitfalls, as we will see throughout this chapter.

DEFINITION OF THE INTERNET
AND ITS COMPONENTS

Loosely defined, the Internet is an international network of computers connected by phone lines, special dedicated lines, microwave relay links, and satellite transmission. Historians generally mark 1969 as the beginning of the Internet, when four university computers were interconnected as part of a research project funded by the U.S. Department of Defense. In 2002, the estimated number of host computers on the Internet was 147,344,723 (Zakon, 2002). Most of this phenomenal growth has taken place since 1990, undoubtedly due in large part to the advent in the early 1990s of the World Wide Web (WWW). The WWW allows instant communication between geographically diverse computers by means of a user-friendly graphical interface called a *browser* – a vast improvement over early text-based methods of accessing the Internet. The number of Web sites has grown exponentially, from 130 sites in 1993 to an estimated 38 million in 2002 (Zakon, 2002).

When we speak of the Internet, we are referring to a collection of components that comprise different ways of accessing and sharing information across computers. In assessing the usefulness of the Internet for research purposes, it is important to know the characteristics of the major components:

- WWW: Network of computers that allow linking of documents by means of *hypertext*, links embedded in one document (a Web page) that provide instant access to files located on different computers.
- USENET/NETNEWS: A worldwide system of discussion groups, with comments passed among hundreds of thousands of machines. USENET is completely decentralized and nearly uncensored, with over 10,000 discussion areas, called newsgroups. Messages are discrete postings to the area; therefore "discussions" may occur over weeks or months. Most Internet service providers include access to USENET discussion groups. The list of current groups and messages can be viewed using

major WWW browsers, with instructions for subscribing to discussion groups contained in their help files.

- Mailing Lists (e.g., LISTSERV®s): A system of exchanging e-mail messages among people who subscribe to the same topical forum. When e-mail is addressed to a LISTSERV® mailing list, it is automatically broadcast to everyone who subscribes to the list. The result is similar to a USENET newsgroup or forum, except that the messages are transmitted as e-mail and are therefore available only to individuals on the list. LISTSERV®s are maintained by many psychological organizations and can be joined by accessing the organization's Web site. Other public LISTSERV®s are catalogued at http://www.lsoft.com/catalist.html.

- Chat Groups/Instant Messaging: Systems that allow nearly instantaneous exchange of messages among individuals located at computers that are widely dispersed geographically. Chat groups are usually topically oriented and can be joined by anyone. One form of chat group, call Multi User Domains (MUDs), involves elaborate role-playing games in imaginary environments. Chat groups on psychological topics can be located through professional organizations and societies, and are an increasingly common component of online conferences. Instant messaging systems allow private and intimate online discussions among a small number of individuals. Current versions of major WWW browsers have instant message systems as a built-in component.

Internet Users: Number and Demographics

In the early years of the Internet users tended to be a homogenous group – mostly young males who were members of the U.S. military or university researchers. The explosive recent growth of the Internet has led to a wider range of user characteristics, though Internet users are still not representative of larger populations. The worldwide number of Internet users in May 2002 was estimated to be 580 million, almost 10% of the world's population (NUA Surveys, 2002). There are significant variations among countries and regions, however, with by far the largest numbers of users being North American (182.67 million), European (186 million), or Asian (168 million) (NUA Surveys, 2002). Within regions there still exist great disparities associated with gender, socioeconomic status, and ethnicity. For example, a recent study in the United States showed that a large proportion of the overall population, almost 60%, were Internet users, but that different ethnic groups exhibited wide variations in proportions of users (U.S.

Department of Commerce, 2002). Whites (60%) and Asian American/ Pacific Islanders (60%) showed the highest proportions of users, with Blacks (40%) and Hispanics (32%) having much lower proportions. Differences such as these stress the need for caution in generalizing the results of Internet research studies.

SEARCHING THE INTERNET

Overview of Internet Searching and Search Engines

The information available on the Internet has been likened to what would happen if the pages in all the books in a library were torn out and thrown into a huge pile. The information would still be available, of course, but locating and organizing material on a particular topic would be extremely daunting. Fortunately, this view is somewhat overly cynical because effective strategies and tools for locating information exist that can make the task more manageable.

The primary tool for finding specific information on the Internet is the search engine, a software program that provides a list of links to documents and web pages that contain the keywords specified by the user. The most popular engines include AltaVista, Google, Hotbot, and Lycos. Each of these can be accessed using a WWW browser and entering the Internet address http:\\www.searchengine.com, where "searchengine" is replaced with the name of the engine you wish to employ. Most users are familiar with one or more of these programs, but few people take full advantage of their features. Here are some tips for effective searching:

> *Carefully construct the search phrase.* The search phrase, or query, can greatly influence the relevance and quality of the results, and creating effective phrases requires careful thought and practice. For example, suppose the topic being investigated was "spouse abuse in rural settings." What would be a good search phrase? The following are suggestions from an excellent online tutorial by the Bright Planet software company (http://www.brightplanet.com/deepcontent/ tutorials/Search/): (a) use nouns or objects rather than verbs (*abuse* versus *abusing*); (b) indicate exact phrases by using quotes ("spouse abuse"); (c) include synonyms of key concepts, using Boolean operators if required by the specific search engine (spouse OR "intimate

partner"; "domestic abuse" OR violence OR assault); (d) order concepts with the main subject first (rural spouse OR "intimate partner," assuming the main focus is on rural settings). Note that the syntax for combining words in a search phrase may vary somewhat from engine to engine – consult the help section of the engine's Web site for details.

Use more than one search engine. Engines differ in the breadth of their search, how they order the search results, how up-to-date the links are that are listed; therefore the same search phrase entered into two engines may not return the same list of links. Also consider using a meta-search engine which automatically queries several search engines and eliminates duplicate links, such as QueryServer, Vivisimo, or Dogpile. You can access any of these by using the same address method suggested above for single-source search engines.

Limit search to certain domains. Most search engines allow the search to be restricted to certain domains (e.g., .org, .edu, or .gov). This can be useful for maximizing the relevance of links that are identified. For example, suppose the researcher wanted to locate government-sponsored reports on the subject of spouse abuse in rural settings. The search phrase could be entered with the restriction that only links with .gov be listed. Check the search engine's help page for the exact format of a restricted search.

Search for links to a specific document. Imagine in the example above that a restricted search of the .gov domain leads to a site that is particularly informative. Other sites that are linked to it might be informative as well, and most search engines allow a search for linked sites. This strategy is the Internet equivalent of using citation indices in searching for printed materials. A related approach involves taking an exact phrase from one document and using it as a search query. For example, a government report on intimate partner violence contained the phrase "Intimate partners committed fewer murders in each of the 3 years 1996, 1997, and 1998." Inserting this phrase as a search query will locate other Internet documents that used the same reference.

Some Specific Types of Useful
Online Research Information

There are several types of valuable online information that might not be located using a general search strategy of the sort described above. Some of these are proprietary but are available through public computer systems at libraries and universities that have paid for access to the information source. Check with a librarian to see what resources may be available in your situation.

Journal articles. Full texts of articles published in major psychology journals can be searched and viewed online using PsycLIT, a database maintained by the American Psychological Association (APA). The database contains journal articles from 1974 to the present, and book chapters and books published from 1987 to the present. The APA also provides PsycINFO, which contains the same information as PsycLIT and in addition has citations to dissertations in psychology and journal references back to 1967. PsycLIT and PsycINFO are purchased by most universities and some public library systems.

Magazine and newspaper articles. Most major magazines and newspapers have Web sites that allow free searches of past articles. The search engines available on these sites function in much the same way as the major search engines, and the same tips for using them effectively apply.

Government databases. Many online databases are maintained by the U.S. government, including archives of the Congressional Record, Supreme Court decisions, crime statistics, and reports of various government agencies. A number of these can be accessed and searched through the U.S. government Web site, Fedworld (http://www.fedworld.gov). The advanced search option allows searches of federal and specific state government databases.

Home pages of specific researchers. A useful source of information can be the individual home page of a researcher in the field of interest. Researchers usually list their own publications and presentations on the topic, and sometimes provide links to other relevant information. You can locate home pages by conducting a general Internet search using a researcher's name as the search phrase, or by going to the individual's academic institution Web site and searching there. Alternatively, many directories of professional society memberships, such as the American Psychological Association and the American Psychological Society, provide Web site addresses for their members.

Popular Internet sites for research resources. There are a number of organizational Web sites that have useful information for researchers. For example, the American Psychological Association's Web site (http://www.apa.org/) can be searched for short research articles on a variety of topics. The American Psychological Society's site (http://www.psychologicalscience.org) contains a compendium of links to university psychology departments, psychology organizations, and sites that provide tips and resources for conducting research and writing reports. The Social Psychology Network (http://www.socialpsychology.org/) maintains links to individual home pages of psychologists as well as links to research and teaching resources, including tips on writing in APA style, conducting data analysis, and so on.

CRITICAL EVALUATION OF
INTERNET-BASED INFORMATION

Relying on information obtained from an Internet search without critically evaluating its quality can be very risky. Much of the information on the Internet has not been subject to the same publishing standards or filters as material found in major scientific journals, books, and newspapers.

Almost anyone can post information to the Internet without checks on its reliability and accuracy. The result is that a great deal of *misinformation* exists on the Internet – information that seems legitimate but is factually incorrect or incomplete. Misinformation is not necessarily intentionally misleading, but more likely the result of the author's carelessness or ignorance. However, the ease and low cost of creating Web sites has also led to many sites where the intent is not so much to provide information as it is to persuade the reader to hold a particular belief or point of view, and the lack of checks on objectivity may make it difficult to tell the difference. Information intended to persuade the audience is called *propaganda.* In some cases attempts to be persuasive may include deliberate distortions or fabrications of information – often referred to as *disinformation.* For online examples and comparisons of misinformation, propaganda, and disinformation, see a Web site maintained by Johns Hopkins Library at http://www.library.jhu.edu/elp/useit/evaluate/counterfeit.html.

The existence of misinformation, propaganda, and disinformation on the Internet means that a researcher must carefully evaluate material that might be used in a particular project. There are several criteria for evaluating information that can be adapted to the Internet (cf. Alexander & Tate, 1999). The following is adapted from online material provided by librarians at Widener University (http://www2.widener. edu/Wolfgram-Memorial-Library/webevaluation/webeval.htm), New Mexico State University (http://lib.nmsu.edu/instruction/eval.html), and Johns Hopkins University (http://www.library.jhu.edu/elp/useit/ evaluate/index.html):

- *Accuracy*: It is difficult to determine the accuracy of information when you are not an expert on the topic. However, certain indicators can help you assess the likelihood that Internet material is accurate. Does the author indicate the source of his information, and is the source public so that it can be accessed and verified? Are there fact checkers and editors who may have screened the document (probably so for an online journal article or newspaper article, probably not for a personal home page)?

- *Authority*: Is the author and publishing body of the Internet document indicated? Are the credentials of the author given or is there a way to locate and evaluate them? If the publishing body is indicated (for example, an organization or educational institution), is it reputable? If the document is found on a university server (i.e., has an .edu domain), is the page one that is sponsored by the institution itself, or is it the personal home page of the author? If the author is not someone you recognize as an authority on the topic, do others refer to the work in a positive way? Can you find links to the document from authors you do know and trust?

- *Objectivity*: What is the point of view or bias of the document or the Web site? Is the author a person or organization with a stake in the issue you are researching? Does the document reside on the server of an organization that has a political or philosophical agenda? Is the author motivated to selectively present information, or perhaps to distort it? Sometimes these questions are easy to answer, but often the motivation and bias in a document may not be clear. For example, do not assume that all documents residing on a university server or authored by Ph.D.s are bias-free. Academics may have strong points of view that influence their interpretation of information just as anyone else does. Perhaps the question is not *whether* a document is objective, but rather *to what degree* is the presentation of information biased, and *in what ways*?

- *Currency*: How recent or up to date is the information that the site provides? In a fast-moving field of research, articles just a few years old may be supplemented by newer findings that change the conclusions about a topic. It can be important, then, to know the currency of the Internet information you are using. Is there a publication or "last modified" date indicated on the document? Are there references within the document to the dates on which data were collected? If the author refers to published works, how recent are the dates?

- *Coverage*: How thoroughly or deeply does the document deal with the topic? Does it provide background information and references that seem appropriately extensive? Has the author demonstrated the connection of his or her work to other research and theory? Assessing coverage allows you to determine the unique contribution and value of the author's document.

It is possible to obtain practice in applying these criteria to Web sites and Internet documents. Alexander and Tate at Widener University have collected examples of Internet documents and Web sites that illustrate variations on each of the criteria (http://www2.widener.edu/ Wolfgram-Memorial-Library/webevaluation/examples.htm). They also provide examples of special types of Web sites, such as those that blend advertising with information, and those that subtly advocate political or philosophical causes. Another excellent source of examples is Susan Beck's Web site, "The Good, the Bad, and the Ugly" (http://lib. nmsu.edu/instruction/eval.html). Beck provides examples of each criterion, as do Alexander and Tate, but also presents sets of links to Internet material on four different topics (e.g., smoking and tobacco use, AIDS, immigration, and drugs). The links within each topic vary in quality, and the viewer must decide which criteria are most relevant – a very realistic exercise. Research by Dietz-Uhler (2002) has shown that students who work through Beck's examples are significantly more confident and critical evaluators of Internet information.

USING THE INTERNET TO CONDUCT RESEARCH

Clearly, the Internet can be a valuable resource when seeking ideas for a research project. But even when you have settled on an idea for a study and are confident that enough resources exist to successfully answer your research question, you still need to discover a way to collect data that will allow you to answer your research question. The Internet can be a valuable tool during the data collection phase of the research process. In this section, we will explore how to use the Internet as a source of data and as a data collection tool. Specifically, we will discuss how to use the Internet to conduct archival research and how to use the Internet to collect original data. We will also discuss some of the advantages and disadvantages of using the Internet to collect data.

Archival Research

Archival research refers to a method of data collection involving the use of records or previously existing information. For example, suppose you wanted to construct a personality profile of a U.S. president, perhaps to examine if a president's personality is related to his performance in office. Although this is an excellent research idea, you are likely to have two problems collecting data. First, the president whose personality profile you want to construct might not be living anymore. Second, even if the president is living, it is unlikely that you will be able to interview him or get him to complete a personality survey for you. It turns out that personality profiles of U.S. presidents can be created without ever talking with a president or having him complete a personality questionnaire. Instead, the personality traits of a president can be inferred from such pieces of information as his speeches, notes and papers he writes, his conversations with other political leaders, interviews, and press conferences. The advantage for a researcher is that all of this material is archived and made available for public consumption. Any research that involves the use of previously existing material, whether it be public records (e.g., crime statistics, census information) or public documents (Supreme Court justices' decisions, presidential speeches) for example, is referred to as archival research. Archival research is a particularly useful research strategy for answering research questions that are difficult or impossible to answer via traditional data collection methods.

The Internet is an especially valuable tool for researchers interested in archival research. As already discussed, the Internet and World Wide Web contain an abundance of information, much of which can be used to conduct research. Below are some ideas and examples for using the Internet to conduct archival research.

Newsgroups. The Internet is full of "discussion boards" on every imaginable topic. Newsgroups allow people from all over the world to engage in asynchronous conversations about a variety of topics. An Internet search of newsgroups yields thousands of virtual discussions (e.g., discussions of a football team's performance, a support group for people who have chronic pain, discussion of the best restaurants on Maui). Most discussion boards are accessible to anyone, as a participant or as an observer. For the purposes of archival research, newsgroups are typically archived, so that a researcher can have access to the transcripts of the discussions (although permission of the moderator is often required, and always advisable). These transcripts can be a valuable source of data to a researcher attempting to answer specific research questions. For example, if a researcher wanted to learn whether fans of winning football teams express more pride in their team than fans of losing football teams, she could analyze the transcripts of a discussion board of a winning team and the discussion board of a losing team. Or, suppose a researcher was interested in examining the extent of depressive symptoms displayed by chronic pain sufferers. He could analyze the discussion board of chronic pain sufferers for evidence of depressive symptoms.

Public records. Public records can be an excellent source of data. The Internet allows one to access most public records with incredible ease. The consequence for a researcher is that innumerable research questions can be answered with the use of these data. For example, the government's Web site (http://www.fedworld.org) includes access to a variety of information, such as the complete transcripts of Supreme Court decisions, transportation fatality statistics, and a list of the current endangered species. Similarly, every state in the United States has a Web page and can be accessed by using the syntax: http://www.state.SA.us, where "SA" stands for the state abbreviation (e.g., http://www.state.oh.us is Ohio's Web page). A state's Web page makes available information such as the incidence of cancer by type, year, and county, the results of a family health survey, and the number of live births by county and year.

Web sites. The format and information contained on a Web site can also be a source of data for a researcher. Suppose a researcher was interested in examining whether females are more likely than males to disclose personal information about themselves. One method of answering this question is to analyze the Web sites of males and

females, paying attention to the amount and type of personal information included on the sites. Or, imagine a researcher who wants
to investigate the correlation between the success (in net profit) of
small businesses and the appearance of the business's Web site. A researcher could analyze the appearance of small business Web sites
and then determine if it is related to the success of the business.

Data Collection via the Internet

The Internet can also be a valuable tool for the collection of original data, because it allows researchers to collect survey data or conduct experiments. There are several methods available to researchers
who wish to collect data using the Internet. First, a researcher can
construct a Web page that permits respondents to answer a survey
or participate in an experiment. Of course, this technique requires a
researcher to have some knowledge of constructing Web pages and
surveys on the Web and to have access to a WWW server. Second, a researcher can send a questionnaire or survey to potential respondents
via e-mail. Third, a researcher can make use of a LISTSERV® to send
potential respondents a survey or questionnaire.

Conducting research via the Internet has a number of important
advantages and disadvantages (Reips, 2000). Some of the advantages
include:

1. Population access. As already discussed, the number of people using
   the Internet is increasing every day. Use of the Internet allows researchers to have access to many more people than would be possible
   using more traditional methods. Further, the Internet allows access to
   more diverse populations.
2. Volunteer bias. One criticism of most research conducted in universities is that participants may not be invested in the research in which
   they are participating. On the Internet, people who participate in a
   study do so because they want to.
3. Statistical power. The large sample size that use of the Internet permits
   also increases the amount of statistical power of a study.
4. Experimenter effects. Face-to-face experiments typically require the
   use of an experimenter. The presence of an experimenter can sometimes (unintentionally) influence the outcome of a study. The Internet
   does not require the physical presence of an experimenter, which eliminates any experimenter effects.

5. Costs. The costs of conducting a study on the Internet are greatly reduced. Internet studies do not require the use of lab space, equipment, experimenters, or paper. The amount of time needed to complete a study on the Internet is also greatly reduced because Internet studies can be conducted 24 hours per day, 7 days per week.

6. Ethical issues. Participation in Internet studies is completely voluntary. A respondent can drop out of the study at any time without penalty.

Of course, there are also some disadvantages of using the Internet to conduct research. These include:

1. Control issues. In non-Internet studies, researchers can exercise a great deal of control over many of the practical issues in research, such as who the participants are, when the study is conducted, and where the study takes place. On the Internet, a researcher gives up this control. Among the control issues that plague Internet research are the fact that people can participate in the study multiple times and that the researcher lacks control over the experimental situation. It is wise to ask participants not to participate more than once or to ask for personal information that can be verified independently.

2. Self-selection. Another issue with Internet studies is that all of the participants are self-selected, rather than randomly assigned. The results, therefore, may not be as generalizable as a randomly selected sample. One solution is to advertise the study widely so that Internet users from a variety of entry points have access to the study.

3. Drop-out. Whenever research is completely voluntary, as is the case in Internet research, there tends to be a high drop-out rate. A participant may decide, in the middle of the study, that she does not have the time to complete it. Or, a participant might decide, after starting a survey, that he is really not interested in this topic. Potential solutions to this problem include offering an incentive for participation, making the Web site as attractive as possible, and providing participants with estimates of the amount of time needed to complete the study.

4. Technical variance. Researchers try very hard to reduce the amount of error variance in their studies. Studies conducted on the Internet can pose some unique challenges to the control of error variance. For example, participants in a study are likely to have different WWW browsers, different monitor sizes, and different Internet connections, all of which can inflate error variance. However, these sources of variance

are likely to be random and may not affect the study in a systematic manner.

5. Interaction with participants. If a participant in an Internet study has a question, he is unable to ask an experimenter. It is a good idea, therefore, to always include an e-mail address or other means of contacting the experimenter if the participant wishes clarification of procedures.

Clearly, the Internet offers a variety of unique ways of conducting research. The Internet can be a valuable source of data to an investigator interested in conducting archival research. Many research questions can be answered via access to public records, public documents, and countless Web sites. The Internet can also be used as a way to collect original research. Minimal knowledge of Web page construction is really all that is needed to collect data via the Internet. And, currently there are several Web sites (e.g., http://survey.psy.buffalo.edu/home.html; http://www.genpsy.unizh.ch/forschungUR/ati/wextor/index.html) that essentially build your survey or experiment for you. Finally, a review of the research (Krantz & Dalal, 2000) suggests that the results of Web experiments are comparable to non-Web experiments, making the conduct of research via the Internet even more attractive.

USING THE INTERNET TO DISSEMINATE RESEARCH FINDINGS

In addition to the use of the Internet to locate ideas for research projects, gather information about a research topic, and collect data, the Internet can be an important and valuable tool for the dissemination of research findings. In this section, we will examine the use of the Internet to disseminate research findings, paying particular attention to the advantages and disadvantages of using the Internet to publicize your research findings. Traditionally, researchers had two outlets to publicize their research: presentations and publications. Researchers can present their research study at a conference, typically in the form of a poster or oral presentation. There are usually a variety of conferences for which a researcher can present his or her study. For example, departments and universities sometimes host conferences to give students and faculty an opportunity to present the results of their research. There are also a number of disciplinary conferences to choose from, such as the Society for Personality and Social Psychology annual conference, the Forum for Behavioral Science in Family Medicine meeting, or the Society for Judgment and Decision Making annual meeting. Finally, there are a number of regional (e.g., Eastern Psychological Association) and national conferences (e.g., American Psychological Society) that are of interest to researchers in any area of psychology. Perhaps the most popular outlet for the dissemination of research is to publish a study in a psychological journal, a topic that is the focus of this book.

In addition to conferences and publications, the Internet can be an outlet for the dissemination of research findings. There are a number of ways of using the Internet to disseminate your research. These include:

- *A research home page.* Many researchers publish a research Web site that typically includes information about their research, biographies of collaborators, highlights of their most important or current research findings, and information about their current projects. Because any Web site can be accessed by any person, at any place, and at any time, a research home page can often attract a good deal of attention.
- *Use of a LISTSERV®.* A LISTSERV® can be a good method of sharing the results of your research with many people. A LISTSERV® can also be used to obtain feedback about your research findings. For example, suppose you obtained an unexpected finding and are at a loss for how to explain it. You can query a LISTSERV® for ideas about how to explain your results.
- *Profile.* Some Web sites include profiles of various researchers. Such profiles typically include information about a researcher's interests and a list of his or her publications. For example, the Social Psychology Network contains hundreds of profiles of various social psychologists.

Advantages and Disadvantages of Publicizing Your Research on the Internet

There are a number of advantages and disadvantages of publicizing your research on the Internet. Some of the advantages include:

1. The Internet allows for the quickest, most efficient way to disseminate your results or obtain feedback. Information about your research can be posted to the WWW instantaneously.
2. Publishing your research on the Internet does not require a reviewer. You can publish anything you want about your project.
3. The Internet allows for immediate feedback on your project. If you

post information about your project on a Web site, it is conceivable that someone reading your Web site will send you an e-mail containing feedback on your project. Or, you can solicit feedback by posting a query to a LISTSERV®, for example.

4. The Internet allows potential for greater visibility. If you present your research at a conference, then only those in attendance will hear about your research. If you publish your research in a journal, then only those who read that particular journal or who obtain a reference to your article will be exposed to it. But on the Internet, you could have an audience of millions!

Of course, there are also some disadvantages of publicizing your research on the Internet. These include:

1. You might get some unintended responses. Remember that if you publicize your research on a Web site, it is accessible to anyone at anytime. It is possible that someone will respond to your research in a negative fashion, such as by sending you an e-mail that is highly critical of your research. Another unintended response is that students might contact you and ask you for information for their term papers or ask you to collect data for them.

2. The information that you provide via the Internet is not reviewed. It is conceivable that your study has a serious flaw of which you are not aware. Publicizing a study with a serious flaw can be embarrassing, among other things.

3. Because information on the WWW is accessible to anyone, there is a possibility that someone will "steal" your idea and present it as their own.

Publishing an Article on the Internet

One purpose of presenting and publishing is to communicate research findings. The popularity of the Internet poses some problems to traditional means of communicating research findings. Among the issues of posting research findings on the Internet that we will consider here is whether published work can be posted on the Internet and whether unpublished work posted on the Internet can be considered a publication. Much of the information presented in this section reflects the position of the American Psychological Association (as of June 1, 2001).

Posting Published Material on the Internet. When a manuscript is published in a journal or a conference presentation is published in a conference proceedings, typically it becomes the property of the publisher. At issue is whether or not the author can post the article to his or her Web site. Ultimately, the decision is up to the publisher, who technically owns the papers. If an article is published in an APA journal, the APA's position (as of June 1, 2001) is (http://www.apa.org/journals/posting.html):

Authors of articles published in APA journals may post a copy of the final manuscript, as a word processing, PDF, or other type file, on their Web site or their employer's server after it is accepted for publication. The following conditions would prevail:

- The posted article must carry an APA copyright notice and include a link to the APA journal home page.
- APA does not permit archiving with any other non-APA repositories.
- APA does not provide electronic copies of the APA published version for this purpose, and authors are not permitted to scan in the APA published version.

Posting Unpublished Material on the Internet. If a manuscript is not yet published, it can be posted to a Web site or disseminated electronically. However, the APA (http://www.apa.org/journals/posting.html) warns that there are a number of risks to disseminating unpublished articles. One risk is that unpublished articles are not copyrighted. The ideas or findings presented in an uncopyrighted article can easily be copied by others. Another risk is that a journal might decide not to review an article because it has been previously posted on the Internet. Finally, the APA warns that the dissemination of unreviewed manuscripts can lead to a lowering of the standards for scientific research.

Another issue is whether an article posted on the Internet is considered a "publication." Although there is no official "rule" on this issue, most psychologists do not consider a manuscript that has not been peer reviewed to be a publication. However, this does not negate the dissemination of an unpublished article via the Internet. The official position of the APA (as of June 1, 2001) is (http://www.apa.org/journals/posting.html):

If a paper is unpublished, the author may distribute it on the Internet or post it on a Web site but should label the paper with the date and with a statement that the paper has not (yet) been published. (Example: Draft version 1.3, 1/5/99. This paper has not been peer reviewed. Please do not copy or cite without author's permission.)

Upon submitting the paper for publication, the author is obligated to inform the editor if the paper has been or is posted on a Web site. Some editors may consider such a Web posting to be prior publication and may not review the paper.

In summary, there are a variety of issues involved in using the Internet to publicize your research findings. The Internet offers a number of outlets for publicizing your research, including a research home page, a LISTSERV®, and a profile on an organization's Web page. Of course, there are a number of advantages and disadvantages of using the Internet to disseminate your research. Advantages include ease and efficiency, freedom from hassle, immediacy of feedback, and greater visibility. Disadvantages include unintended responses, lack of reviewers, and theft. In terms of posting published and unpublished articles on the Internet, issues to consider include ownership of the article, crediting the publisher, theft of ideas, and lowering of standards if articles are disseminated prior to review.

INCREASING THE EFFICIENCY OF PUBLISHING VIA THE INTERNET

The popularity of the Internet has also made publishing articles a more efficient process, a welcome situation for researchers who often wait years until they see their article in print. In this section, we will discuss the use of the Internet to communicate with research collaborators, locate potential journal outlets, submit manuscripts, and review articles.

Communicating with Collaborators

Prior to the popularity of the Internet, most researchers communicated via telephone, face-to-face meetings, or via surface mail. For example, if a researcher wanted a collaborator to have access to a data file, generally he would send a diskette via surface mail. Even collaborations with colleagues in the same department typically involved placing edited copies of a manuscript in the colleague's mailbox. The use of the Internet increases the efficiency with which collaborators can communicate. Discussions about research can be conducted via e-mail or virtual chats, data files can be sent via e-mail, and manuscripts can be sent via e-mail, whether collaborators are 3,000 miles away or in the next room. In addition, many word-processing programs have an editing feature that allows coauthors to see what changes have been made to a manuscript. Clearly, many features of the Internet including e-mail, instant messaging, and discussion boards have increased the ease and efficiency of communication with research collaborators.

Locating Journal Outlets

Most researchers have a clear sense of what journals are the most popular in their field and which journals are likely outlets for their research. But a quick search of the Internet may uncover other journals you may not have known existed. Searching the WWW for journals relevant to your research topic may yield some new or interesting outlets. Additionally, most journals now have Web sites that include, among other things, instructions for contributors. Typically, this information is available in the print version of journals. However, if your library does not subscribe to that journal, then obtaining submission information can be difficult. Journal Web pages can make the submission process easier and more efficient. Finally, many journals now make articles available electronically, especially if one's library subscribes to that journal. If an article that you publish is available on the publisher's Web site in an electronic format, it can make dissemination of your article easier.

Submitting Manuscripts

Many conferences and journals either allow, recommend, or require electronic submission of conference papers or journal manuscripts. Electronic submission is advantageous for a number of reasons. First, it greatly improves the speed and efficiency of article submissions. Second, it reduces the amount of paper typically required of nonelectronic submissions. Third, you are likely to receive instant confirmation of receipt of your manuscript.

Electronic Reviews

Finally, the publication process is greatly improved with the use of the Internet because manuscripts are sent out for review electronically, thereby increasing the speed with which a reviewer receives the manuscript. In addition, reviewers can send their reviews to the editor via e-mail, which increases the speed with which an author receives a decision about his or her article.

CONCLUSIONS

In this chapter, we have explored the use of the Internet to aid the research process. We have seen how the Internet can be used to search for information relevant to a research project, to collect data, to disseminate results, and to speed the publication process. For researchers, the Internet is full of potential:

- The Internet allows access to unlimited, often novel, pieces of information. On your desktop, at any time of the day or night, you can have access to court briefs, the incidence of diseases in your county, and up-to-date sports statistics! The potential of the Internet to answer previously unanswerable research questions is limitless.
- The Internet increases the speed and efficiency of the research process in ways that were previously unimaginable. Every stage of the research process, from idea creation to publication, benefits from the speed and ease of the Internet.
- The Internet holds more information than any resource that we have ever had access to previously. It is true that information on the Internet can be disorganized and at times, difficult to access. Nonetheless, a little Internet-search savvy can go a long way to uncovering enormous amounts of information. Additionally, the Internet allows us to collect enormous amounts of data from more diverse samples than was ever possible before.

Of course, the Internet can also be a source of pitfalls:

- The amount of information available on the Internet can be overwhelming and tempting. For example, say you were searching for information on breast cancer. The amount of information available makes it impossible to thoroughly review. On the other hand, because so much information is available, it is tempting to not only study the incidence of breast cancer in various counties in one state, for example, but to study the incidence of breast cancer in all 50 states.
- Anything on the Internet can be made to look credible. Yet, we know it is not. Always keep in mind that *anyone* can publish *anything* on the

Internet. It is important when gathering information on the Internet to verify the credibility of the sources. And, when using the Internet to collect data, steps can be taken to exert more control over the types of information that are collected. It is wise to always be skeptical of any information collected via the Internet.

- Because the Internet is so easy and efficient to use, it is tempting to avoid consulting non-Internet sources. However, it is important to remember that the library still includes information that is not available on the Internet. Your professors and colleagues have information that likely will never be found on the Internet. As tempting as it is to rely exclusively on the Internet to conduct research, keep in mind that you might be leaving out important information or ideas.

Chapter Six

Commonly Misused Words

This chapter explains the meanings of some of the most commonly misused words in student papers. The chapter is divided into two parts. The first part deals with meanings of nontechnical terms. Strunk and White (1979) provide a longer list, and Fowler (1965) provides a complete dictionary of English usage. The second part of the chapter deals with meanings of technical terms. The psychological dictionaries and encyclopedias described in Chapter 9 provide much more extensive lists of psychological terms.

NONTECHNICAL TERMS

1. *adapt, adopt.* To adapt is to accommodate, to adjust, to bring into correspondence. To adopt is to embrace, to take on, to make one's own.
   a. Organisms adapt to their environment.
   b. Children adopt the attitudes of their peers.
2. *adopt.* See (1).
3. *affect, effect.* Both words can be used either as nouns or as verbs. An affect is an emotion or something that tends to arouse an emotion. An effect is a result or outcome of some cause. To affect is to influence or to have an effect upon something. To effect is to accomplish or to achieve.
   a. His display of affect in response to the TAT picture seemed artificial and contrived to gain the psychologist's sympathy.
   b. The effect of the experimental treatment was negligible.

c. Shoddy procedures affect the outcome of an experiment.

d. She was able to effect a change in behavior by desensitizing the patient to snakes.

4. *aggravate, irritate.* To aggravate is to intensify, to heighten, or to magnify. To irritate is to annoy, to inflame, to provoke.

a. Don't aggravate his frustration by telling him that he answered all the questions incorrectly.

b. Experimenters who deceive subjects often irritate the subjects.

5. *allusion.* An allusion is an indirect reference. An explicit statement about *X* is not an allusion to *X*.

a. The first experimenter made an allusion to a reward for exceptional performance, but she never came out and directly told the subject that the subject would receive a reward.

b. The second experimenter told the subject he would receive a reward for exceptional performance. (He did not allude to a reward.)

6. *among, between.* A relation is between two things and among more than two things. The term *between* can be used for a relation involving more than two things if reciprocity is involved in the relation. When in doubt regarding relations among more than two things, use *among.*

a. The subject had to decide between the button on the left and the button on the right.

b. The subject had to decide among the left, middle, and right buttons.

c. The agreement between the three members of the group broke down quickly when the experimental manipulation was introduced.

7. *amount of, number of.* An amount of something is a sum total or aggregate. A number of something is a quantity of it. Use *amount of* when dealing with quantities that can't be counted. Use *number of* when dealing with quantities that can be counted. Monetary terms are exceptions to this generalization.

a. The amount of liquid in the tall jar was the same as the amount in the fat jar.

b. The number of stimuli was too small.

c. The subject was dissatisfied with the amount of money she received for participating in the experiment.

8. *and/or.* Avoid this expression, which means that a relation is either conjunctive (*and*) or disjunctive (*or*). The expression disrupts the flow of prose, is ambiguous, and often indicates that the author couldn't decide which conjunction to use, so he used both simultaneously.

9. *as to whether.* Avoid this expression. Say *whether.*

10. *between.* See (6).

11. *bring, take.* To bring something is to carry it toward the speaker or listener. To take something is to carry it away from the speaker or listener.

    a. Take this incomprehensible book back to the library.

    b. Bring me a better book from the library.

12. *certainly.* Use the word *certainly* only if you mean "With 100% probability." Don't use the word loosely to connote near-certainty.

    a. She certainly won't eat her hat.

13. *compare to, compare with.* To compare to is to point out or emphasize similarities between different things. To compare with is to point out or emphasize differences between similar things.

    a. The student compared the predictions of the continuous learning model to those of the discrete learning model, and showed that they were indistinguishable.

    b. The student compared Freud's conception of the ego with Erikson's conception and showed that the two conceptions differed in fundamental respects.

14. *comprise.* To comprise is to consist of or to embrace. This word has the dubious distinction of being misused more often than it is properly used in student papers. A whole comprises its parts; parts constitute (form or compose) a whole.

    a. This book comprises 14 fascinating chapters.

15. *continual, continuous.* Continual means often repeated. *Continuous* means without stop.

    a. Continual interruptions forced the experimenter to terminate the session early.

    b. Continuous background music improved employees' morale.

16. *continuous.* See (15).

17. *data. Data* is a plural noun and requires a plural verb. The singular form is *datum.* This form is used infrequently.

    a. The professor's data were far from perfect.

    b. One datum was inconsistent with all the rest.

18. *different from, different than.* If two things differ, they are different from each other. The expression *different than* is incorrect.

19. *discover, invent.* To discover something is to find something that was there before. To invent something is to create something new.

    a. No one has discovered a single gene for intelligence.

    b. Some people would like to invent a pill to increase intelligence.

20. *disinterested, uninterested.* To be disinterested is to be impartial. To be uninterested is to be lacking in interest.

   a. There seem to be few disinterested investigators studying the heritability of intelligence. Most of them have obvious biases.

   b. Psychoanalysts are generally uninterested in stimulus–response explanations of behavior.

21. *effect.* See (3).

22. *enormity, enormousness.* The former word refers to extreme wickedness, the latter to extreme size or volume.

   a. The enormity of the tyrant's crimes could not be simulated in an experimentally controlled setting.

   b. The enormousness of the giant scared the children.

23. *enormousness.* See (22).

24. *fact.* A fact should be directly verifiable either empirically or logically. Do not refer to judgments or probable outcomes as facts.

25. *factor.* Because this word has at least two technical meanings in psychology (see the next section of this chapter), it is best not to use it in a loose, nontechnical sense. Instead of saying, for example, that "several factors contributed to the subject's euphoria," say that "the subject was euphoric for several reasons."

26. *farther, further.* The word *farther* should be used to refer to greater distance; the word *further* should be used to refer to quantity or time.

   a. Further jokes were to no avail; the subject refused to laugh.

   b. The patient explained to the psychologist that the farther he traveled from his home, the more anxious he felt.

27. *fewer, less. Fewer* refers to number, *less* to amount or degree.

   a. The patient had fewer nightmares after she began therapy.

   b. The patient's nightmares became less frightening after she began therapy.

28. *former, latter. Former* refers to the first item in a series, *latter* to the second. These words are applicable when the series consists of just two items or when a longer series is divided into two parts. In series with more than two items, refer to the endpoints of the series as the first and last items.

   a. The male and female confederates entered the room together, the former carrying a live alligator and the latter carrying a dead rattlesnake.

   b. Of the three people who interviewed for the job, only the first was qualified but only the last was willing to take the job after finding out what it entailed.

29. *fortuitous, fortunate.* A fortuitous event is one that occurs by chance. A fortunate event is one that is favored by fortune.

  a. The simultaneous appearance of the two rivals was made to appear fortuitous, but it was in fact contrived.

  b. The appearance of all the subjects at the testing session was most fortunate, because the machine controlling the testing exploded at the end of the session and thereafter was incapable of further use.

30. *fortunate.* See (29).

31. *further.* See (26).

32. *hopefully.* This word means *full of hope.* It does not mean *it is to be hoped.* Today, this word is more often used incorrectly than correctly.

  a. He started the experiment hopefully, but ended it discouraged.

33. *imply, infer.* To imply something is to suggest it indirectly. To infer something is to conclude or deduce it from the information available. The two words are not interchangeable.

  a. The patient implied that she still felt like strangling anyone who got in her way.

  b. The therapist thus inferred that the patient was not yet cured.

34. *infer.* See (33).

35. *interesting.* This word is overused. Saying that something is interesting is not a substitute for making it interesting.

36. *invent.* See (19).

37. *irregardless.* This word does not exist in English. The proper word is *regardless.*

  a. The rat receives a sugar pellet after pressing the bar, regardless of how long the rat takes to press it.

38. *irritate.* See (4).

39. *its, it's.* The word *its* means *belonging to* or *pertaining to.* The word *it's* means *it is* or *it has.*

  a. The investigator knew the fear manipulation had failed when the monster shook its tail and the children laughed in response.

  b. After seeing the children's response, the investigator thought to himself: "It's all over."

40. *latter.* See (28).

41. *lay, lie. Lay* and *lie* both have a number of meanings. Confusion regarding which word to use arises from one meaning of each word. For *lay,* this meaning is *to put or place something.* For *lie,* this meaning is *to recline.* The past tense of *lay* is *laid,* and the present perfect is *have laid.*

The past tense of *lie* is *lay*, and the present perfect *is have lain*. *Lay* always takes an object; *lie* never does.

a. i. When the experimenter enters the room, he lays the booklets on the table.

ii. The experimenter laid the booklets on the table.

iii. The experimenter has laid the booklets on the table.

b. i. The patient lies down on a couch when she enters the therapist's office.

ii. The patient lay down on a couch after she entered the therapist's office.

iii. After the patient has lain down, the therapist begins the session.

42. *less*. See (27).

43. *lie*. See (41).

44. *literally*. If something is literally true, then it is true in fact. Use *literally* only if you mean it. Do not use the expression *literally true* if you mean figuratively true or almost true.

45. *number*. See (7).

46. *one*. Do not follow *one* by *his*. Follow it by *one's*.

a. One must organize one's papers carefully in order for them to communicate effectively.

47. *only*. Careless placement of *only* in a sentence can change the meaning of the sentence. Place *only* immediately before the word or clause it modifies. Do not say, for example, "I only tested 5 subjects" if you mean, "I tested only 5 subjects." Consider how the meaning of a sentence changes, depending upon the placement of *only:*

a. Only I will treat the patient in my office tomorrow.

b. I only will treat the patient in my office tomorrow.

c. I will only treat the patient in my office tomorrow.

d. I will treat only the patient in my office tomorrow.

e. I will treat the only patient in my office tomorrow.

f. I will treat the patient only in my office tomorrow.

g. I will treat the patient in only my office tomorrow.

h. I will treat the patient in my only office tomorrow.

i. I will treat the patient in my office only tomorrow.

j. I will treat the patient in my office tomorrow only.

48. *principal, principle*. Used as an adjective, *principal* means *chief, dominant, main, major*. Used as a noun, it means a *person* or *thing of importance* or *rank*. *Principle* can be used only as a noun, and it refers to *a general truth or law*.

a. The principal reason for not scoring the subject's test was that the subject had cheated in answering the last two problems.

b. This book presents many principles for writing psychology papers.

49. *principle.* See (48).

50. *relevant.* Use this word only if you can specify a precise relationship. Do not use it to express a vague connection to everyday life or your experience, as in "Clinical psychology is relevant." If you make the connection clear, then the word is appropriate:

a. Clinical psychology is relevant to everyday life.

51. *since.* Use this word only in its temporal sense, not as a substitute for *because.* If you mean *because,* use *because.*

a. Since leaving therapy, the patient has shown no recurrence of symptoms.

52. *take.* See (11).

53. *that, which. That* is used for restrictive clauses, *which* for nonrestrictive clauses. Clauses using *which,* therefore, are surrounded by commas. The use of *which* for *that* is common in psychological (and other) writing but is inadvisable. Excessive use of *which* makes sentences cumbersome and difficult to read. The advice of Strunk and White (1979) is most appropriate: "The careful writer, watchful for small conveniences, goes *which*-hunting, removes the defining *whiches,* and by doing so improves his work" (p. 53).

a. The experiment that he designed is a gem. (This sentence tells which experiment is a gem.)

b. The experiment, which he designed, is a gem. (This sentence tells something about the one experiment in question.)

54. *try.* Say "try to," not "try and."

a. Before she showed the picture of the snake to the patient, the therapist told the patient to try to relax.

55. *uninterested.* See (20).

56. *unique.* Something that is unique is one-of-a-kind. It is not merely unusual or extraordinary. There can be no degrees of uniqueness.

a. The psychologist employed a unique combination of therapeutic techniques in treating his patients.

57. *utilize. Use* is simpler, and usually serves just as well.

a. The subject used the process of elimination to answer the multiple-choice test questions.

58. *which.* See (53).

59. *while.* This word is best used to mean "at the same time that." It is frequently used as a substitute for *whereas, but,* and *although.* The word does not serve well as a substitute, because it is not clear whether the author intends to imply simultaneity. The sentence, "I went east while he went west," is unambiguous if the reader knows that the author uses *while* only to mean *at the same time that.* But if the author sometimes uses *while* to mean *whereas,* the sentence is ambiguous: The reader does not know whether the two individuals went in opposite directions at the same time. Similarly, in reading the sentence "the subject answered test questions while the examiner scored them," the reader will want to infer that answering and scoring occurred simultaneously.

    a. The experimenter appeared nonchalant while the subject finished the task.

60. *Whom.* This word is often used incorrectly before expressions like *he said,* when *who* should serve as the subject of the verb following the expression.

    a. The graduate student who the professor said would come to Yale went to Squeedunk instead. (*Who* is the subject of *would come.*)

61. *Whose.* This word can serve as the possessive case of either *who* or *which.* Hence, it can refer to inanimate as well as animate objects.

    a. The subject was upset when the machine whose buttons she pressed disintegrated in less than five seconds.

    b. The experimenter, however, knew whose fault the disintegration was, and had trouble holding back a smile.

TECHNICAL TERMS

1. *ability, capacity.* Capacity is innate potential. Ability is developed capacity. One's ability may not reflect one's capacity if environmental circumstances have been unfavorable to the development of that capacity. Only ability can be measured; hence, we cannot assess the degree to which one's ability reflects one's capacity.

    a. The child's test scores indicated only marginal ability to succeed in school work.

    b. The child's unhappy childhood suggested to the psychologist that the child's capacity for school work might not be reflected in his scores on ability tests.

2. *algorithm, heuristic.* An algorithm is a systematic routine for solving a problem that will eventually solve the problem, even if the solution involves consideration of all possible answers to the problem. A heuristic is a short-cut or informal routine for solving a problem that may or may not eventually solve the problem. An algorithm may be slow, but it is guaranteed eventually to reach an answer. A heuristic is relatively fast, but does not guarantee solution. Some problems can be solved only by heuristics. No algorithm is available, for example, that guarantees that a given move in a game of chess is the optimal move.

a. The subject discovered an algorithm for solving the jigsaw puzzle, but the algorithm required 752,964 arrangements of the pieces of the puzzle to guarantee a solution.

b. Another subject discovered a heuristic for solving the puzzle that she estimated gave her a 75% chance of solving the puzzle after only 55 arrangements of the pieces.

3. *anxiety, fear.* Anxiety is a state (or trait) of apprehension or uneasiness with no well-defined object. Fear is a state of apprehension in response to a well-defined threat.

a. The executive felt a constant sense of anxiety and yet was unable to pinpoint anything in his environment that threatened his well-being.

b. The hunter was filled with fear when her rifle failed to fire and the bear started charging toward her.

4. *applied research, basic research.* Applied research strives for findings of practical value, regardless of whether or not they have theoretical value. Basic research strives for findings of theoretical value, regardless of whether they have practical value. Applied research may yield findings of theoretical value, and basic research may yield findings of practical value, although such findings are incidental to the major goals of each type of research.

a. Research on consumer preferences for different kinds of cosmetic products has been almost exclusively applied research.

b. Research on serial learning of nonsense syllables has been primarily basic research.

5. *artificial intelligence, simulation.* Artificial intelligence researchers seek to build machines or instructions for machines that solve in an optimal way problems usually thought to require intelligence. Little or no attempt is made to have these machines or instructions correspond to the human mind or to the strategies used by the human mind. Simulation research seeks to build machines or instructions for machines

that solve problems in ways analogous to those used by humans. Little or no attempt is made to achieve optimal performance. Indeed, if human performance is suboptimal, then an attempt is made to imitate this suboptimal performance.

a. Using the techniques of artificial intelligence, the computer scientist was able to program a computer to solve algebra problems far more efficiently than human beings solve them.

b. The psychologist wrote a simulation program that closely matched the techniques of Algebra I students in solving algebra problems.

6. *average.* As a statistical term, this word is used in two ways. The more specific way is as a synonym for *mean.* Used in this way, the average is the sum of a set of values divided by the number of values. The more general way is as a generic term for all measures of central tendency (cf. mean, median, mode). Used in this way, the average is the central value, however defined. In order to avoid confusion, the word *average* is best used only in its more specific meaning.

a. The five children taking the test had scores of 2, 4, 4, 6, and 14, giving an average of 6.

7. *avoidance learning, escape learning.* Avoidance learning is motivated by avoidance of punishment. The learner is punished only if learning does not take place. Escape learning is motivated by escape from punishment. The learner is punished until learning takes place.

a. After being suspended from school for a third time, the mischievous child learned not to play practical jokes on his classmates. (This situation provides an example of avoidance learning.)

b. The rat learned to jump on the pedestal whenever the floor to its cage was electrified. (This situation provides an example of escape learning.)

8. *basic research.* See (4).

9. *classical conditioning, operant conditioning.* In classical conditioning, an originally neutral stimulus is repeatedly paired with a stimulus that evokes a certain response. This latter stimulus is called the unconditioned stimulus or US. The response given to the stimulus is called the unconditioned response or UR. As a result of the repeated pairing, the originally neutral stimulus eventually starts to evoke the same response as the unconditioned stimulus, even if it is not paired with the US any more. At this point, the originally neutral stimulus becomes a conditioned stimulus or CS. The response given to this stimulus is called the conditioned response or CR. In operant conditioning,

a learner is rewarded (reinforced) each time a desired response takes place. Eventually, the learned response occurs even without paired presentation of the reward.

a. Every time the salesman visited his Southeast Asian client, the salesman became ill from the change in climate; the salesman was surprised, though, when the client came to visit him and he became sick without exposure to the different climate. (This situation provides an example of classical conditioning.)

b. As a child, she was given a lollipop every time she took her vitamins without complaining, and as an adult, she continued to take her vitamins without complaining, even though the lollipop no longer accompanied the vitamins. (This situation provides an example of operant conditioning.)

10. *compulsion, obsession.* A compulsion is an irresistible urge to perform repeatedly a stereotyped act that serves no apparent purpose. An obsession is a recurrent thought that the thinker is powerless to control.

a. The therapist suggested to the patient that the patient's desire to wash her hands every 15 minutes might be a compulsion rather than a reasonable wish for cleanliness.

b. As a soldier during the Korean War, he had seen a little girl shot to death on the battlefield. Since then he was obsessed: A vision of the little girl being shot plagued him at least twice every waking hour.

11. *control group, experimental group.* A control group is one that does not receive the experimental treatment of interest. An experimental group is one that does receive the treatment. The effect of the treatment can then be assessed by comparing performance in the experimental group with that in the control group. The term *experimental group* is sometimes used in a more general sense to refer to any group in an experiment. In order to avoid confusion, the term is better restricted to the more limited, contrastive usage.

a. Members of the experimental group were told that they had been selected because their teachers had rated them unusually likely to succeed in difficult reasoning tasks.

b. Members of one control group were told that they had been selected at random, whereas members of a second control group were not told anything about selection procedures. The first group served as a control for telling subjects that they were rated unusually likely to succeed, and the second group served as a control for telling subjects anything at all about selection procedures.

12. *culture-fair test, culture-free test.* A culture-fair test is one that attempts to minimize the *differential* effects of different cultural experiences upon performance. A culture-free test is one that attempts to minimize the *absolute* effects of any cultural experiences upon performance. Construction of a culture-fair test is a sensible goal, although one that probably can be only approached. Construction of a culture-free test is not a sensible goal, (a) because the very act of taking a test is culture-bound and (b) because we have no culture-free baseline against which to assess the success of a culture-free test. In other words, we have no way of knowing what *culture-free* means.

    a. By using only pictures of naturally and commonly occurring objects, the investigator hoped to attain a culture-fair test.

    b. The investigator set out to make a culture-free test by stripping away from her culture-bound test everything that in any way reflected cultural experiences; when she finished her task, she realized she had nothing left.

13. *culture-free.* See (12).

14. *deduction, induction.* Deduction is reasoning from the general to the specific. Given general principles, one deduces specific outcomes. A characteristic of deduction is that one can attain certainty in one's conclusions. If the premises are valid and the reasoning correct, then the conclusions must be valid. Mathematical and logical proofs are usually deductive. Induction is reasoning from the specific to the general. Given specific outcomes, one induces general principles. A characteristic of induction is that one can never attain certainty in one's conclusions. One can disconfirm but never confirm with certainty an inductive argument.

    a. From just a few basic axioms, Euclid was able to deduce all the theorems that constitute what we now call Euclidean geometry.

    b. A jeweler observed that all emeralds he had ever seen were green. He induced on the basis of his extensive observations that all emeralds are green, regardless of whether he had ever seen them. He realized, though, that the induction could be disconfirmed by the subsequent appearance of just a single nongreen emerald, but that the induction could not be confirmed because the next emerald he saw might be nongreen.

15. *delusion, hallucination, illusion.* A delusion is a false belief. A hallucination is a sensory experience in the absence of an appropriate external stimulus. An illusion is a misperception of a stimulus.

a. The psychologist tried to convince the patient that her belief that her friends were secretly plotting against her was a delusion.

b. After 3 days without water in the desert, the explorer saw an oasis ahead; but when he reached the point where he had seen the oasis, and saw only dry sand, he realized he had suffered a hallucination.

c. The clever student knew that her perception of the train tracks as meeting each other on the horizon was an illusion.

16. *dependent variable, independent variable.* A dependent variable is one whose value is affected by (is dependent upon) the value of some other variables(s). These other variables, which are the variables under experimental control, are the independent variables.

a. The dependent variable in the experiment was reaction time to a visually presented stimulus.

b. The independent variables in the experiment were length of stimulus presentation and clarity of the visual stimulus.

17. *descriptive statistics, inferential statistics.* Descriptive statistics summarize data. They include indices such as the mean, median, standard deviation, and correlation coefficient. Each of these statistics tells us some important property of the data under consideration. Inferential statistics provide tests of hypotheses about data or simply permit generalizations about populations from sample data. They include such indices as t, z, and F. Each of these statistics is used to test hypotheses about differences between one value (or set of values) and another.

a. The author first presented descriptive statistics so that readers could get a feeling for the data.

b. Then he presented inferential statistics so that readers could see the extent to which the data were consistent with his hypotheses.

18. *deviation IQ, ratio IQ.* The IQ, or intelligence quotient, was originally conceived of as a ratio of mental age to chronological age. This ratio (or quotient) was soon perceived to have several disadvantages. First, it seemed to assume that mental age kept increasing as long as chronological age increased, whereas in fact mental age increases very slowly after a person reaches a chronological age of 16, and eventually it begins to decrease. Second, the ratio assumed that increases in mental age are continuous in the same way that increases in chronological age are continuous, although the research of Piaget (1952) and others indicates that this assumption is not the case. In order to correct for these undesirable properties of the ratio IQ, deviation IQs were introduced. These IQs are not actually quotients, although the designation "IQ" was retained. The concept of mental age is not used in the calculation of deviation IQs. Instead, the IQs are fixed at a certain mean, usually 100, as is a certain standard deviation, usually 15 or 16. IQs are then computed on the basis of each person's standardized deviation from the mean. If the mean IQ is set to 100 and the standard deviation to 15, the deviation IQ is equal to {[(Raw Score – Mean Score)/(Standard Deviation)] × 15} + 100.

a. The child's raw score on the intelligence test was 50. Because the mean on the test was 40, and the standard deviation was 10, her deviation IQ was {[(50 – 40)/10] × 15} + 100, or 115.

b. The child's raw score of 50 corresponded to a mental age of 12 years, 0 months. Because her chronological age was 10 years, 0 months, her ratio IQ was (12/10) × 100 = 120.

19. *escape learning.* See (7).

20. *empiricism, nativism.* Empiricism is a view that behavior is learned primarily as a result of experience. In its extreme form, it claims that all behavior is acquired through experience. Nativism makes the claim that most behavior is innately determined. In its extreme form, it claims that all behavior is innately determined.

a. Empiricists such as Skinner claim that language acquisition can be explained by operant conditioning.

b. Nativists such as Chomsky claim that language acquisition can be understood only if one postulates an innate competence for learning (sometimes called a language acquisition device).

21. *experimental group.* See (11).

22. *experimental psychology.* This term is used in two different ways. Properly used, it refers to a methodology – the use of experiments to collect data. Thus, psychologists who collect data via experiments are referred to as experimental psychologists. A second and less desirable use of the term is as referring to a substantive area of psychology embracing sensation, perception, learning, memory, and thinking. This latter usage developed because researchers interested in these processes have long (although not always) used experimental methods.

Because investigators in other areas of psychology (e.g., personality, social, developmental) may also use experimental methods, the term experimental psychology is better used in its first meaning.

a. Using experimental methods, the investigator concluded that introverts were more likely to complete his boring task than were extroverts.

23. *extrinsic motivation, intrinsic motivation.* Extrinsic motivation is motivation controlled by the possibilities of reward or punishment other than those directly achieved by engaging in a behavior or by the outcome of that behavior. Intrinsic motivation is motivation controlled by the possibilities of reward or punishment that are achieved directly by engaging in a behavior or by the outcome of that behavior.

a. The student's motivation to learn geometry was extrinsic: She wanted to receive an A in her geometry course.

b. Her friend's motivation to learn geometry was intrinsic: He enjoyed learning how all of geometry could be deduced from a few simple axioms.

24. *factor.* This word has two common technical meanings in psychology. First, it can refer to an independent variable in an experiment. A three-factor experiment is one with three independent variables. In such cases, you are better off referring to *variables* rather than *factors* in order to avoid confusion with the second meaning of *factor*. Second, the word can refer to a mathematical representation of a hypothetical psychological construct. This mathematical representation is obtained through a statistical technique called factor analysis.

a. The student manipulated two factors in her experiment, attractiveness and sex of the confederate.

b. According to Spearman's theory of intelligence, intelligence comprises one general factor common to performance on all intellectual tasks and many specific factors, each limited to performance on a single intellectual task.

25. *fear.* See (3).

26. *fixation, regression.* Fixation refers to arrested development at some stage, usually a stage earlier than the one an individual should be in. Regression refers to a return to an earlier stage of development.

a. The 5-year-old child's continual sucking of anything she could get into her mouth suggested to the psychologist that the child had fixated at the oral stage of development.

b. The soldier seemed perfectly normal until he entered the battlefield, at which time he showed regression toward infantile behaviors that he had not exhibited for more than two decades.

27. *genotype, phenotype.* A genotype is a set of inherited characteristics that may or may not be displayed. A phenotype is the set of characteristics that is displayed.

   a. The woman's phenotype revealed brown eyes.

   b. When the brown-eyed woman had a child with blue eyes, it became apparent that her genotype included the recessive gene for blue eyes as well as the dominant gene for brown eyes.

28. *hallucination.* See (15).

29. *heritability.* Heritability is the proportion of the total variance of a trait in a population that is attributable to genetic differences among individuals in that population. Heritability is thus the ratio of (variance due to genetic causes)/(total variance). (See item 68.)

   a. Height is a characteristic with high heritability, whereas temperament is a characteristic with low heritability.

30. *identification, imitation.* In identification, a person (often a child) acquires the social role of another person by modeling the behavior of that person. In imitation, the person models the behavior of another person, not necessarily acquiring that person's social role.

   a. Because the man identified with his lazy and irresponsible father, he found himself unable to cope with any of his family responsibilities.

   b. The young boy often imitated the actions of his mother, but he eventually identified with his father.

31. *illusion.* See (15).

32. *imitation.* See (30).

33. *independent variable.* See (16).

34. *induction.* See (14).

35. *inferential statistics.* See (17).

36. *intrinsic motivation.* See (23).

37. *latent content, manifest content.* The latent content of a dream is its deeper, hidden meaning. The manifest content of a dream is its apparent meaning.

   a. The manifest content of the dream consisted of the patient's being chased out of a luxurious palace across a moat by an angry older man wielding a big stick.

b. The psychologist believed the latent content of the dream was sexual, and that the man exhibited through the dream an unresolved Oedipal conflict.

38. *learning, maturation, performance.* Learning is often distinguished both from maturation and from performance. Learning is an increment in knowledge that occurs as a result of practice. Maturation is a change in behavior resulting from a growth process that is independent of practice. Performance is overt behavior. Note that learning takes place only with practice; maturation takes place regardless of whether or not it is preceded by practice. Note also that learning may occur without showing itself through a change in performance.

a. The child repeatedly failed to understand that the amount of liquid in the tall jar was the same as the amount obtained when the contents of the tall jar were poured into the fat jar. Eventually, her cognitive abilities matured to the point at which she could understand the principle of conservation, and thus the equality between the two amounts of liquid.

b. Although the subject had learned all the words in the list, his recall performance was far from perfect; it was not until the subject was given a test of recognition performance that he showed that he was familiar with all of the words.

39. *manifest content.* See (37).

40. *maturation.* See (38).

41. *mean, median, mode.* The mean (average) is the sum of a set of values divided by the number of values. The median is the middle value: Half the values are higher and half are lower. The mode is the most frequently occurring value.

a. The mean of the numbers 2, 2, 4, 6, and 16 is 6.

b. The median of the numbers 2, 2, 4, 6, and 16 is 4.

c. The mode of the numbers 2, 2, 4, 6, and 16 is 2.

42. *median.* See (41).

43. *mode.* See (41).

44. *nativism.* See (20).

45. *nature–nurture.* The nature–nurture distinction refers to the relative proportions of variance in traits or behaviors attributable to heredity (*nature*) versus environment (*nurture*).

a. In the nature–nurture debate, hereditarians favor nature and environmentalists favor nurture as the primary source of differences in behavior.

46. *neurosis, psychosis.* A neurosis is a minor disorder in which a person exhibits maladaptive behavior patterns (symptoms) that avoid rather than cope with underlying problems. A psychosis is a major disorder in which a person exhibits severely maladaptive behavior patterns that usually require treatment in a hospital.

   a. The neurotic woman counted her money every hour-on-the-hour to make sure it hadn't fallen out of her pocket.

   b. The psychotic man continually saw robbers reaching out to grab his wallet, but when he chased the robbers, they always disappeared into thin air.

47. *null hypothesis.* The null hypothesis is a hypothesis of no difference. It is not *no* hypothesis.

   a. The investigator's null hypothesis was that the treatment would produce no effect on the experimental group relative to the control group.

48. *obsession.* See (10).

49. *operant conditioning.* See (9).

50. *parameter, statistic.* A parameter is a constant value that describes a characteristic of a population. A statistic is a variable value that describes a characteristic of a sample from a population.

   a. A psychologist tested the IQs of all 25 students in Ms. Blakeley's 1977 fourth-grade class. He found that the mean IQ was 105. If this class were the population of interest, then the mean of 105 would be a population parameter. (See item 53 for definition of *population.*)

   b. If, in the above example, Ms. Blakeley's 1977 fourth-grade class were viewed as a sample of fourth-grade classes throughout the United States, then the mean of 105 would be a sample statistic. (See item 53 for the definition of *sample.*)

51. *performance.* See (38).

52. *phenotype.* See (27).

53. *population, sample.* A population is the universe of cases to which an investigator wants to generalize his results. A sample is a subset of a population.

   a. If an investigator views Ms. Blakeley's 1977 fourth-grade class as a population, then any generalizations he makes from data obtained from the class will be limited to that class only.

   b. If an investigator views Ms. Blakeley's 1977 fourth-grade class as a sample, then generalizations he makes from data obtained from the class will be to the population of which Ms. Blakeley's class is a subject. The more diverse the population, the less likely is Ms. Blakeley's class to be representative of the population and, thus, the less likely are the data to be generalizable. One could have more confidence in generalizations to the entire fourth grade at Ms. Blakeley's school than in generalizations to the fourth grades of the entire United States.

54. *primacy, recency.* Primacy effects are effects that occur at the beginning of some temporal sequence. Recency effects are effects that occur at the end of some temporal sequence.

a. The primacy effect in free recall is the tendency for people to remember items from the beginning of a list better than they remember items from the middle of a list.

b. The recency effect in free recall is the tendency for people to remember items from the end of a list better than they remember items from the middle of a list.

55. *ratio IQ.* See (18).

56. *recency.* See (54).

57. *regression.* See (26).

58. *reliability, validity.* Reliability refers to how well or consistently a test measures whatever the test measures. Validity refers to how well a test measures what it is supposed to measure. Thus, a perfectly reliable test can be completely invalid if it measures something well but not what it is intended to measure. A perfectly valid test, however, must be perfectly reliable, because if the test measures what it is supposed to measure perfectly, it must measure what it does in fact measure perfectly.

a. The test of finger-tapping speed proved to be highly reliable, providing consistent estimates of people's finger-tapping abilities. The test of intelligence proved to be only moderately reliable, providing only somewhat consistent estimates of people's measured intelligence.

b. The highly reliable test of finger-tapping speed proved to be invalid as a predictor of school achievement. The moderately reliable intelligence test proved to be moderately valid as a predictor of school achievement. In this case, the more reliable test was less valid for a specific purpose to which it was poorly suited. Although reliability places an upper bound on validity, it is no guarantee of validity.

59. *repression, suppression.* Repression is a defense mechanism whereby a thought or feeling is removed from consciousness. Suppression is a defense mechanism whereby a thought or feeling remains in consciousness but is not overtly expressed. People are aware of suppressed but not repressed material.

   a. The patient had long ago repressed all memories of his brutal grandfather. At the therapy sessions, he honestly denied ever even having known his grandfather.

   b. The psychologist's therapy sessions with the student were getting nowhere, because the student suppressed any information that she thought might embarrass her in the psychologist's eyes.

60. *significant.* A statistically significant result is one that enables an investigator to reject a null hypothesis (see item 47). Statistical significance is sometimes contrasted with practical significance. A result can be statistically significant but not practically significant. Whenever the term *significant* is used by itself, it should be used only to refer to the technical meaning of *statistical significance.* Do not use the word to refer to any result that you think is important.

   a. The large difference between means in the two groups was statistically significant, enabling the psychologist to reject the null hypothesis of no difference between the groups.

61. *simulation.* See (5).

62. *state, trait.* A state is a temporary mood or frame of mind. A trait is a permanent disposition.

   a. Anxiety as a state refers to a temporary frame of mind in which the individual feels uneasy or apprehensive for no clear reason.

   b. Anxiety as a trait refers to a permanent disposition of an individual to feel uneasy or apprehensive for no clear reason.

63. *preconscious, unconscious.* The preconscious contains cognitions that are not conscious but can be brought into consciousness with little or no effort. The unconscious (subconscious) contains cognitions and feelings of which we are unaware and that can be brought into consciousness only with difficulty.

   a. As she completed the first sentence of her paper, the ideas for her second sentence glided from her preconscious to her conscious thoughts.

   b. The girl's desire to excel over her three sisters was unconscious and showed itself only in her behavior and in her repeated dreams of athletic conquests over three familiar but not quite recognizable opponents.

64. *suppression.* See (59).

65. *trait.* See (62).

66. *unconscious.* See (63).

67. *validity.* See (58).

68. *variability, variance.* The variability of a set of observations refers to the amount of dispersion or spread in the observations. The variance of a set of observations refers to a specific measure of the amount of dispersion: $\Sigma(x^2)/N$, where x is the deviation of each score from the mean and N the number of cases. The term *variance* should be used only to refer to this specific measure, not to refer loosely to the amount of dispersion in the observations.

    a. The scores in the sample showed very little variability.

    b. The variance of the scores in the sample was only 4 points.

69. *variance.* See (68).

70. *white noise.* White noise is noise composed of sounds of all frequencies. It is called white noise as an analogy to white color, which is composed of colors of all wavelengths. It otherwise has no relation to white or any other color.

    a. White noise was piped into the testing room in order to distract subjects from the difficult memory task.

Chapter Seven

American Psychological Association Guidelines for Psychology Papers

This chapter summarizes the guidelines for preparing a psychology paper presented in the *Publication Manual of the American Psychological Association*, Fifth Edition (2001). This manual should be consulted for a complete list of guidelines. If you intend to submit a paper for publication, then you cannot afford to be without this manual. It can be obtained from Publication Sales, American Psychological Association, 750 First Street, NE, Washington, DC, 20002-4242.

Journals of the British Psychological Society (BPS), and many other non-APA journals, will accept papers prepared in accordance with APA guidelines, even though there are minor differences in style. Some examples of the main differences between BPS and APA styles are given in Appendix B.

All examples used to illustrate principles in this chapter are fictitious.

WORD-PROCESSING THE PAPER

Rules of Format

Paper. Print your paper on one side only of heavy, white, 8½ × 11 inch paper. Do not use onionskin, which lacks durability, or erasable paper, which smudges easily. Do not paste or glue together pieces of pages. Reprint those pages that otherwise would require pasting.

Margins. Set your margins to leave 1 inch at the top, bottom, and both sides of each page. Allow for a 6½ inch line. This length is obtained by allowing 65 characters of pica (large) typeface, or 78 characters of

119

elite (small) typeface. Do not right-justify lines (i.e., use a uniform printed right margin, as in printed pages) or use proportional spacing (i.e., different spacings between words on different lines). In other words, the right margin should be "ragged." Do not hyphenate words at ends of lines.

Vertical Spacing. Double space between all lines, without exception. There may be times when you are tempted to single space – in writing references, footnotes, block quotations, tables, and the like. Do not succumb to the temptation. Your paper should be double spaced throughout.

Horizontal Spacing. Begin each new paragraph by indenting five spaces, or using a standard computer default indentation; type all other lines starting from a uniform left margin. Leave (a) no space after internal periods in abbreviations (e.g., U.S.A., U.K.), (b) one space after commas and semicolons, (c) one space after internal periods in first and middle initials (e.g., H. B. Hinkelmeyer), (d) two spaces after colons, except in ratios, where there are no spaces, and (e) one space after periods ending sentences.

Numbering Pages. Number pages consecutively, starting with the title page. Use arabic numerals. The only pages after the abstract that are not numbered are the figures. Each figure should be numbered consecutively on the back of the page. Number pages in the upper right-hand corner. Above each page number, write the first few words of the title, so that if pages become separated from the manuscript, they can be returned to it later.

Font. For the text, use a 12-point font size with an easily readable font such as Times New Roman or Courier. For figures, use a sans-serif typeface.

Rules of Legibility

Printed Output. Make sure that your printer, word processor, or typewriter produces clear, sharp, black type. Faint copy is difficult to read and annoying to the reader. Avoid using colored (e.g., red, green, blue) print, as it often does not reproduce well during the duplicating process. Do not submit articles generated by a dot-matrix printer; the quality is insufficient.

Erasures. Erasure is best produced by correction fluid, paper, or tape. Do not strike over letters, type insert pages (e.g., page 15a to be inserted in the middle of or after page 15), or write in the margins. If there are large numbers of corrections on a page, retype the page. If possible, use a word processor so that erasures are unnecessary.

Additions. If lengthy additions are required on a page, the page should be retyped. If a brief addition is required, it can be typed or printed in pencil above the word or line to be corrected. Insert a caret in the appropriate place. In general, it is preferable simply to reprint the page.

GRAMMAR

Punctuation
Comma. A comma should be used

1. before *and* and *or* in a series of three or more items
  The subject, confederate, and experimenter all entered the room together.
2. before and after a nonrestrictive clause (i.e., a clause that is nonessential to the sentence)
  An empty box, which had been rigged to look like a lie detector, was placed on a table next to the subject.
3. to separate two coordinate clauses joined by a conjunction
  The experimenter pretended to activate the lie detector, and the confederate disappeared into an adjoining room with a one-way mirror.

A comma should not be used

1. before or after a restrictive clause (i.e., a clause that limits or further defines the word it modifies)
  The button that the experimenter pushed served only to impress the subject.
2. between two parts of a compound predicate
  The experimenter attached two fake electrodes to the subject's wrists and told the subject that the truth or falsity of each response would be recorded by the machine.
3. to separate two independent clauses not joined by a conjunction
  First the subject was asked to answer each question; then he was told that he would receive double pay at the end of the experiment if he succeeded in fooling the "lie detector."

Semicolon. A semicolon should be used to

1. separate two independent clauses that are not joined by a conjunction
   The experimenter then proceeded to ask the subject a series of embarrassing questions; she pretended to be surprised at the subject's responses.
2. separate items that already contain commas
   The sets of questions asked by the experimenter dealt with sex, swearing, bathroom habits; masculinity, undressing habits, thumbsucking; or private fantasies, nightmares, academic failures.

Colon. A colon should be used

1. before a final phrase or clause that amplifies the material that comes before it
   Most subjects initially hesitated to answer the questions: They stared at the experimenter in disbelief.
2. in ratios and proportions
   The proportions of subjects answering the questions honestly were 15:25, 13:37, and 18:26 in the three groups receiving the different sets of questions.

Hyphen. A hyphen should be used in

1. a compound with a participle if the compound precedes a noun it modifies
   The truth-telling subjects showed less fidgeting than the lie-telling ones.
2. a phrase used as an adjective if the phrase precedes a noun it modifies
   A subject-by-subject analysis of the results showed strong differences in the honesty with which various individuals answered the questions.
3. an adjective–noun compound that precedes and modifies another noun unless the adjective is a comparative or superlative
   High-anxiety subjects were less honest in their answers than were low-anxiety subjects.
4. all compounds involving *self*
   Self-report data indicated that high-anxiety subjects were more worried than low-anxiety subjects that honest answers would later be used against them.

5. all compounds involving a number as the first element in which the
   compound precedes a noun
   Second-session results showed the same trends, although in this
   session the trends failed to reach significance.

A hyphen should not be used in

1. a compound with an adverb ending in -*ly*
   A widely expressed fear was that the subjects' responses would
   not really be kept confidential.
2. a compound involving a comparative or superlative
   A less common fear was that the experimenter would know from
   the "lie detector" which responses were truthful and which
   were not.
3. a modifier with a letter or numeral as the second term
   The Session 2 data seem to have been affected less by these fears
   than were the Session 1 data.

Dash. A dash should be used to indicate an interruption in the
continuity or flow of a sentence.

> The subjects who lied in answering every question—all of them
> members of the high-anxiety group—confessed that they thought
> the "lie detector" was nothing more than an empty box. [Note
> that there is no space between the dash and the text.]

Double Quotation Marks. Double quotation marks should be
used

1. to introduce a word or phrase used in a special or unusual way (Use
   quotation marks only the first time a word is used.)
   The experimenter divided the subjects into two groups: the "con
   artists" and the "apple polishers."
2. to reproduce material that is quoted verbatim
   The con artists had taken to heart the experimental instruction
   that "you should lie whenever you think you can get away with
   it." The apple polishers seem to have ignored or disbelieved this
   instruction and almost always told the truth.
3. for names of articles
   The experimenter planned to name the article, "An Experimental Investigation of Con Artistry."

Quotation marks should not be used

1. to qualify statements or to hedge bets
   The apple polishers were relieved when the experiment was
   over; the con artists begged for more (not "begged" for more).
2. for long quotations; use block format
   The experimenter debriefed the subjects at the end of the
   experiment:

   > The purpose of this experiment was to provide a source of ex-
   > amples for *The Psychologist's Companion.* The experiment it-
   > self made no sense and had no purpose other than to provide
   > the examples. I hope you enjoyed this meaningful activity.

Observe the following rules in using quotation marks:

1. Omission of material within a sentence of a quotation is indicated by
   the use of three ellipsis points (. . .). Omission of material between sentences of a quotation is indicated by four ellipsis points. Ellipsis points
   should not be used at the beginning or end of a quotation.

   According to McGoof (1974), "The difference between groups
   . . . was statistically but not practically significant" (p. 303).

   As he left the room, the subject said to the experimenter, "I hope
   I wasn't really supposed to write down the words in the order
   in which they were read. . . . I know the instructions said to, but
   I didn't see the point."
2. Insertion of material within a sentence of a quotation is indicated by
   brackets. Such insertions are usually used to clarify the quotation for
   the reader or to make the grammar of the quotation consistent with
   the sentence or paragraph in which it is embedded.

   According to the instructions, "this test [should be] timed for
   30 minutes."
3. Two kinds of changes are permissible in quotations without any indication to the reader: (a) The first letter of the first quoted word may be
   changed from a capital to a small letter or vice versa, and (b) the punctuation mark at the end of the quotation may be changed to fit the
   syntax of the sentence in which you have embedded the quotation. All
   other changes must be indicated by ellipses or brackets.

   The sentence, "She ate the cheese," may be cited as, "she ate the
   cheese."
4. The source of a direct quotation should always be cited. Include in the
   citation the author(s), year, and page number(s) of the quotation. If the
   quotation is (a) in the middle of a sentence, cite the source of the quo-

tation in parentheses immediately after the quotation; (b) at the end of a sentence, cite the page number in parentheses after the end of the quotation, but before the final punctuation mark; (c) in block format, cite the page number in parentheses after the end of the quotation and after the final punctuation mark.

> According to the author, "None of the mice ate the cheese until they had finished the task" (Rattan, 1976, p. 108), so they were hungry.

> Rattan (1976) found that "none of the mice ate the cheese until they had finished the task" (p. 108).

> According to Rattan (1976),

> > None of the mice ate the cheese until they had finished the task. After they ate the cheese, six mice proceeded to redo the task, while the other nine mice marched back to their cages. (p. 108)

5. In general, commas and periods are placed inside quotation marks and other marks of punctuation are placed outside, unless they are part of the quoted material, in which case they are placed inside.

> "Eat the banana," he screamed at the monkey.

> Did he scream at the monkey, "Eat the banana"?

6. Long quotations may require permission from the owner of the copyright on the material. APA policy permits use of up to 500 words without permission. Copyright owners vary in the number of words permitted, however, and so for quotations of 100 or more words it is wise to check the policy of the copyright owner. Even if the copyright owner is a journal or book company, it is a common courtesy to request permission from the author as well as the company. If multiple authors are involved, request permission only of the senior author.

Single Quotation Marks. Single quotation marks should be used for quotations within quotations.

> The experimenter, as if to emphasize the pointlessness of the experiment, said to the subjects, "Remember the well-known proverb: 'All's well that ends well.'"

Parentheses. Parentheses should be used to

1. set off items that are structurally independent from the rest of the sentence

> After debriefing, subjects were given a questionnaire in which they were asked their reactions to the experiment (see Table 1).

2. enclose the date of references cited in the text or references
   The questionnaire was adopted with minor modifications from one used by Bozo (1971).
   Bozo, B. B. (1971). A questionnaire for measuring slap-stick tendencies. *Humor, 3,* 26–31.
3. enclose abbreviations for previously cited items
   Subjects were also given the Toliver Test of Tolerance for Trauma (TTTT).
4. enclose letters or numbers enumerating items in a series
   Finally, subjects were given three ability tests: (a) the Penultimate Test of Pencil-Pushing Power, (b) the Scofield Scale of Hand–Foot Coordination, and (c) the Williams Test of Will Power.
5. enclose the page number of a cited quotation
   The Williams test seemed particularly appropriate for this experiment, because it is described in the manual as "an invalid test of practically anything an investigator might want to measure" (p. 26).
6. group terms in mathematical expressions
   On the Williams test, there is a correction for guessing, so that overall score is a function of both right and wrong answers:
   $$R - (W/4).$$
7. enclose enumeration of equations
   The overall score on the Williams test can be converted to a standard score
   $$z = (X - \bar{X})/SD. \tag{1}$$
   In this notation, z is the standard score, X the overall score, $\bar{X}$ the mean of the scores, and SD the standard deviation of the scores.

Brackets. Brackets should be used to

1. enclose material inserted in a quotation by someone other than the quoted writer or speaker
   A subject remarked as he left the experiment, "This is the most pointless [experiment] I've ever been in."
2. enclose parenthetical material within parentheses
   (The confederate [see *Method* section] was inclined to agree.)

Capitalization
When to Use Capitals. A capital letter should be used for the first letters of

1. nouns followed by numerals or letters indicating membership in an enumerated series (except for enumeration of pages, chapters, rows, and columns)

    In Session 1 of a new experiment on pencil pushing, subjects were asked to copy on page 1 of their booklets a paragraph of printed material.

2. trade and brand names

    Subjects used a Pengo Permapencil to do their copying.

3. exact, complete titles of tests

    Three tests of pencil pushing were administered: (a) the Penultimate Test of Pencil-Pushing Power, (b) the Staley Push-a-Pencil Test, and (c) the Pennsylvania Pencil Inventory.

4. names of factors from a factor analysis

    A factor analysis of the tests revealed just one reliable factor, which the experimenter called Pencil-Pushing Speed.

5. names of university departments referring to specific departments within specific universities

    The experiment was conducted under the auspices of the Department of Psychology, Zingo University.

6. major words in titles of books and journal articles mentioned in the text of a psychology paper

    The article reporting the experiment was to be entitled, "A Factor Analysis of Pencil-Pushing Power."

7. the first word in titles of books and articles cited in the references of a psychology paper

    Muddlehead, M. M. (1976). A factor analysis of pencil-pushing power. *Journal of Junky Experiments, 5,* 406–409.

8. all major words of journal names appearing in the references of a psychology paper

    (see above example)

9. major words of table titles

    Table 1

    Loadings of Ability Tests on Pencil-Pushing Speed Factor

10. first words of figure captions

    Figure 1. A typical sample of copied material.

When Not to Use Capitals. A capital letter should not be used for first letters of

1. names of conditions or groups in an experiment

    Subjects in the experiment were divided into two groups, fast pencil pushers and slow pencil pushers.

2. names of effects taken from analyses of variance

An analysis of variance revealed no difference in school achievement as a function of pencil-pushing speed.

3. shortened or inexact titles of tests or titles of unpublished tests

Scores on the Staley test showed no practice effect.

4. nouns preceding a variable

Scores in session n were no higher on the average than were scores in session $n - 1$.

5. names of laws, theories, and hypotheses

The experimenter used a unifactor theory of pencil pushing to explain her results.

Boldface

Use boldface type as symbols for vectors (e.g., **V**).

Italics

When to Use Italics. If you are using a typewriter, indicate italics by underlining. Otherwise format the italic text as italic. Italics should be used for

1. titles of books, periodicals, and microfilms

The article relating bumps on the head to claustrophobia was published in the journal *Phrenology Today.*

The author didn't think a book titled *Bump It or Lump It* would sell enough copies to make writing the book worthwhile.

2. introducing new, technical, or important terms

All subjects in the experiment were told the meaning of the word *phrenology.*

3. letters, words, phrases, or sentences cited as linguistic examples

Some subjects did not even realize that *phrenology* was a noun.

4. letters used as statistical symbols or algebraic variables

The difference in number of bumps on the head between claustrophobic and nonclaustrophobic subjects was not significant, $t(32) = 0.26, p > .05$.

The phrenologist still argued that the relation between degree of claustrophobia (y) and number of bumps on the head (x) could be expressed by the equation $y = 7x + 2$.

5. volume numbers in reference lists

Bumpo, B. P. (1921). The relation between bumps on the head and claustrophobia. *Phrenology Today, 13,* 402–406.

When Not to Use Italics. Italics should not be used for

1. common foreign words and abbreviations

    The a priori likelihood of a relation between number of bumps on the head and degree of claustrophobia seemed remote. The remarks of Zootz et al. (1949) vis-à-vis errors in counting number of bumps are still relevant today.
2. names of Greek letters

    Zootz and his colleagues noted that there are two kinds of bumps, alpha (α) bumps and beta (β) bumps, and that only alpha bumps should be counted.
3. emphasis unless the emphasis would be lost without italics

    Zootz and his colleagues emphasized that there was no known relation between number of beta bumps and claustrophobia.
4. abbreviations

    The National Phrenological Society (NPS) dissociated itself from the work of both Bumpo and Zootz.

Spelling

The standard reference used by American Psychological Association journals for spelling is *Merriam-Webster's Collegiate Dictionary*, 10th ed. (1993). *Webster's Third New International Dictionary* (1976) should be consulted for spellings of words not in the collegiate volume. In cases where two or more spellings are acceptable, use the first, preferred spelling. You can also consult *www.apastyle.com* for the latest information on certain spellings not found in the dictionary.

Abbreviations

When to Use Abbreviations. Use abbreviations sparingly. Explain each abbreviation the first time it is used, except in the case of (1) below. Abbreviations may be used

1. without explanation if they are listed as word entries (i.e., are not labeled *abbr*) in *Webster's New Collegiate Dictionary* (1985)

    The subject scored 108 on the IQ test.
2. even if they are not in the dictionary but are frequently used in a relevant journal

    The subject's average response time (RT) in responding to test items was 6.52 S.

3. for standard Latin terms, statistics, and reference terms
   Blimpey et al. (1966) had full confidence in the IQ test they used.
4. for metric units
   To give readers an idea of the length of the test, the authors
   noted that the test booklet was two cm thick.

When to Use Periods in Abbreviations. Periods should be used with

1. initials of names
   A. C. Acney discovered the little known Acney effect.
2. abbreviations of state and territory names
   He discovered the effect in his little lab in Washington, D.C.
3. Latin abbreviations
   The discovery was made at exactly 8:00 A.M.
4. reference abbreviations
   The effect is described in Vol. 3 of the *Autobiography of A. C. Acney.*

When Not to Use Periods in Abbreviations. Periods should not be used with

1. capital-letter abbreviations, including acronyms
   The now discredited Acney effect relates IQ to facial complex-
   ion. Acney was unsuccessful in getting the report of his findings
   into any APA journal.
2. abbreviations of metric units
   Expressed in metric units, the weight of Vol. 3 of Acney's autobiography is 1.4 kg, 1.4 kg more than the book is worth.
3. abbreviations of nonmetric measurement
   This lengthy book weighs 3 lb, and can be used to press leaves.

When Not to Use Abbreviations. Do not use nonstandard abbreviations or abbreviations that you make up. Do not use the abbreviations *S* for subject, *E* for experimenter, or *O* for observer. Although
these abbreviations were once standard, they are no longer used.

HEADINGS

APA editorial guidelines make provision for five levels of headings:

1. a centered heading typed all in capitals;
2. a centered heading with initial letters of main words capitalized;
3. an italicized centered heading with main words capitalized;
4. an italicized heading flush with the left margin, with initial letters of major words capitalized;
5. an indented italicized paragraph heading with the initial letter of the first word capitalized and the last word followed by a period.

The complete set of five headings is usually needed only in very long articles, for example, reports of multiple experiments. The rules for headings are these:

Rule 1. If you use only one level of heading, as in short articles, use the second (2) level described above.

Rule 2. If you use two levels of headings, as in articles of average length, use the second (2) and fourth (4) levels described above.

Rule 3. If you use three levels of headings, as in longer articles, use the second (2), fourth (4), and fifth (5) levels described above.

Rule 4. If you use four levels of headings, as in long articles and monographs, use levels 2, 3, 4, and 5, as described above.

This book does not follow this sequence of headings.

An example using all five levels of headings is the following:

EXPERIMENT I

Collection of Norms

Method

Design

    Independent variables.

QUANTITATIVE ISSUES

Units of Measurement

The American Psychological Association has adopted the metric system in all APA journals, and other journals have generally followed suit. Authors therefore should express measurements in metric units wherever possible. If measurements are expressed in other kinds of units, metric equivalents should be given.

Statistics

Statistics can be presented in the text, in tables, or in figures. The author of a paper must choose the means that most effectively communicates his data. Frequently used statistics (e.g., the mean, t, F) can be used without explanation. Infrequently used statistics (e.g., c_p) should be explained, and a reference for the statistic cited. A reference should also be given for use of a statistic in a controversial way (e.g., the F statistic when sample variances are widely discrepant).

The standard format for presentation of inferential statistics in text calls for inclusion of the name of the statistic, the degrees of freedom for the statistic (if relevant), the value of the statistic, and the probability level associated with the statistic. This information is presented in the following way:

Subjects informed of the relation between lists recalled significantly more words than subjects not informed of this relation, $t(68) = 2.93$, $p < .01$. The personality scale did not differentiate among compulsive, hysterical, and normal subjects, $F(2, 28) = 1.18$, $p > .05$.

Note that the use of the less-than sign ($<$) indicates a significant difference, but the use of the greater-than sign ($>$) indicates a nonsignificant difference. It is preferable, when possible, to give an exact p-value (e.g., $p = .02$). Authors are expected, when possible, to report effect sizes as well as significance levels.

Equations

General Principles. Several general principles apply to the presentation of equations:

1. Space mathematical expressions as you would space words, keeping in mind that the primary consideration is legibility.
$$y = a/(b + c)$$
2. Align mathematical expressions carefully. Subscripts generally precede superscripts, but primes occur immediately following the primed letter or symbol.
$$y = x_p 3 + x_q' 2$$
3. Punctuate all equations, however presented, as you would any expression, mathematical or not.
   The standard formula was used for computing IQ:
$$IQ = MA/CA.$$

4. Parentheses ( ), brackets [ ], and braces { } should be used in that order to avoid ambiguity.

$$y = a/(b + c)$$
$$y = a/[(b + c) \cdot (d - e)]$$
$$y = \{a/[(b + c) \cdot (d - e)]\} + f$$

5. Use the percentage symbol (%) only when it is preceded by a number. Otherwise, use the word *percentage*.

Only 18% of the sample responded to the questionnaire.

The percentage of respondents was disappointing.

Equations Merged with Text. Short and simple equations that will not have to be referred to later in the text can be placed in the midst of a line of text. Follow these rules:

1. Fractions presented in the midst of a line of text should be indicated by use of a slash.

The data indicated that for any values of *a* and *b*, $y = a/b$.

2. The equation should not project above or below the line. If it does, use the format for equations described below.

Equations Separated from Text. Equations should be separated from the text if (a) they are referred to later, (b) they are complex, or (c) they project above or below a single line of text. Equations separated from the text should be numbered consecutively, with the number enclosed in parentheses and near the right margin of the page.

$$RT = 5x^2 + \frac{y + 8}{2n} + \frac{z^3 + 5}{y} \tag{1}$$

Numbers

General Principles. Several general principles apply to the use of numbers in text:

1. Rules for cardinal numbers (e.g., *two)* and ordinal numbers (e.g., *second)* are the same (see below), except for percentiles and quartiles. Percentiles and quartiles should always be expressed in figures.

The boy's score placed him in the 5th percentile.

2. Use arabic rather than roman numerals wherever possible. Use roman numerals, however, where convention calls for their use.

The probability of a Type I error was less than 5%.

3. For numbers greater than or equal to 1,000, use commas between every group of three digits.
   Her response was timed at 1,185 ms.
4. In writing decimals, place a zero before the decimal point if the number is less than one, unless the number *must* be less than one.
   The average score on the test was a pitiful 0.73.
   The proportion of subjects finishing the task was .86.
5. Use decimal notation instead of mixed fractions wherever possible. Do not use decimals, though, if their use is awkward.
   The maximum score on the test was 8.5 out of 10.
   The oldest child in the experimental group was 5½ years old.
6. Round numbers, in most cases, to two decimal digits, not more (e.g., a correlation of .53, not .5297).

Numbers Expressed in Words. Numbers should be expressed in words if

1. they are between zero and nine inclusive (with exceptions described in the next section)
   There were only six children in the sample.
2. they begin a sentence, regardless of whether or not they are less than 10
   Eleven children were tested.

Numbers Expressed in Figures. Numbers should be expressed in figures if they satisfy any of the following conditions. Notice that all conditions except the first are exceptions to rule (1) above for expressing numbers in words. Express numbers in figures if they are

1. greater than or equal to 10
   There were 18 adults in the sample.
2. ages
   All of the adults were over 21 years of age.
3. times and dates
   The experiment took place between the hours of 8 A.M. and 10 A.M. on April 6, 1976.
4. percentages
   Over 90% of the subjects finished the task.
5. ratios
   This was a ratio of 9:1.

6. fractions or decimals
   The corresponding fraction was ⁹⁄₁₀, and the corresponding decimal, .9.
7. exact sums of money
   Subjects were each paid $3 for participation in the experiment.
8. scores and points on scales
   The student received a score of 8.32 on a scale ranging from 0 to 9.
9. references to numerals as numerals
   The numeral 0 was placed next to each true item; the numeral 1 was placed next to each false item.
10. page numbers
    The students were told to write their identification numbers on page 1.
11. series of four or more items
    Students were assigned consecutive identification numbers: The first four students, for example, were assigned the numbers 1, 2, 3, and 4, respectively.
12. numbers grouped for comparison either between or within sentences if any of the numbers is 10 or greater.
    There were 11 subjects in the first group, but only 9 subjects in the second group.
13. sample or population sizes
    The experiment involved 8 subjects, half of them male and half of them female.

Seriation

Within a Paragraph. Seriation within a paragraph is indicated by lowercase letters written in parentheses. Do not italicize the letters.

The five categories of words to be recalled were (a) fruits, (b) animals, (c) nuts, (d) countries, and (e) oceans.

Of Paragraphs. Seriation of paragraphs is indicated by arabic numerals followed by periods. Do not enclose the numbers in parentheses.

The experimenter used a three-step procedure:
1. The experimenter greeted the subject as the subject entered the room.
2. A confederate entered the room and asked for the time of day. He appeared to be in a state of great confusion.

3. The confederate noticed the subject, and struck up a conversation with him.

(Note that neither of these seriation conventions has always been followed in the present book.)

REFERENCES

Citations in Text
Standard Formats. References that are generally available may be cited either directly or indirectly:

1. If the author is cited directly, the date follows the author citation in parentheses.
   Nimbus (1962) found that cloud formations can be used to predict persons' moods.
2. If the author is cited indirectly, both the author's name and the date are placed in parentheses.
   It has been found that cloud formations can be used to predict persons' moods (Nimbus, 1962).
   This result has since been replicated (Nimbus, 1963; Stratus, 1964).
3. If the date is mentioned in the text, it need not be repeated in parentheses.
   In 1962, Nimbus found that cloud formations can be used to predict people's moods.
4. If a work is cited more than once on the same page or within a few pages, the date need not be repeated if there is no resulting ambiguity.
   Nimbus's (1962) work on cloud formations and mood has received little attention. The lack of attention may be due to Nimbus's opening sentence: "Only a fool would take the work reported here seriously" (p. 1).
   If you are citing an Internet source and no page numbers are available, you may use a heading and paragraph number instead (e.g., Bighead, 2003, Introduction Section, ¶3).
5. Multiple references to work of the same author published in the same year are assigned lowercase letters to distinguish them when they are cited. The letters should be assigned alphabetically, by title name.
   Snow (1964a) has concluded that precipitation can dampen

people's spirits. Snow (1964b) has argued that frozen precipitation is most demoralizing.

Multiple Authors. Follow these rules in citing work of multiple authors:

1. If a work has just two authors, cite both names and the date every time you make a citation.

   McLeod and O'Dowd (1962) found an artifact in Nimbus's (1962) study. (First citation)

   McLeod and O'Dowd (1962) corrected the artifact. (Later citation)

2. If a work has more than two authors, cite all names up to the sixth author and the date the first time you make the citation – in later citations, you need only cite the first author, followed by "et al." and the date. Authors beyond the sixth may be incorporated into the "et al." statement, regardless of how many there are. If two different pieces of work shorten to the same form, then always cite the full references to avoid confusion.

   McLeod, O'Dowd, and Giroud (1967) found no relation between cloud formations and mood. (First citation)

   McLeod et al. (1967) did not investigate cloud formations during tornadoes or hurricanes, however. (Later citations)

3. If citations with multiple authors are made directly, the names of the authors are connected by "and." If citations are made indirectly (that is, parenthetically), the names of the authors are connected by "&":

   McLeod and O'Dowd (1962) found the artifact.

   An artifact was discovered (McLeod & O'Dowd, 1962).

No Author. If you cite a reference with no author, use the first two or three words of the entry as described in the references. In this case, the entry will usually be cited by title.

   The pamphlet suggests ways of improving one's memory ("Tips on Memory," 1931).

Corporate Author. A corporate author may be cited instead of a personal one. Lengthy corporate names should be abbreviated only if they are readily identifiable in the reference list.

   The book presented 15 ways to make friends (Golden Friendship Society, 1968).

Authors with the Same Surname. If you refer to more than one author with the same surname, include each author's initials each time you cite the author.

> S. Jones (1973) disagreed with the interpretations drawn by E. Jones (1970).

The Reference List

The References section of a paper contains an alphabetical list of the generally available references cited in the text of the paper. References to more than one work of the same author are arranged by order of date of publication, with earlier works listed first. Each reference should include the author(s), title, and facts of publication. Details regarding format are given in Chapter 2: The format for the references is the same as the format for the author cards described in that chapter. Note the use of the hanging indent, whereby the first line of each reference is flush with the left margin and other lines are indented. Here are some examples of different kinds of references:

REFERENCES

Balderdash, H. Q. (1969). *Writing for meaning.* Los Angeles: Perfection Press.

Crumpet, C. D., & Donut, D. C. (1975). *Sugar tastes good and is good for you* (Vol. 1). Honolulu: Sugar Promotion Press.

Finn, D., Jr. (1970). Breathing in fish. In G. Trout & H. Bass (Eds.), *The physiology of fish.* San Francisco: Fisherman's Press.

Firestone, N. Z. (1974). You can prevent pyromania. *Journal of Exotic Ailments, 15,* 63–68.

Gamboling for fun and profit. (1958). Las Vegas: American Exercise Institute.

Lemon, B. J. (1974). *Vitamin C in your diet* (2nd ed.). Miami: Citrus Press.

Lohne, E. Z., & Sharke, P. P. (in press). Should usury be a crime? *Money Minder's Digest.*

Pompus, V. Q. (Ed.) (1970). *Encyclopedia of knowledge* (16 vols.). San Francisco: Worldwide.

It is not possible to include here all possible kinds of reference formats. Please consult the APA manual for a complete list of formats.

AUTHOR NOTES

This kind of note (a) acknowledges the basis of a study, (b) acknowledges financial support for a study, (c) acknowledges assistance in preparing, conducting, analyzing, or reporting a study, (d) reports on any potential conflict of interest, (e) elaborates upon or notes a change of an author's affiliation, or (f) provides an address for correspondence, including an e-mail address if possible. Combinations of these four functions may be combined in a single author note. The example below combines all these functions. Author identification notes are not numbered. They are placed after the references and before the footnotes.

This study is based upon a doctoral dissertation submitted in partial fulfillment of the requirements for the Ph.D. degree at Prestige University. The research was supported by grant G107H5 to the author from the National Institute of Rodent Research. I thank Whyte Meise for assistance in conducting the study.

The author is now at Rocky Ridge State College. Correspondence regarding this article should be sent to Phineas Phlom, Department of Psychology, Rocky Ridge State College, Small Town, Vermont. e-mail: *pphlom@rrsc.edu*.

FOOTNOTES

Kinds of Footnotes

Content Footnotes. Content footnotes are used for material that elaborates upon the text but is not directly relevant to it. When citing a footnote in the text, place the note citation after all punctuation (except dashes).

Because these footnotes can distract the reader, they should be used sparingly. Before using such a footnote, you should decide whether the material might be better incorporated into the text or deleted.

[1] The only ill effect upon the subject resulting from the treatment was a deep fear of furry animals, a fear we hope eventually to eradicate.

Reference Footnotes. Reference footnotes are used only rarely in psychological reporting. Almost all citations should be made through references. Reference footnotes may be used, however, for legal citations and copyright permissions.

[1] Copyright 1971 by Peanut Press, Inc. Quoted by permission.

Table Footnotes. Table footnotes amplify information contained in tables. These footnotes are of three kinds.

1. *General notes.* A general note provides further information about the table as a whole. In the example on p. 103, the general note informs the reader about the subjects.
2. *Specific notes.* A specific note provides further information about one or more entries in the table. Such notes are indicated by letter superscripts attached to the appropriate entries. In the example on p. 103, there are two specific notes. Because there is more than one note, the notes are ordered horizontally by rows.
3. *Probability levels.* Probability levels are used to ascertain the significance of statistical tests. A single asterisk should be used for the highest probability level, and an additional asterisk should be used for each lower probability level.

The number of asterisks used for a given probability level need not be consistent across tables. The most common use of asterisks is for one to represent $p < .05$, two to represent $p < .01$, and three to represent $p < .001$. When possible, authors should report exact p values (e.g., $p = .03$) rather than ranges (e.g., $p < .05$)

When more than one kind of footnote appears in a single table, general footnotes precede specific ones, and specific ones precede probability levels. The footnotes to a single table might look like this:

Note. All subjects were veterans.
[a] Two subjects were caught copying from each other, and were eliminated from this group. [b]One subject in this group refused to finish the task, and was eliminated.
*$p < .05$ **$p < .01$ ***$p < .001$

Observe that multiple footnotes of a given kind follow each other on a single line, where possible.

Numbering of Footnotes

Content and reference footnotes are numbered consecutively throughout a paper. Footnotes are indicated by arabic numeral superscripts. If a footnote is referred to more than once, subsequent references should use a parenthetical statement rather than a superscript. Footnotes to a table should be lettered consecutively within each table.

Jones (1958) found that subjects suffered from few ill aftereffects.[1]
Critics have lambasted Jones's (1958) alleged insensitivity to subjects (see Footnote 1).

Placement of Footnotes

In papers to be submitted for publication, footnotes are placed on a separate page after the author notes (see Chapter 3). In student papers, however, it is often more convenient for the reader if the footnotes are placed at the bottom of the page on which each footnote is cited.

PERMISSIONS

All direct quotations need to be accompanied by a reference citation, regardless of the length of those quotations. If you quote, you must supply an exact citation, including page numbers, even for short quotes. You also need permission from the rights holder for longer quotes. The length of the quote for which you need to express permission varies by copyright holder. Hence you may need to check whether written permission is needed. The same rules apply to use of electronic material and for use of material in an electronic medium. APA requires permission for quotes of over 500 words in length.

CONFLICT OF INTEREST

When you go to publish an article, you may be asked to sign a form either stating that no conflicts of interest are involved in the research or else stating what they are or may be. For example, if you are funded by a drug company to test the psychological effects of a drug that company produces, you are in a potential conflict of interest situation. You *must* report all such conflicts or potential conflicts fully and accurately.

A FINAL WORD

You should adhere to these rules diligently, whether you submit your paper to a course instructor or to a journal editor. In the former case, your instructor will appreciate your concern for correct format, even if he has not explicitly requested it. In the latter case, a journal editor will expect strict adherence to the rules and may send back a paper that does not conform to them. A sample student paper typed according to the APA rules is presented in Appendix A.

Chapter Eight

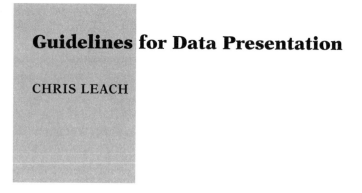

Guidelines for Data Presentation

CHRIS LEACH

This chapter draws heavily on three sources to which readers are referred for more details. For the presentation of data in the form of tables, Andrew Ehrenberg's *Data Reduction* and *A Primer in Data Reduction* contain much good sound advice. For the use of figures, William Cleveland's *The Elements of Graphing Data* is a style guide that is required reading for anyone considering using a graph, from the most junior undergraduate to the most experienced researcher. Good advice is also available in Tufte (1983) and Wainer (1984).

Tables and figures allow large amounts of material to be presented concisely. Well presented, they often enable a reader to understand at a glance patterns of data and exceptions that would be obscured if presented in the text. Tables and figures are expensive for journals to produce, however, so if you plan to submit a paper for publication, you should present in this form only your most important sets of data. Do not duplicate data from one table or figure to another unless it is essential for comprehension. Extensive sets of data should be reported in appendixes rather than in the body of the paper.

The same principles apply to the effective presentation of tables and figures as apply to effective scientific writing. The basic rule is to aim for simple, direct presentation, with no unnecessary clutter. Stylistic excesses like the moiré pattern graphics that appear on many histograms hinder rather than help, because they often direct attention away from the data. Edward Tufte (1983) uses the term "chartjunk" to refer to such unnecessary elements of graphs and has good advice on how to avoid it.

Care in preparing tables and figures helps you understand your data. As you produce better versions, you are exploring your data and teasing out meanings as well as choosing how best to communicate the data. For this reason, tables and figures should be constructed first. Together with their captions, they should be able to communicate alone much of the information in the paper.

RELATION BETWEEN TABLES OR FIGURES AND TEXT

Three common mistakes in the use of tables and figures are (a) duplication in the text of material presented in tables and figures, (b) presentation of tables and figures that are unintelligible without reference to the text, and (c) presentation of tables and figures with no or minimal discussion. First, data presented in tables and figures should be discussed in the text, not re-presented. Give brief verbal summaries to lead readers to the main patterns and exceptions, but do not repeat values that can easily be read from the tables or figures. Second, construct each table and figure and the caption accompanying it so that readers are able to understand it without reference to the text. Third, remember that even if readers are able to understand the table or figure by itself, they may not see what conclusions you want to draw. If data are important enough to present in tabular or graphical form, they are important enough to discuss.

TABLES

When to Use Tables

Tables are preferable to figures for many small data sets. For larger, more complex data sets, a good choice of graph may do a better job of showing the patterns and exceptions. Tables may also be preferable if it is important to show precise values.

Four Rules for Constructing Tables

Compare Tables 1 and 2, which show the same unemployment figures for 15 states over a 4-year period. Table 2 was produced using four guiding principles suggested by Andrew Ehrenberg that make it

Table 1.
The Number of Unemployed by States: 1971–1974 (The first 15 states)

	Unemployed			
	Number (1,000)			
	1971	1972	1973	1974
Alabama	72	62	62	78
Alaska	12	13	14	15
Arizona	32	32	34	49
Arkansas	40	36	34	40
California	737	652	615	670
Colorado	37	35	36	43
Connecticut	116	121	89	88
Delaware	13	11	12	15
D.C.	34	44	59	62
Florida	135	127	132	208
Georgia	76	83	81	109
Hawaii	21	25	24	27
Idaho	19	20	19	22
Illinois	240	245	203	223
Indiana	128	103	101	123

Source: Adapted from Ehrenberg, 1982, Table 16.1. Reprinted by permission of John Wiley & Sons, Ltd.

much easier to understand than Table 1. (See Ehrenberg, 1982, for a fuller account of this example.)

1. *Order rows and columns by size.* Table 2 has the rows ordered by the four-year average for each state. In Table 1, they are ordered alphabetically. The only advantage of alphabetical ordering is that it is easier to find a given state. The columns have not been reordered because the yearly averages do not differ much, and there is some interest in year-to-year fluctuation. It is clear from Table 2 that the ordering of the unemployment figures is similar to the ordering of the states' population sizes. Although it may seem obvious that the larger states would have higher unemployment, this fact is not obvious from Table 1. Rather than using the row averages to order the table, we could have used population size. Using such an external criterion is helpful if a number of

Table 2.
Unemployed: States Ordered by 4-Year Averages

	Unemployed ('000)				
	'71	'72	'73	'74	Av.
California	740	650	610	670	670
Illinois	240	250	200	220	230
Florida	130	120	130	210	150
Indiana	130	100	100	120	110
Connecticut	120	120	90	90	105
Georgia	76	83	81	110	88
Alabama	76	62	62	78	69
D.C.	34	44	59	62	50
Colorado	37	35	36	43	38
Arkansas	40	36	34	40	38
Arizona	33	32	34	49	37
Hawaii	21	25	24	27	24
Idaho	19	20	19	22	20
Alaska	12	13	14	15	14
Delaware	13	11	12	15	13
Average[a]	110	110	100	120	110

[a]For the 15 states.
Source: Adapted from Ehrenberg, 1982, Table 16.2. Reprinted by permission of John Wiley & Sons, Ltd.

tables are to be compared, because the same fixed order can be used for each table. Of course, the external criterion should be one that is likely to be of help in making sense of the data, as population size is here.

2. *Use averages to summarize or provide a focus.* Table 2 has both row and column averages. Where the individual numbers do not differ much, the average provides a good summary. For example, the average of 110,000 unemployed per year summarizes the numbers for Indiana in this period quite well. Where the numbers differ, the average provides a focus for comparison, as with the column averages. In Table 2, we can see that unemployment was fairly stable over this period, and that this stability applies equally to states with high and low unemployment. We can also see exceptions clearly. The numbers are, on average,

lower in 1973 and higher in 1974, although Connecticut remained low in 1974, whereas Florida, Georgia, and Arizona were higher than might be expected.

3. *Round numbers to two effective digits.* Rounding numbers drastically is practically always helpful, because it saves on memory load, making it easier to do quick calculations. For example, we can quickly see that 740 is about three times 250, but comparing 737 and 245 takes longer. We also rarely need the greater accuracy. Rounding to two effective digits gives sufficient accuracy for most purposes. "Effective digits" means digits that vary in that sort of number. Numbers like percentages vary in tens and units, so 18.3 and 35.8 are rounded to 18 and 36. With numbers like 1836.7, 1639.3, 1234.2, and 1122.8, the initial ones are not "effective" in distinguishing the numbers. The first two effective digits are the hundreds and the tens, so the rounded versions are 1840, 1640, 1230, and 1120.

When the numbers in a table differ greatly, variable rounding often helps. In Table 2, the numbers at the top have been treated as a block in which the hundreds and the tens are the first two effective digits, so they are rounded to the nearest ten. The numbers in the middle and the bottom are a separate block, rounded to the nearest unit. Variable rounding helps keep the large numbers simple enough to enable quick mental arithmetic, but keeps the rounding errors of the low numbers small. When you round, you must say you have done so, and say how you have done it.

4. *Table layout should make it easy to compare relevant numbers.* The main principle of table layout is that numbers to be compared should be close together. In Table 2, it is easier to compare the numbers in any column than in any row. This is because the leading digits are close to each other, making for quicker calculations. The larger numbers have also been put at the top, as we are more used to doing subtractions that way. Other aspects of table layout are also important. Widely spaced rows prevent easy comparison, as does irregular spacing of rows and columns. On the other hand, occasional regular gaps help emphasize the patterns, as in Table 2. If tables need to be compared to each other, put them next to each other.

Placement of Tables

In articles submitted for publication, tables are placed after footnotes (see Chapter 3). Use the following notice at the place in the text where you want the table inserted:

Insert Table 1 about here

In student papers, it is often more convenient to insert the tables at the appropriate places in the text for easier reading.

Table Numbers

Tables are numbered consecutively with arabic numerals, starting with Table 1. Suffixes (e.g., Tables 5 and 5a) should not be used. Tables should have numbers only, so Tables 5 and 5a should be numbered Table 5 and Table 6. If you present tables in an appendix, identify them with capital letters, starting with Table A. The table number is written at the top of the table, as in Table 2. It is typed flush against the left side of the page.

Table Titles

The title of a table should describe concisely what the table is supposed to show and should be understandable without reference to the text. Type it below the table number, flush against the left side of the page.

Ruling of Tables

Table 1 has both vertical and horizontal rules, whereas Table 2 has only horizontal rules. Most journals have standard formats. For example, vertical rules are almost never used in APA or BPS journals. Ehrenberg's (1982) version of Table 2 has a vertical line separating the main data from the row averages. The variable spacing in Table 2 achieves the same effect without reducing the clarity of the table.

FIGURES

When to Use Figures

A figure is any type of illustration other than a table. Unlike tables, which are typeset, figures are photographed, so they must be of high artistic and technical quality. Figures include stem-and-leaf displays, graphs, photographs, and drawings. Before making a figure, consider which type of figure will present your information most effectively. Figures should be sized at 100% of the size they will occupy on the page. Minimum type size is 8 points; maximum is 14 points.

Figures, like tables, allow large amounts of data to be presented concisely. Their advantage over tables is that they often enable the reader to see at a glance trends that otherwise would not be readily apparent. With the exception of stem-and-leaf displays, figures have the disadvantage, however, that they do not convey precise values of data.

Use figures when they augment rather than duplicate the text, and only to convey essential facts. Omit visually distracting details. Make sure your figures are easy to read and understand and that you use a consistent style for presenting figures throughout the paper.

Stem-and-Leaf Displays, Boxplots, and Quartile Plots

Stem-and-Leaf Displays. Table 3 shows the scores on the General Health Questionnaire (GHQ) of 30 mothers 6 weeks after giving birth to their first child. They were obtained by Lorna Cameron (1984) in a study of maternal feelings for the newborn. The distribution is skewed to the right, as frequently occurs with psychological data (e.g., scores on a test, magnitudes, reaction times). This skewness makes it misleading to report just means and standard deviations as summary statistics. Both will be heavily influenced by the two or three unusually high scores (or outliers). In this case, the outliers are particularly interesting, raising questions about why some women score extremely high on the GHQ, one of the central questions for Cameron. Reporting robust estimates of location and spread (e.g., median and interquartile range instead of mean and standard deviation) will reduce the impact of the outliers. However, a fuller report of the data, rather than just summary statistics, would be more informative, particularly if outliers are seen as potentially interesting cases rather than just as nuisance values that mess up the calculation of summary statistics.

The frequency distribution given in Table 3 is one compact way of presenting all the data. A better way is to use a stem-and-leaf display, which combines the advantages of tables and graphs by retaining all the numerical information as well as showing clearly the shape of the distribution of numbers. Stem-and-leaf displays were developed by John Tukey (1977). The simplest type is produced by first rounding the numbers to two effective digits (see above). The 30 scores in Table 3 are already in this form. Each score is now broken into two parts, the part up to and including the first effective digit (the tens in this case) forming the stem and the second effective digit (the units) forming

Table 3.
General Health Questionnaire (GHQ) Scores for 30 Mothers
6 Weeks Postnatally

GHQ score	0	1	2	3	4	5	6	7	8	10	11	14	18	20
Frequency	3	2	4	3	4	4	3	1	1	1	1	1	1	1

Source: Data from Cameron (1984).

the leaf. So 18 has 1 as stem and 8 as leaf. The stems determine which row of the display the score appears in and the leaves are written alongside the appropriate stem to identify the individual scores, as shown in Figure 1a. This display makes clear the skewness of the distribution, but it is too short and fat to give a clear view of the bulk of the distribution. In this case, it helps to have narrower stems to spread out the display. Figure 1b uses stem widths of 5 GHQ points, with the *s containing leaves between 5 and 9 and the ·s containing leaves between 0 and 4. The 14 is therefore placed alongside the 1· stem, whereas the 8 goes with the 1* stem.

Figure 1c gives an even more spread-out display, drawing attention to the outliers more effectively than do the other displays. Here the stem widths are 2 GHQ points, with the stems identified by · (for leaves 0 and 1), t (for *two* and *three*), f (for *four* and *five*), s (for *six* and *seven*), and * (for 8 and 9). So 4 and 8 now go in stems 1f and 1*. These displays are helpful for exploring data and also give a compact way of communicating complete data sets when summary statistics are not sufficient. For further variations, see Tukey (1977), Velleman and Hoaglin (1981), or Seheult (1986).

Box Plots and Quartile Plots. For cases where the data are too extensive to report the full stem-and-leaf display, Tukey's box plot is a convenient way of reporting summary statistics. Tufte's (1983) quartile plot is a more compact version of a box plot. The quartile and box plots both plot a five-number summary of the data, including the two extremes (highest and lowest scores), the first and third quartiles (called lower and upper hinges by Tukey), and the median. For the GHQ data, the extremes are 0 and 20, the hinges are 2 and 6, and the median is 4.

These five values can be obtained easily from the stem-and-leaf display. First, it helps to add a cumulative count from either end in

```
2 | 0
1 | 0148
· | 00011222233344445555566678
        (a)
```

```
2· | 0
1* | 8
1· | 014
 * | 555566678
 · | 0001122223334444
        (b)
```

```
 1   2· |  0
 2   1* |  8
     1a
 3   1f |  4
     1t
 5   1· |  01
 6    * |  8
10    s |  6667
 8    f |  44445555
12    t |  2222333
 5    · |  00011
        (c)
```

Figure 1. Stem-and-leaf displays of GHQ scores: (a) stem widths of 10 GHQ points; (b) stem widths of 5 GHQ points; (c) stem widths of 2 GHQ points, with a cumulative count from either end to the middle.

toward the middle of the display, as has been done in Figure 1c. From this panel, we can see that there are 10 scores of 6 or higher, 12 of 3 or lower, and eight in the middle stem with values of 4 or 5. The lowest and highest scores, 0 and 20, can be read off immediately.

The median is the unique score in the middle if there is an odd number of scores, or the average of the two middle scores if there is an even number of scores. To see how deep we have to count in from either end to hit the median, the general rule is

depth of median = (1 + number of scores)/2.

Here, there are 30 scores, so the median depth is (1 + 30)/2 = 15½. The half shows that there is no unique middle score, so the median is

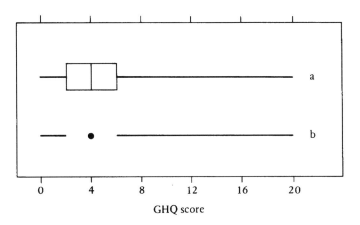

Figure 2. (a) Box plot; (b) quartile plot of GHQ scores.

the average of the 15th and 16th scores in from either end. Counting
from low to high, the cumulative count tells us that there are 12 scores
of 3 or less and eight in the middle stem, so the 15th and 16th scores
will be the third and fourth entries in the middle stem. Both these
scores are 4, so the median is 4.

The hinges are the scores in the middle of the two halves of the data
from the median to the extremes. The middle half of the data lies between the two hinges, so the hinges give a good indication of the
spread of the bulk of the data. The simplest general rule for the depth
of the two hinges is

depth of hinges = (1 + depth of median)/2.

For an even number of scores, the half that crops up on the end of the
median depth should be removed before calculating the hinge depth.
For this case, with a median depth of 15½, the hinge depth will be (1 +
15)/2 = 8, so the two hinges are eight in from either end, with values 2
and 6.

Figure 2a shows the box plot of this five-number summary. The two
hinges form the outer edges of a box, with a line inside the box where
the median is. Outside the box, whiskers are extended to the extremes.
(Tukey's original term was "box-and-whisker plot," now contracted to
box plot.) From this plot, it can quickly be seen that the middle half of
the data lies between scores 2 and 6 – the two hinges – with a median

Figure 3. Quartile plot of GHQ scores with outliers marked.

score of 4. The fact that the right whisker is longer than the left one suggests the skewness that is actually present in the data.

Figure 2b gives the more compact quartile-plot version, with a filled circle for the median, the boxes omitted, but the whiskers the same. This version is the preferred one, particularly when several plots are to be compared.

Outliers. Information about outliers can be added to these plots very straightforwardly. Tukey (1977) suggests a simple general procedure for detecting outliers. Calculate the midspread (or interquartile range), which is just the difference between the hinges. Outliers are those scores more than 1½ midspreads beyond the hinges. Extreme outliers are scores more than 3 midspreads beyond the hinges. In this example, the midspread is $6 - 2 = 4$, so scores lower than -4 [$= 2 - (1½ \times 4)$] or higher than 12 [$= 6 + (1½ \times 4)$] are outliers, whereas scores lower than -10 or higher than 18 are extreme outliers. The three high scores of 14, 18, and 20 noted earlier now count as outliers, with 20 being an extreme outlier. On this criterion, none of the low scores is low enough to count as an outlier.

The outliers can be marked on the quartile plot or box plot, using ×s to represent outliers, ⊗s to represent extreme outliers, and extending the whiskers only to the highest (or lowest) scores not counted as outliers. The quartile plot in Figure 3 shows the three high outliers, with the whisker extending to 11, the highest score in Figure 1c that is not an outlier.

There are many other methods of detecting outliers. The method given here is a general purpose rough-and-ready approach that works well in many cases. For information on other methods, see Lovie (1986).

Comparing Data Sets. Stem-and-leaf displays and quartile plots

Immediate		Delayed
	2*	
	2·	0123
9876	1*	79
33311100	1·	2334
98765	*	68
332	·	0

Figure 4. Back-to-back stem-and-leaf display of neuroticism scores for 20 mothers showing immediate affection and 13 showing delayed affection. (Data from Cameron, 1984.)

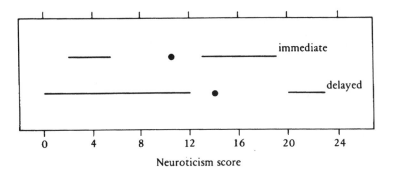

Figure 5. Quartile plots of neuroticism scores for mothers showing immediate or delayed affection.

are also helpful in comparing two or more sets of data. Figure 4 shows the neuroticism scores for 20 mothers in Cameron's study who showed immediate affection for their newborn child, back-to-back with scores from 13 mothers who showed delayed affection. Figure 5 shows the two quartile plots of these data. From each display, it can be seen that the scores for the delayed group are slightly higher, on average, and more spread out than the scores of the immediate group. Although there are no outliers here, these displays are much more informative than a table of means and standard deviations.

Graphs

"Above all else show the data" (Tufte, 1983, p. 105). This is the best single principle of graph presentation. William Cleveland's rules, listed

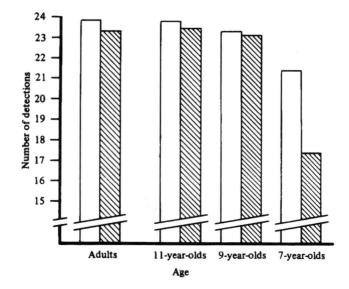

Figure 6. Bar chart of mean number of apparent movement detections made by four age groups in mid and extreme periphery; ☐ mid periphery; ▨ extreme periphery. (Reprinted, with permission, from David et al., 1986.)

in the next section, are good ways of following this advice, aiding both your own understanding and your ability to communicate the data. Before looking at these rules, two examples of published graphs will illustrate some of the main points. I have chosen two graphs that already do a reasonable job of communicating the data and suggest some improvements. Most published graphs could be improved; many have worse problems than these two; and many are quite dreadful. For some examples of the dreadful ones, see Wainer (1984).

Figure 6 shows a grouped bar chart, as reported by David, Chapman, Foot, and Sheehy (1986) in a study of peripheral vision in child pedestrian accidents. It shows quite clearly the mean number of detections of apparent movement by each of four age groups in mid and extreme periphery. The main points being communicated are that the 7-year-olds made fewer detections than did the other groups and had a larger difference between the mid and extreme periphery.

The first thing to note is that the figure communicates only eight numbers, so a table is likely to do a better job than a graph. In the

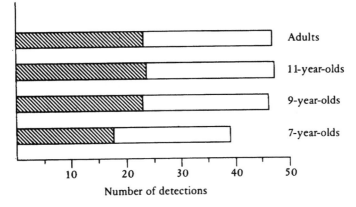

Figure 7. Divided bar chart version of the data in Figure 6: ☐ mid periphery; ▨ extreme periphery.

David et al. paper, though, there are many tables and a figure was chosen to highlight these data.

How can we do worse than these authors in presenting the data? A common choice is to use a divided bar chart, as in Figure 7. This chart makes it difficult to compare the mid-periphery values, because non-aligned length judgments are involved. The only thing worse than a divided bar chart is a pie chart, because such a chart involves judging areas, which people find hard to do accurately. And the only thing worse than a pie chart is several pie charts.

Cleveland (1985) reports the results of a number of studies in graphical perception, examining the performance of people at the elementary tasks required for understanding graphs. He reports the following ordering of elementary tasks, from most to least accurate:

1. position along a common scale
2. position along identical, nonaligned scales
3. length
4. angle/slope
5. area
6. volume
7. color hue/color saturation/density

When choosing which type of graph to use, it helps to choose one involving judgments as high up in this ordering as possible. Divided bar

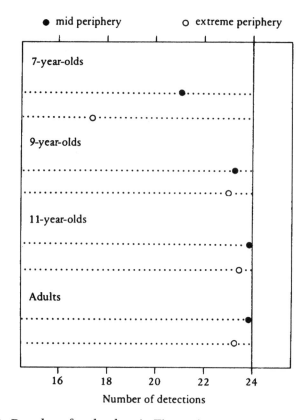

Figure 8. Dot chart for the data in Figure 6.

charts and pie charts involve judgments low down in the ordering. They can always be replaced by a dot chart of the type shown below, which involves judgments of position along a common scale. For this reason, divided bar charts and pie charts should never be used.

How can we improve on Figure 6? First, the scale break is unnecessary. Second, there is no need to use boxes to represent the numbers. If anything, these boxes might be misleading, as they invite viewers to make area judgments and the areas contain no information about the numbers, particularly as the scale does not start at zero. Figure 8 shows a dot chart for these data. Here the eight dots are visually prominent, with light dotted lines extended across the display up to the maximum value of 24 for easier comparison. Because the scale does not start at zero, it would be misleading to stop the dotted lines at the data points;

Figure 9. Cluttered graph of mean scores and standard deviations by sessions of daily anxiety ratings: ▲–▲ CBT; ■ – - – ■ AMT; X – - – X BZ; ● – - – ● WL. (Reprinted, with permission, from Lindsay et al., 1987.)

this procedure would invite viewers to compare lengths rather than positions. The data region is enclosed in a rectangle, with a pair of scale lines marked in, again for easier comparison.

Figure 9 gives a comparison of four treatments for generalized anxiety as reported by Lindsay, Gamsu, McLaughlin, Hood, and Espie (1987). The data are ratings of anxiety by clients in three groups receiving either cognitive behavior therapy (CBT), anxiety management training (AMT), or benzodiazepines (BZ), together with a waiting-list control group (WL). Means and standard deviations for each group on each of nine occasions are presented. The main problem with this graph is that it is incredibly cluttered. With some effort, it is possible to see what is going on. The BZ group shows a rapid reduction in anxiety, which is not maintained. The WL group stays basically the same, whereas the other two groups show a gradual reduction in anxiety, with a slight advantage to the CBT group.

The error bars show a fair bit of variation. It is likely, but not absolutely clear, that sample standard deviations rather than standard deviations of the mean (or standard errors) are reported – standard errors would be shorter. Many published graphs incorporating error bars give less information than in this case, making it difficult to decide whether sample standard deviations, standard errors, or confidence intervals are shown. It is important to state which is being used, because which is used will affect judgments of group differences.

Figure 10 shows one way of reducing the clutter. At the top, only the group means are plotted, for easier comparisons between groups. The means and error bars for each group are then shown in four separate aligned displays. As in Figure 8, the data region is enclosed in a rectangle, with two scale lines for each variable. The light reference line highlighting the baseline measures is an optional extra.

Rules for Constructing Graphs

The rules given below are the main principles offered by William Cleveland (1985), with minor modifications. Some are very general (e.g., the first six), whereas others give specific advice (e.g., rule 10). For fuller information and many examples, see Cleveland's Chapter 2.

1. *Make the data stand out.* The data in Figure 9 do not stand out well. Figure 10 improves on this situation, although the baseline points are not well discriminated. Using different plotting symbols for the four groups may help a little. See Figure 11 for examples of plotting symbols.
2. *Avoid superfluity.* Getting rid of unnecessary elements would improve many graphs. The boxes in Figure 6 do not hinder communication, but serve no useful purpose beyond what is provided by the dots in Figure 8. For the same reason, quartile plots (Figure 2b) are often better than box plots (Figure 2a).
3. *A large amount of data can be packed into a small region.* Although clutter and superfluous elements should be avoided, there are many examples of clear graphs with large amounts of data. Computer graphics allow clear graphics to be produced more easily. See Cleveland (1985) and Tufte (1983) for examples.
4. *Graphing data should be an iterative, experimental process.* Graphing data in several different ways is a good method for exploring the data.
5. *Graph data two or more times when necessary.* If the error bars in Figure 9 are worth having, it is better to present them in separate graphs, as in Figure 10, rather than to clutter up the display.
6. *Many useful graphs require careful, detailed study.* The messages in the

Figure 10. Redrawing of Figure 9 to remove the clutter.

graphs presented here are all straightforward and fairly easy to see. Straightforwardness is not the most important criterion for a good graph. A more important one is whether we can see something using a graph that would have been difficult or impossible to see without a graph. Some of the graphs in Cleveland (1985) or Tufte (1983) reward careful study.

7. *Use visually prominent graphical elements to show the data.* Many published graphs have the data points obscured by lines connecting the data, or background grids, or in other ways, simply because the plotting symbols are not prominent enough.

8. *Use a pair of scale lines for each variable.* Make the data region the interior of the rectangle formed by the scale lines. Put tick marks outside the data region. Using two scale lines, as in Figures 8 and 10, makes it easier to compare points. In addition, Poulton (1985) gives evidence of distorted judgments when only one scale line is used. All the figures here have the tick marks outside the data region, which helps prevent them from obscuring data points.

9. *Do not clutter the data region.* Figure 9 is too cluttered.

10. *Avoid using too many tick marks.* Figure 9 has overdone the number of tick marks. Using half as many, as in Figure 10, still allows data values to be judged well. From 3 to 10 tick marks usually suffice to give a broad sense of the measurement scale.

11. *Use a reference line when there is an important value that must be seen across the entire graph, but do not let the line interfere with the data.* The reference line highlighting the baseline measures in Figure 10 is helpful but not essential.

12. *Do not allow data labels in the data region to interfere with the data or to clutter the graph.* The labels in Figure 10 do not get in the way of the data. Added to Figure 9, they would have increased the clutter.

13. *Avoid putting notes and keys in the data region.* Put keys to symbols just outside the data region and put notes in the figure caption or the text.

14. *Overlapping plotting symbols must be visually distinguishable.* In Figure 10, the baseline measures overlap a little, but are distinguishable. Using different symbols for the four groups would help in worse cases. Figure 11 shows two sets of plotting symbols recommended by Cleveland. The top set is for times when there is little overlap among data points, and the bottom set is for times when overlap makes it difficult to distinguish the data points. For each set, Cleveland suggests using

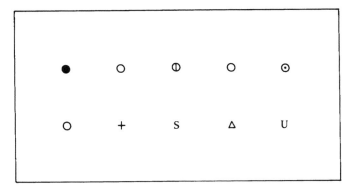

Figure 11. Plotting symbols (from Cleveland, 1985). The top set is for cases when there is little overlap; the bottom set is for cases when overlap causes problems. Use the first two symbols on the left when there are two categories, the first three when there are three categories, and so on.

the first two symbols on the left if there are two categories, the first three if there are three categories, and so on.

15. *Superimposed data sets must be readily visually discriminated.* The four groups are clearly discriminable in Figure 10, although there is a slight problem with the AMT and CBT scores in Session 1. Use different plotting symbols where there is poor discrimination.

16. *Put major conclusions in graphical form. Make captions comprehensive and informative.* Readers quite often look first at the tables and figures. With their captions, they should communicate most of the major points. Captions should briefly describe what is in the display, bringing attention to the important features and the main conclusions you wish to draw.

17. *Error bars should be clearly explained.* Error bars are useful ways of indicating variability in the data, but only if they are described unambiguously. Say clearly whether you are using (a) sample standard deviations of the data, (b) standard errors of the statistic graphed, or (c) confidence intervals for the statistic graphed.

18. *Choose the scales so that the data fill up as much of the data region as possible.*

19. *Choose appropriate scales when graphs are to be compared.* The graphs in Figure 10 are all on the same scale, making it easy to compare

them. In some cases, using the same scale results in poor resolution, however.

20. *Do not insist on zero always being included on a scale showing magnitude.* Including zero often helps comparisons, but it is not necessary to include it if this inclusion results in poor resolution of the data. Clearly labeled tick marks are essential, though.

21. *Use a logarithmic scale when it is important to understand percentage change or multiplicative factors.* When magnitudes are converted to logarithms, percentage change and multiplicative factors are easy to understand because equal percentage or multiplicative factors have equal distances on a logarithmic scale. (See Cleveland, 1985, pp. 104–114, for explanation and examples.)

22. *Showing data on a logarithmic scale can improve resolution.* Many data sets in psychology are skewed to the right. Plotting the data on the original scale will often result in graphs with most of the data bunched together at the low end and just a few points at the high end. This bunching can cause poor resolution. Using logarithms reduces the skewness and improves resolution.

23. *Use a scale break only when necessary.* If a break cannot be avoided, use a full scale break. Do not connect numerical values on two sides of a break. The scale break in Figure 6 is unnecessary, as there is no reason why the scale cannot start at 15. In some cases, scale breaks are needed to improve resolution, although transforming the data (logarithms, again, for data skewed to the right) often removes the need for a break.

Preparing Figures for Publication

If you plan to submit your paper for publication, remember that figures may be reduced in size, so that detail becomes harder to see. Be sure, then, to make your figures especially sharp and legible. Follow the particular journal or book publisher's instrucitons regarding the submission format for electronically prepared figures. If you draw you figures by hand, use black india ink on bright white drawing paper.

Graphs. When plotting values of a dependent variable against values of an independent variable, place the independent variable on the horizontal axis and the dependent variable on the vertical axis. It is usually helpful for the vertical axis to be about two-thirds as long as the horizontal axis (see Tufte, 1983, pp. 186ff).

Drawings. Drawings are most effective when kept simple. Drawings with shades of gray, like photos, require halftone processing, which is more expensive than regular processing. Avoid the added expense, when possible, by using patterns of lines or dots to create a shaded effect.

Photographs. Submit professional-quality black-and-white photographs with high contrast. If necessary, crop the photograph to remove unwanted material. If it is a photograph of a person, obtain written permission to use it.

Placement of Figures

In articles submitted for publication, figures are placed at the end of the article (see Chapter 3). Use the following notice at the place in the text where you want a figure inserted:

Insert Figure 1 about here

Figure captions, along with the figure numbers, are typed double-spaced on a separate page, which is placed before the figures. In student papers it is often more convenient to insert the figures at the appropriate places in the text, with the figure captions directly underneath each figure.

Figure Legends

Many figures require a legend or key to symbols. The legend appears within the figure itself, and is photographed as part of the figure. The legend should thus be consistent in style and proportion with the rest of the figure. Put the legend just outside the data region so as not to interfere with the data.

Figure Numbers

Figures are numbered consecutively with arabic numerals, starting with Figure 1. In articles submitted for publication, write the figure number lightly on the back, not on the front, of the figure.

Figure Captions

A figure caption should describe concisely what the figure is supposed to show. It should be understandable without reference to the text. If you need to include any further information, add it in parentheses after the figure caption. If you use a figure that is not original, obtain written permission to reprint the figure, and cite the source in the figure caption.

Submitting Figures

For APA journals, figures should be submitted as electronic files (for those journals that permit electronic submissions), as hardcopy laser-printer printouts (not dot matrix), or as 20 × 25 cm glossy photographs. Glossy prints smaller than 20 × 25 should be mounted on 22 × 28 cm paper. For other journals, follow the publisher's instructions. On the back of each figure write "TOP" to show which side is the top of the figure, and also write the figure number and the article's short title. On a photograph, write lightly in pencil so as not to damage it. Do not use staples or paper clips. Protect prints by covering them with tissue paper and separating them with cardboard if necessary. Before submitting figures, carefully proofread them.

Chapter Nine

References for the
Psychology Paper

Authors of psychology papers should be aware of the references available to them. This chapter, which is divided into two parts, contains a list of such references. The first part briefly describes general references that may be useful in all areas of psychology, whereas the second part briefly describes many of the journals psychologists read and consult when writing papers. Wherever possible, descriptions of the journals have been paraphrased from those provided in the journals themselves. The publisher's name and address are supplied at the end of each journal description and can be used to request further information about the journal and for subscriptions. This address is not appropriate for submission of manuscripts, because manuscripts are submitted to the editor of a journal, not the publisher. Because the editorship of a journal usually changes on a fairly regular basis, I do not provide here the names and addresses of editors, but they can be obtained by consulting recent issues of each journal. In addition, the journals usually contain useful information on style, specifications for articles, deviations from APA guidelines, and so on.

GENERAL REFERENCES

A Comprehensive Dictionary of Psychological and Psychoanalytical Terms: A Guide to Usage

A Comprehensive Dictionary of Psychological and Psychoanalytical Terms: A Guide to Usage contains many of the technical terms most frequently used in psychology and psychoanalysis. The book, published in 1958, is now somewhat out of date. The book is by H. B. English and A. C. English and is published by Longmans, Green, and Company.

Concise Encyclopedia of Psychology: Abridged

Editors Raymond J. Corsini et al. have distilled the four-volume *Corsini Encyclopedia* (above) into just over 2,000 articles in this abridged volume. It is widely praised as an essential resource for quick references and was named Reference Book of the Year by the American Library Association. Published by John Wiley & Sons, it was last revised in 1998.

The Corsini Encyclopedia of Psychology and Behavioral Science, Third Edition

This four-volume encyclopedia offers detailed discussion on 10 areas of psychology: applied, clinical cognitive, developmental, educational, measurement, personality, physiological, social, and history/theory. The volumes, edited by W. Edward Craighead and Charles B. Nemeroff, were last revised in 2002. The publisher is John Wiley & Sons.

Dictionary of Behavioral Science

Dictionary of Behavioral Science, second edition, published in 1989, defines technical terms in all of the behavioral sciences. It was edited by B. B. Wolman and is published by Academic Press.

Dictionary of Psychology

Dictionary of Psychology, by J. P. Chaplin, defines technical psychological terms. It also includes appendixes containing abbreviations commonly used in psychology; Hull's major symbolic constructs; common Rorschach scoring symbols; Greek letter symbols commonly used in psychology; prefixes, suffixes, and combining forms commonly used in psychological terminology; and commonly used statistical formulas. The book was published in 1991 by the Dell Publishing Company.

Dictionary of Psychology

The Penguin *Dictionary of Psychology*, third edition, by A. S. Reber and E. S. Reber, resolves some of the problems raised by psychological terms. It focuses on what a given technical term means, and shows how the term is actually employed, its connotations, and how it has been used and abused. The book was published in 2002 by Penguin Books Ltd.

Dissertations and Theses from Start to Finish: Psychology and Related Fields

Dissertations and Theses from Start to Finish discusses some of the nuts and bolts needed to put together a thesis and a dissertation. It was written by J. D. Cone and S. L. Foster and published in 1993 by the American Psychological Association.

Encyclopedia of Human Behavior (Four-Volume Set)

These four volumes, edited by V. S. Ramachandran, offer a sweeping view of human behavior with 250 articles. Each article has an outline, glossary, and bibliography. The encyclopedia includes a comprehensive index. The set was published in 1994 by the Academic Press.

Encyclopedia of Psychology

This encyclopedia includes more than 1,500 entries. Editor Alan Kazdin designed the encyclopedia to cover all approaches and all issues in psychology, while keeping an eye on past history, current practice, and future development. A sampling of encyclopedia topics are: research methods, study design and analysis, assessment, biological and cognitive processes, interactive systems, life-span development, cultural psychology, and clinical psychology. The relationship between psychology and other fields, including medicine, sociology, law, and philosophy, is described in detail. Also included are more than 400 biographies. The "Synoptic Outline of Contents" in the final volume provides a field guide to exploring specific topics using the encyclopedia, guiding the reader to principal entries, field surveys, and entries on related issues. The *Encyclopedia of Psychology* was published by the Oxford University Press in 2000 in collaboration with the American Psychological Association.

Encyclopedic Dictionary of Psychology

Edited by R. Harre and R. Lamb, *Encyclopedic Dictionary of Psychology*, a reference source, offers short articles on topics, problems,

and people. It was published in 1983 by Basil Blackwell in England
and simultaneously in the United States by MIT Press/Bradford Books.
Revised and updated sections on physiological and clinical psychology,
ethology, animal learning, developmental and educational psychology,
and personality and social psychology were published as separate
paperback books in 1986.

Ethical Principles of Psychologists and the Code of Conduct

Ethical Principles of Psychologists and the Code of Conduct contains principles and discussions of issues in research with human participants. Some of the issues dealt with are informed consent, freedom
from coercion, anonymity and confidentiality, and use of research
results. The original book was published in 1992 by the American Psychological Association (reprinted from *American Psychologist*, 1992, 47,
1597–1611). The APA ethics code is available at http://www.apa.org/
ethics/code.html *Graduate Study in Psychology and Associate Fields*.
The most recent version was published in December 2002.

Ethics for Psychologists: A Commentary on the APA Ethics Code

A practical resource for psychologists to learn to apply the APA
Ethical Principles and Code of Conduct. The book examines the code
(revised in 1992) in-depth. Edited by Mathilda B. Canter et al., the book
was published by the American Psychological Association in 1994.

Ethics in Plain English: An Illustrative Casebook for Psychologists

The APA Ethics code is presented in everyday language. Case
studies illustrate how the code applies in practice. Edited by Thomas
Nagy, this book was published by the American Psychological Association in 1999.

Graduate Study in Psychology

Graduate Study in Psychology, a standard reference that is updated
every year, provides complete and current information on more than
600 graduate programs in both the United States and Canada. The book
includes information regarding application procedures, admission re-

quirements, degree requirements, tuition, financial assistance, and considerations of special relevance to applicants from underrepresented groups. The book is published by the American Psychological Association.

Guide to Reference Books

Guide to Reference Books, eleventh edition, by R. Balay, is a standard annotated bibliography for all disciplines. The guide includes both author and subject entries. It functions as a central reference in which most other references are documented. The book was published in 1996 by the American Library Association.

Information Sources in the Social Sciences

This textbook is intended as a guide to references for library-science students and reference librarians. Edited by David Fisher et al., and published by K. G. Saur, the book was last revised in 2002. The first edition appeared in 1990.

International Encyclopedia of the
Social & Behavioral Sciences

These 26 volumes represent an ambitious project to describe the state of the art in all the fields within the social and behavioral sciences. It includes over 4,000 articles, indexed by name and subject, in 52 sections. The set is edited by N. J. Smelser and P. B. Baltes and was published by Pergamon Press in 2001.

Is Psychology the Major for You?
Planning for Your Undergraduate Years

Is Psychology the Major for You?, designed to help undergraduates decide whether a degree in psychology would be valuable in preparing for careers, provides information on how to decide on psychology as a major, the variety of careers available, how to make use of career counseling, how to find a job, and how to survive as a newly hired employee. It was published in 1987 by the American Psychological Association.

Journal Supplement Abstract Series

Journal Supplement Abstract Series (*JSAS*) provides access to psychological materials not available through conventional channels.

Manuscripts are submitted to the service and reviewed for possible inclusion. If a manuscript is accepted, an abstract of the manuscript appears in the *JSAS Catalog of Selected Documents in Psychology*, which is published quarterly. Accompanying the abstract are the length, price, and ordering information for the document. Documents are reproduced both in standard size and in microfiche format. The service and catalogue of documents are provided by the American Psychological Association.

Journals in Psychology: A Resource Listing for Authors, Fifth Edition

Journals in Psychology, APA's directory written exclusively for psychology authors, is designed to answer questions about where to submit papers for publication. It provides information on more than 350 U.S. periodicals in the behavioral and social sciences, including the editors' names, addresses, editorial policies, circulation, publishers, selective notes on submissions, and so on. This edition was published in 1997 by the American Psychological Association.

Library Research in Psychology: Finding it Easily

This pamphlet was created by the American Psychological Association (APA) to help students and nonpsychologists find relevant research on psychological topics of interest. Topics range from newspaper articles on current topics to detailed articles found in scientific journals. It provides a head start in finding where psychological research is published, how it is indexed, and where to go in the library to find different resources. It is available on the Web at *http://www.apa.org/science/lib.html*.

Mastering APA Style: Instructor's Resource Guide

This *Instructor's Resource Guide* is designed to improve students' understanding and use of APA's points of style in their writing before they begin the research paper. The guide contains eight multiple-choice assessment surveys, correction keys, and answer sheets along with informative instructions to incorporate this material into a teaching curriculum. The guide was published in 2001 by the American Psychological Association.

Mastering APA Style: Student's Workbook and Training Guide

Used in collaboration with the *Publication Manual of the APA, Fifth Edition, Mastering APA Style* is a self-pacing, self-teaching workbook that can be used to learn APA style quickly and effectively. The volume contains groups of instructional exercises on various aspects and features of the *Publication Manual*, including references and citations, headings, serialization, statistical and mathematical copy, italics and capitalization, number style, and table format. It was published in 2001 by the American Psychological Association.

Membership Directory of the American Psychological Association

Membership Directory of the American Psychological Association lists for each member of the APA his or her name, address, telephone number, education, present major field, areas of specialization, certification as a psychologist, diplomate status, and membership status in each relevant division; the association bylaws; a list of present and past officers of the association; ethical standards; and current data on laws governing the practice of psychology. The directory is published every four years by the American Psychological Association. It was most recently published in 2001.

Membership Register of the American Psychological Association

Membership Register of the American Psychological Association is published to provide an up-to-date listing of the current association membership, including addresses, telephone numbers, membership status, and divisional affiliations. The register is published annually by the American Psychological Association.

Preparing for Graduate Study in Psychology: 101 Questions and Answers

Written by William Buskist and Thomas Sherburne, this book addresses questions for applicants to graduate psychology programs. It was published by Allyn & Bacon in 1995.

PsycINFO

PsycINFO is an information retrieval service that provides a computer-assisted search of the *Psychological Abstracts*. Use of the system is described in detail in a *User's Reference Manual* that is updated frequently. The service and manual are supplied by the American Psychological Association. More information on *PsycINFO* can be found at *www.apa.org/psycinfo/*.

Psychological Abstracts

Psychological Abstracts is probably the single most valuable general psychological general reference. It contains subject and author indexes for more than 850 journals, technical reports, monographs, and other documents, and it provides a brief, non-evaluative summary of each article. The *Abstracts* are published monthly by the American Psychological Association.

Psychological Reader's Guide

Psychological Reader's Guide is a bibliographic source reproducing tables of contents from more than 200 journals in psychology. The guide is published monthly by Elsevier Sequoia S.A.

Psychology: A Guide to Reference and Information Sources (Reference Sources in the Social Sciences)

This book is a bibliographical guide for undergraduate and graduate students. Editor Pam Baxter devotes half of the book to sources in general psychology and special topics in psychology. Included within the 24 special topics are perception, intelligence, personality, consumer behavior, research methods, and motivation. The end of the book includes a subject index and an author–title index. It was published by Libraries Unlimited in 1993.

Publication Manual of the American Psychological Association, Fifth Edition

Publication Manual of the American Psychological Association, Fifth Edition, is an indispensable guide to the writing of psychology papers for publication. The manual contains chapters on content and organization of a manuscript, writing style, APA editorial style, typing, mailing, proofreading, and the journals of the APA. It also includes a useful bibliography. The manual was revised and published by the American Psychological Association in 2001.

Science Citation Index

Science Citation Index is an index of who has cited whom in the natural science literature. It includes the fields of natural sciences, medicine, agriculture, technology, and the behavioral sciences. (Because of its inclusion of the behavioral sciences, psychologists will find it largely overlapping with the *Social Science Citation Index*, described below.) The index is published quarterly and is bound into an annual volume. It is published by the Institute for Scientific Information. The index is available on the Web at *http://www.isinet.com/isi/products/citation/sci/*.

Social Science Citation Index

Social Science Citation Index is an index of who has cited whom in the social-science literature. It is organized both by author and by subject cited. Under each author or subject is a list of persons who have made the citation, and the location of the citation. The index is updated annually and is published by the Institute for Scientific Information. The index is available on the Web through *http://www.isinet.com/isi/products/citation/sci/*.

Standards for Educational and Psychological Testing

Standards for Educational and Psychological Testing establishes guidelines for the development, use, and sale of standardized tests. The standards were revised in 1999 by the American Psychological Association.

Thesaurus of Psychological Index Terms, Ninth Edition

Thesaurus of Psychological Index Terms contains a compilation of the vocabulary used in psychology and related fields. It is a useful source for those encountering technical terms with which they are unfamiliar. The ninth edition of the book was published in 2001 by the American Psychological Association.

JOURNAL REFERENCES

Acta Psychologica: International Journal of Psychonomics

Acta Psychologica publishes research in the field of psychonomics, a field defined by the journal as fundamental rather than applied and oriented toward quantitative models rather than toward verbal theories. Psychonomics is closest to what is usually called experimental psychology, but it also overlaps with the fields of biophysics, physiology, neurology, systems analysis, and computer science. The journal is published bimonthly by Elsevier Science Publishers B.V., Journal Division, P.O. Box 211, 1000 AE Amsterdam, The Netherlands.

Adolescence

Adolescence contains articles dealing with a broad range of issues relevant to the study of adolescent psychology. The journal relies heavily on solicited material, but ideas and suggestions are welcome. The journal is published quarterly by Libra Publishers, Inc., 3089C Clairmont Drive, Suite 383, San Diego, CA 92117.

American Behavioral Scientist

American Behavioral Scientist publishes general articles in the behavioral sciences. Each issue is devoted to a specific topic. Some recent topics have included military ethics and professionalism, social science data archives, social policy research, and age in society. The journal is published bimonthly by Sage Publications, Inc., 2455 Teller Road, Newbury Park, CA 91320.

American Journal of Community Psychology

American Journal of Community Psychology is devoted to theory and research concerned with interactions between individuals, organizations, and social structures. The journal especially seeks articles dealing with topics such as the promotion of mental health, early detection and prevention of behavioral disorders, effectiveness of mental health consultations, new techniques for the delivery of psychological services, and the creation of social environments that facilitate human growth and development. The journal is published bimonthly in association with the Division of Community Psychology of the American

Psychological Association by Plenum Publishing Corporation, 233 Spring Street, New York, NY 10013.

American Journal of Psychology

American Journal of Psychology contains original research articles dealing with problems in experimental psychology. It also contains notes, discussions, and book reviews. The journal is published quarterly by the University of Illinois Press, 54 East Gregory Drive, Champaign, IL 61802.

American Journal on Mental Retardation

American Journal on Mental Retardation contains original articles extending our knowledge of mental retardation. The journal is published bimonthly by the American Association on Mental Retardation at the Boyd Printing Company, 49 Sheridan Avenue, Box 1413, Albany, NY 12201-413.

American Psychologist

American Psychologist, the official journal of the American Psychological Association, contains archival documents relating to business of the APA and also publishes theoretical, empirical, and practical articles of interest to a broad spectrum of psychologists. The journal is published monthly by the American Psychological Association, 750 First Street, NE, Washington, DC 20002-4242.

Animal Learning and Behavior

Animal Learning and Behavior contains experimental, theoretical, and review articles in conditioning, motivation, developmental processes, social and sexual behavior, and sensory processes. Studies involving human subjects are published only if they deal with principles of learning and behavior that do not apply exclusively to humans. The journal is published quarterly by the Psychonomic Society, 1710 Fortview Road, Austin, TX 78704.

APA Monitor

APA Monitor is a newspaper containing new stories about current developments in psychology. Additionally, it contains information about current APA activities and about legislative activity pertaining to psychology. The newspaper also carries classified advertisements that publicize job openings in the various fields of psychology. The newspaper is published monthly by the American Psychological Association, 750 First Street, NE, Washington, DC 20002-4242.

Applied Psychological Measurement

Applied Psychological Measurement publishes empirical research on the application of techniques of psychological measurement to substantive problems in all areas of psychology and related disciplines. The journal is published quarterly by Sage Publications, Inc., 2455 Teller Road, Thousand Oaks, CA 91320.

Behavior Research Methods, Instruments, and Computers

Behavior Research Methods, Instruments, and Computers publishes articles dealing with methods, techniques, and instrumentation in experimental psychological research. The journal also contains a section on computer technology. It is published quarterly by the Psychonomic Society, 1710 Fortview Road, Austin, TX 78704.

Behavior Therapy

Behavior Therapy is an interdisciplinary journal devoted to original research on the theory or practice of behavior therapy or behavior modification. Occasionally it publishes theoretical or review articles in addition to experimental and clinical research articles. The journal also contains critical notices of new books, tapes, and films of relevance to the behavior-therapy and -modification fields. The journal is published four times a year under the auspices of the Association for Advancement of Behavior Therapy, 305 Seventh Avenue, Suite 16A, New York, NY 10001.

The Behavioral and Brain Sciences

The Behavioral and Brain Sciences is an international journal that seeks articles in psychology, neuroscience, behavioral biology, and cognitive science. *BBS* operates a service called "Open Peer Commentary," by which accepted articles are circulated to a large number of commentators who provide substantive criticism, interpretation, elaboration, and pertinent supplementary material from a full cross-disciplinary perspective. The article, the commentaries, and the author's response to the commentaries then appear simultaneously in the journal. *BBS* is published bimonthly by Cambridge University Press, Edinburgh Bldg., Shaftesbury Road, Cambridge CB2 2RU, United Kingdom.

Behavioral Neuroscience

Behavioral Neuroscience considers its primary mission to be the publishing of original research papers in the broad field of the biological bases of behavior. The journal also entertains occasional review articles and theoretical papers. The journal is published bimonthly by the American Psychological Association, 750 First Street, NE, Washington, DC 20002-4242.

Behavioral Science

Behavioral Science publishes original articles concerning living and nonliving systems: atoms, molecules, crystals, viruses, cells, organs, organisms, groups, organizations, societies, supranational systems, ecosystems, planets, solar systems, galaxies. The journal also publishes articles on mechanical, conceptual, and abstracted systems. The journal is published quarterly by Behavioral Sciences and the General Systems Science Foundation, P.O. Box 40, Fallbrook, CA 92088-0040.

Brain and Cognition

Brain and Cognition is devoted to theory and research concerning any aspect of human neuropsychology other than language. The journal especially seeks articles dealing with movement, perception, praxis, emotion, memory, and cognition, in relationship to brain structure and function. The journal is published nine times a year by Academic Press, 525 B Street, Suite 1900, San Diego, CA 92101-4495.

British Journal of Developmental Psychology

British Journal of Developmental Psychology publishes empirical, theoretical, review, and discussion papers in child development, abnormal development, educational implications of child development, parent-child interactions, social and moral development, and effects of aging. The journal is published quarterly by the British Psychological Society, St. Andrews House, 48 Princess Road East, Leicester LEI 7DR, United Kingdom.

British Journal of Educational Psychology

British Journal of Educational Psychology accepts articles that deal with any of a broad range of topics relevant to educational psychology, from psychometrics to motivation to cognitive systems and styles. The journal is published quarterly by the British Psychological Society, St. Andrews House, 48 Princess Road E, Leicester LE1 7DR United Kingdom.

British Journal of Mathematical and Statistical Psychology

British Journal of Mathematical and Statistical Psychology publishes papers on all aspects of quantitative psychology, including mathematical psychology, statistics, psychometrics, decision making, psychophysics, and relevant areas of mathematics, computing, and computer software. The journal is published twice a year by the British Psychological Society, St. Andrews House, 48 Princess Road East, Leicester LEI 7DR, United Kingdom.

British Journal of Psychology

British Journal of Psychology considers a broad range of topics for publication. Reports of empirical studies, literature reviews, and theoretical contributions are welcome. The journal is published quarterly by the British Psychological Society, St. Andrews House, 48 Princess Road East, Leicester LEI 7DR, United Kingdom.

British Journal of Social Psychology

British Journal of Social Psychology publishes original contributions to the methodological and theoretical issues confronting the discipline. The journal is published four times a year in February, June, September, and November by the British Psychological Society, St. Andrews House, 48 Princess Road East, Leicester LEI 7DR, United Kingdom.

Canadian Journal of Experimental Psychology

Canadian Journal of Experimental Psychology publishes empirical and theoretical papers in general experimental psychology. The journal is published quarterly by the Canadian Psychological Association, 151 Slater Street, Suite 205, Ottawa, ON K1P 5H3, Canada.

Canadian Psychology/Psychologie Canadienne

CP is a general, professional, and applied journal, publishing a wide spectrum of articles relevant to the field of psychology. *CP* is published quarterly by the Canadian Psychological Association, 151 Slater Street, Suite 205, Ottawa, ON K1P 5H3, Canada.

Child Development

Child Development reports empirical research, theoretical articles, and reviews having theoretical implications for developmental psychology. It welcomes contributions from all disciplines that bear on developmental processes. The journal is published bimonthly for the Society for Research in Child Development by Blackwell Publishers Ltd., 108 Cowley Road, P.O. Box 805, Oxford OX4 1FH, United Kingdom.

Clinical Psychology Review

Clinical Psychology Review publishes substantive reviews of all topics germane to clinical psychology. The journal is published eight times a year by Pergamon Press, Inc., The Boulevard, Langford Lane, East Park, Kidlington, Oxford OXB 1GB United Kingdom.

Cognition

Cognition contains theoretical and experimental papers on the study of the mind, book reviews, notes, and discussions on current trends in scientific, social, or ethical matters. The journal is published monthly by Elsevier Science Publishers B.V., Journal Division, P.O. Box 211, 1000 AE Amsterdam, The Netherlands.

Cognitive, Affective, and Behavioral Neuroscience

Cognitive, Affective, and Behavioral Neuroscience publishes articles in physiological psychology, and in the neurosciences in general, as long as the articles are relevant to behavior. The journal contains theoretical and empirical papers, as well as reviews. The journal is published quarterly by the Psychonomic Society, 1710 Fortview Road, Austin, TX 78704.

Cognitive Neuropsychology

Cognitive Neuropsychology publishes papers on cognitive processes from a neuropsychological perspective. It is published eight times a year by Psychology Press, 27 Church Road, Hove, E Sussex BN3 2FA, United Kingdom.

Cognitive Psychology

Cognitive Psychology publishes original empirical, theoretical, and tutorial papers; methodological articles; and critical reviews in the fields of language processing, memory, perception, problem solving, and thinking. The journal accepts articles from disciplines related to psychology as long as the articles are interesting to and understandable by cognitive psychologists. The journal is published by Academic Press, 525 B Street, Suite 1900, San Diego, CA 92101-4495.

Cognitive Therapy and Research

Cognitive Therapy and Research is a broadly conceived interdisciplinary journal whose main function is to stimulate and communicate research and theory on the role of cognitive processes in human adaptation and adjustment. It is published bimonthly by Kluwer Academic/ Plenum Publishers, 233 Spring Street, New York, NY 10013.

Contemporary Psychology

Contemporary Psychology publishes reviews of books in psychology and also, occasionally, of films, tapes, and other media relevant to psychology. Reviews are written by invitation, although all readers may submit brief letters pertaining to reviews that have appeared in the journal. The journal is published bimonthly by the American Psychological Association, 750 First Street, NE, Washington, DC 20002-4242.

The Counseling Psychologist

The Counseling Psychologist contains articles on all aspects of counseling psychology. It is published quarterly by Sage Publications, Inc., 2455 Teller Road, Newbury Park, CA 91320.

Creativity Research Journal

Creativity Research Journal publishes research capturing the full range of approaches to the study of creativity: behavioral, clinical, cognitive, cross-cultural, developmental, educational, genetic, organizational, psychoanalytic, and psychometric. Interdisciplinary research is also published, as is research within specific domains (e.g., art, science). Integrative literature reviews and theoretical pieces that appreciate empirical work are therefore extremely welcome, but purely speculative articles will not be published. The journal is published quarterly by Lawrence Erlbum Associates, Inc., 10 Industrial Avenue, Mahwah, NJ 07430-2262.

Current Directions in Psychological Science

Current Directions in Psychological Science is a bimonthly journal of the American Psychological Society that publishes brief (2,000 to 2,500 words) scholarly reviews that focus on emerging trends, controversies, and issues of enduring importance to the science of psychology. It is published by Blackwell Publishers Ltd., 108 Cowley Road, P.O. Box 805, Oxford OX4 1FH, United Kingdom.

Developmental Psychology

Developmental Psychology publishes empirical research dealing with all phases of growth and development. The journal is published bimonthly by the American Psychological Association, 750 First Street, NE, Washington, DC 20002-4242.

Developmental Review

Developmental Review is an international and interdisciplinary journal, publishing original articles that bear on conceptual issues in psychological development. The journal is published quarterly by Academic Press, 525 B Street, Suite 1900, San Diego, CA 92101-4495.

Educational and Psychological Measurement

Educational and Psychological Measurement publishes discussions of problems in the measurement of individual differences, research on the development and use of tests and measurements, descriptions of testing programs, and miscellaneous notes pertaining to measurement.

The journal is published bimonthly by Sage Publications, Inc., 245 Teller Road, Thousand Oaks, CA 91320.

European Journal of Social Psychology

European Journal of Social Psychology publishes theoretical and empirical papers in social psychology. It is published eight times a year by Wiley Europe, Ltd. Baffins Lane, Chichester, Sussex, United Kingdom.

Family Process

Family Process is a multidisciplinary journal that publishes material in the broad area of family studies, with particular emphasis on family mental health and family psychotherapy. It is published quarterly by Family Process, Inc., P.O. Box 23980, Rochester, NY 14692-3980.

Genetic, Social and General Psychology Monographs

Genetic, Social and General Psychology Monographs is devoted to developmental and clinical psychology. It is published quarterly by Heldref Publications, 1319 Eighteenth Street, NW, Washington, DC 20036-1802.

Gifted Child Quarterly

Gifted Child Quarterly publishes articles on the identification, teaching, and assessment of gifted children. It is published in January, April, July, and October by the National Association for Gifted Children, 1707 L Street, NW, Suite 550, Washington, DC 20036-4201.

Human Development

Human Development publishes articles on theory and research pertinent to development across the lifespan. It is published bimonthly by S. Karger AG, Allschwilerstr 10, Basel 4009, Switzerland.

Human Performance

Human Performance publishes articles that deal with all aspects of human performance in jobs as well as in non-occupational settings. It is published by Lawrence Erlbaum Associates, Inc., 10 Industrial Avenue, Mahwah, NJ 07430-2262.

Intelligence

The journal *Intelligence* publishes papers reporting work that makes a substantial contribution to an understanding of the nature and function of intelligence. Varied approaches are welcome. The journal is published six times a year by Elsevier Science Ltd., The Boulevard, Langford Lane, Kidlington, Oxon OX5 1GB, United Kingdom.

International Journal of Psychology

The *International Journal of Psychology* publishes papers in all fields of general psychology, including perception, learning, cognitive processes, language, child psychology, and social psychology. The journal especially seeks comparisons of experimental results obtained in different countries, replications in new cultural contexts, and international discussions of theories and methods. Emphasis is on basic research and theory rather than on technical and applied problems. The journal is published bimonthly for the International Union of Psychological Science by Psychology Press, 27 Church Road, Hove, E Sussex BN3 2FA, United Kingdom.

Journal of Abnormal Psychology

Journal of Abnormal Psychology publishes articles on basic theory and research in the field of abnormal behavior. It covers topics such as psychopathology, normal processes in abnormal individuals, pathological features of the behavior of normal persons, and group effects on pathological processes. Experiments, case histories, and theoretical papers are all welcome. The journal is published quarterly by the American Psychological Association, 750 First Street, NE, Washington, DC 20002-4242.

Journal of Adolescent and Adult Literacy

Journal of Adolescent and Adult Literacy serves those interested in the teaching of reading to adolescents and adults. It is intended as a forum to reflect current theory, research, and practice for a broad audience of reading professionals and to encourage effective instruction. The journal is published by the International Reading Association, 800 Barksdale Road, P.O. Box 8139, Newark, DE 19714.

Journal of Applied Behavior Analysis

Journal of Applied Behavior Analysis publishes original reports of experimental research involving applications of the experimental analysis of behavior (behavioristic techniques) to problems of social importance. Also included in the journal are technical articles and discussions of issues relevant to such research. This journal is published quarterly by Society for the Experimental Analysis of Behavior, Inc., c/o Department of Human Development, University of Kansas, Lawrence, KS 66045.

Journal of Applied Behavioral Science

Journal of Applied Behavioral Science publishes articles that develop or test theoretical and conceptual approaches to planned change, including reports on social interventions, evaluations of attempts at social interventions, and evaluations of the underlying values and biases inherent in attempts at social change. The journal is published for the NTL Institute for Applied Behavioral Science by Sage Publications, Inc., 2455 Teller Road, Thousand Oaks, CA 91320.

Journal of Applied Developmental Psychology

Journal of Applied Developmental Psychology is intended as a forum for communication between researchers and practitioners working in life-span human development fields. The journal is published bimonthly by Elsevier Science Ltd., Langford Lane, Kidlington, Oxon OX5 1GB, United Kingdom.

Journal of Applied Psychology

Journal of Applied Psychology publishes original articles dealing with all areas of applied psychology except clinical psychology. The orientation of the journal is primarily empirical, although a theoretical or review article may be accepted if it presents a special contribution to an applied field. Some of the applied settings covered by the journal are universities, industry, and government. The journal is published bimonthly by the American Psychological Association, 750 First Street, NE, Washington, DC 20002-4242.

The Journal of Community Psychology

The Journal of Community Psychology is devoted to research, evaluation, assessment, intervention, and review articles that deal with human behavior in community settings. The journal is published bi-monthly by John Wiley & Sons, Inc., Journals, 111 River Street, Hoboken, NJ 07030.

The Journal of Comparative Psychology

The Journal of Comparative Psychology publishes laboratory and field studies of the behavioral patterns of various species as they relate to evolution, development, ecology, control, and functional significance. The journal is published quarterly by the American Psychological Association, 750 First Street, NE, Washington, DC 20002-4242.

Journal of Consulting and Clinical Psychology

Journal of Consulting and Clinical Psychology publishes original research on techniques of diagnosis and treatment in disordered behavior, characteristics of populations of clinical interest, cross-cultural and demographic trends in behavioral disorders, and personality assessment as they pertain to consulting and clinical psychology. The orientation of the journal is primarily empirical, although theoretical articles are also published from time to time. The journal is published bimonthly by the American Psychological Association, 750 First Street, NE, Washington, DC 20002-4242.

Journal of Counseling Psychology

Journal of Counseling Psychology contains articles on theory, research, and practice concerning counseling and the activities of counselors and personnel workers. Contributions dealing with developmental aspects of counseling and with diagnostic group, remedial, and therapeutic approaches to counseling are particularly welcome. The journal publishes occasional reviews of research and of tests used by counselors. The journal is published quarterly by the American Psychological Association, 750 First Street, NE, Washington, DC 20002-4242.

Journal of Cross-Cultural Psychology

Journal of Cross-Cultural Psychology deals exclusively with cross-cultural behavioral and social research. Its main concentration is on empirical reports concerning how and why, if at all, psychological phenomena are differentially conditioned by culture and ecology. The focus of the journal is on individual rather than on societal differences. The journal is published for the Center for Cross-Cultural Research by Sage Publications, Inc., 2455 Teller Road, Thousand Oaks, CA 91320.

Journal of Educational Psychology

Journal of Educational Psychology publishes original empirical and theoretical papers dealing with learning and cognition as they relate to instruction, and with the psychological development, relationships, and adjustment of individuals. Articles report findings that for the most part are obtained in various kinds of educational settings. The journal is published quarterly by the American Psychological Association, 750 First Street, NE, Washington, DC 20002-4242.

Journal of the Experimental Analysis of Behavior

Journal of the Experimental Analysis of Behavior contains original reports of experiments and theoretical positions relevant to the behavior of individual organisms. The journal maintains a behavioristic orientation. It is published bimonthly by the Society for the Experimental Analysis of Behavior, Department of Psychology, Indiana University, Bloomington, IN 47405.

Journal of Experimental Child Psychology

Journal of Experimental Child Psychology is devoted primarily to empirical research dealing with children. It also includes critical reviews, theoretical contributions, and short notes on methodological issues and innovative apparatuses pertaining to child psychology. The journal is published monthly by Academic Press, Inc., 525 B Street, Suite 1900, San Diego, CA 92101-4495.

Journal of Experimental Psychology: Animal Behavior Processes

Journal of Experimental Psychology: Animal Behavior Processes contains experimental reports of the perception, learning, motivation, and performance of infrahuman animals. Articles are expected to make a substantial contribution to general behavior theory. The journal is published quarterly by the American Psychological Association, 750 First Street, NE, Washington, DC 20002-4242.

Journal of Experimental Psychology: General

Journal of Experimental Psychology: General contains articles in all areas of experimental psychology. The journal solicits long, integrative reports of general interest to all experimental psychologists. The journal is published by the American Psychological Association, 750 First Street, NE, Washington, DC 20002-4242.

Journal of Experimental Psychology: Human Perception and Performance

Journal of Experimental Psychology: Human Perception and Performance is devoted to experimental reports of human information-processing operations and their relation to experience and performance. The journal is published bimonthly by the American Psychological Association, 750 First Street, NE, Washington, DC 20002-4242.

Journal of Experimental Psychology: Learning, Memory, and Cognition

Journal of Experimental Psychology: Learning, Memory, and Cognition contains experimental articles on acquisition, retention, and transfer in human behavior. It is published bimonthly by the American Psychological Association, 750 First Street, NE, Washington, DC 20002-4242.

Journal of Experimental Social Psychology

Journal of Experimental Social Psychology contains primarily experimental research on social interaction and phenomena. Also included are occasional theoretical papers, literature reviews, and methodological notes. The journal is published bimonthly by Academic Press, 525 B Street, Suite 1900, San Diego, CA 92101-4495.

Journal of General Psychology

Journal of General Psychology publishes articles in the fields of experimental, physiological, and comparative psychology. It also contains briefly reported replications, refinements, and comments on previous work. The journal is published quarterly by Heldref Publications, 1319 Eighteenth Street, NW, Washington, DC 20036-1802.

Journal of Genetic Psychology

Journal of Genetic Psychology is devoted to research in developmental and clinical psychology. In addition to standard empirical reports, it includes briefly reported replications and refinements of previous work, as well as occasional book reviews. The journal is published quarterly by Heldref Publications, 1319 Eighteenth Street, NW, Washington, DC 20036-1802.

Journal of the History of the Behavioral Sciences

Journal of the History of the Behavioral Sciences contains articles on the history of all the behavioral sciences. The journal is published quarterly by John Wiley & Sons, Inc., Journals, 111 River Street, Hoboken, NJ 07030.

Journal of Humanistic Psychology

Journal of Humanistic Psychology publishes experiential reports, theoretical papers, personal essays, research studies, applications of humanistic psychology, humanistic analyses of contemporary culture, and occasional poems. The journal especially solicits articles on the topics of authenticity, encounter, self-actualization, self-transcendence, search for meaning, creativity, personal growth, psychological health, motivation, values, identity, and love. The journal is published quarterly by Sage Publications, Inc., 2455 Teller Road, Thousand Oaks, CA 91320.

Journal of Mathematical Psychology

Journal of Mathematical Psychology publishes original theoretical and empirical research in all areas of mathematical psychology. The journal is published quarterly by Academic Press, Inc., 525 B Street, Suite 1900, San Diego, CA 92101-4495.

Journal of Memory and Language

Journal of Memory and Language contains original experimental, theoretical, and review papers dealing with problems of verbal learning, human memory, psycholinguistics, and related verbal processes. The journal is published eight times a year by Academic Press, 525 B Street, Suite 1900, San Diego, CA 92101-4495.

Journal of Nonverbal Behavior

Journal of Nonverbal Behavior publishes original theoretical, empirical, and methodological research in the areas of nonverbal behavior, including proxemics, kinesics, paralanguage, facial expression, eye contact, face-to-face interaction, nonverbal emotional expression, and other areas that add significantly to our understanding of nonverbal processes, communication, and behavior. The journal is published quarterly by Kluwer Academic/Plenum Publishers, 233 Spring Street, Floor 7, New York, NY 10013-1522.

Journal of Occupational and Organizational Psychology

Journal of Occupational and Organizational Psychology publishes conceptual and empirical papers in industrial and organizational psychology that aim to increase understanding of people at work. It is published quarterly by the British Psychological Society, St. Andrews House, 48 Princess Road East, Leicester LEI 7DR, England.

Journal of Parapsychology

Journal of Parapsychology primarily contains original reports of experimental research in parapsychology. It also contains reviews, theoretical and methodological articles, book reviews, comments, and letters. The journal is published quarterly by the Parapsychology Press, 402 N Buchanan Boulevard, Durham, NC 27701-1728.

Journal of Personality

Journal of Personality publishes investigations in the field of personality. The emphasis is on experimental studies of behavior dynamics, character structure, personality-related consistencies in cognitive processes, and the development of personality in its cultural context. The journal is published bimonthly by Blackwell Publishers Ltd., 108 Cowley Road, P.O. Box 805, Oxford OX4 1FH, United Kingdom.

Journal of Personality and Social Psychology

Journal of Personality and Social Psychology contains original research in social psychology and personality dynamics. Among the topics included are social motivation, attitudes and attitude change, social interaction, verbal and nonverbal communication processes, group behavior, person perception, conformity, and personality dynamics. The journal is published monthly by the American Psychological Association, 750 First Street, NE, Washington, DC 20002-4242.

Journal of Psychoeducational Assessment

Journal of Psychoeducational Assessment specializes in articles relevant for practicing psychologists, educational diagnosticians, special educators, academic trainers, and others interested in psychoeducational assessment. It especially welcomes papers that describe innovative assessment strategies, relationships between existing instruments, diagnostic procedures, the relationship between assessment and instruction, and review articles of assessment techniques, strategies, and instrumentation. The journal is published quarterly in March, June, September, and December by the Psychoeducational Corporation, 505 22nd Street, Knoxville, TN 37916.

Journal of Psychology

Journal of Psychology contains articles covering all areas of psychology. It is published bimonthly by Heldref Publications, 1319 Eighteenth Street, NW, Washington, DC 20036-1802.

Journal of Research in Personality

Journal of Research in Personality contains experimental and descriptive research in personality and related fields. Articles cover the relationship to personality of genetic, physiological, motivational, learning, perceptual, cognitive, and social processes, in both normal and abnormal humans and in animals. The journal is published six times a year by Academic Press, 525 B Street, Suite 1900, San Diego, CA 92101-4495.

Journal of Social and Personal Relationships

Journal of Social and Personal Relationships prints articles on all aspects of social and personal relationships from any academic discipline, specializing in empirical, review, and theoretical articles as well as overviews of research programs. It is published bimonthly by Sage Publications, Inc., 6 Bonhill Street, London EC2A 4PU, United Kingdom.

Journal of Social Psychology

Journal of Social Psychology contains studies of persons in group settings, and of culture and personality. It gives special attention to cross-cultural articles and notes, and to field research. The journal includes briefly reported replications and refinements of previous work. The journal is published bimonthly by Heldref Publications, 1319 Eighteenth Street, NW, Washington, DC 20036-1802.

Learning and Motivation

Learning and Motivation publishes original experimental and theoretical papers dealing with basic phenomena and mechanisms of learning and motivation, including papers on biological and evolutionary influences upon learning and motivational processes. Articles deal with behavior in both animals and humans. The journal is published quarterly by Academic Press, 525 B Street, Suite 1900, San Diego, CA 92101-4495.

Memory and Cognition

Memory and Cognition contains articles covering a broad range of topics in human experimental psychology. Included in the journal are empirical, theoretical, and review papers. The journal is published eight times a year by the Psychonomic Society, 1710 Fortview Road, Austin, TX 78704.

Merrill-Palmer Quarterly: Journal of Developmental Psychology

Merrill-Palmer Quarterly publishes original experimental, theoretical, and review papers that are concerned with issues of human development. The primary focus of the journal is on infant, child, and adolescent development and contexts of development, such as the family and school. The journal is published in January, April, July, and October by Wayne State University Press, The Leonard N. Simons Building, 4809 Woodward Avenue, Detroit, MI 48201-1309.

Motivation and Emotion

Motivation and Emotion publishes theoretical, state-of-the-art, and synoptic reviews, position papers, and original research reports from any area of psychology and behavioral science, provided that the focus is on motivation or emotion. General theory papers are given special consideration. The journal is published quarterly by Kluwer Academic/ Plenum Publishers, 233 Spring Street, New York, NY 10013.

Multivariate Behavioral Research

Multivariate Behavioral Research publishes substantive, methodological, and theoretical articles using or dealing with multivariate statistical techniques. The journal is published quarterly by Lawrence Erlbaum Associates, Inc., 10 Industrial Avenue, Mahwah, NJ 07430-2262.

Multivariate Experimental Clinical Research

Multivariate Experimental Clinical Research publishes original investigations in personality and clinical psychology that use multivariate experimentation and theory. The journal emphasizes experimental research but contains occasional theoretical and review articles. The journal is published three times a year by Psychology Press, 325 Chestnut Street, Suite 800, Philadelphia, PA 19106.

Perception

Perception publishes experimental and theoretical reports in the fields of animal, human, and machine perception. The journal includes full experimental reports, preliminary reports, accounts of new phenomena, theoretical discussions, and descriptions of novel apparatus. The journal is published monthly by Pion Limited, 207 Brandesbury Park, London NW2 5JN, United Kingdom.

Perception and Psychophysics

Perception and Psychophysics publishes experimental investigations of sensory processes, perception, and psychophysics. Reviews and theoretical articles are also sometimes accepted. Articles deal with human and occasionally animal subjects. The journal is published eight times a year by the Psychonomic Society, 1710 Fortview Road, Austin, TX 78704.

Perceptual and Motor Skills

Perceptual and Motor Skills contains articles dealing with perception and motor skills, especially as affected by experience. It also includes articles on general methodology and reviews. The journal is published bimonthly by Dr. C. H. Ammons, Editor and Publisher, P.O. Box 9229, Missoula, MT 59807.

Personality and Individual Differences

Personality and Individual Differences is an international journal of research devoted to the structure and development of personality and the causation of individual differences. The journal is published 16 times a year by Pergamon, The Boulevard, Langford Lane, East Park, Kidlington, Oxford OXB 1GB, United Kingdom.

Personality and Social Psychology Bulletin

Personality and Social Psychology Bulletin publishes a variety of articles dealing with all areas of personality and social psychology. The journal is published monthly by Sage Publications, Inc., 2455 Teller Road, Thousand Oaks, CA 91320.

Personnel Psychology: A Journal of Applied Research

Personnel Psychology contains articles reporting research methods, research results, and application of research results to the solution of personnel problems in business, industry, and government. The journal also includes occasional literature reviews. The journal is published quarterly by Personnel Psychology, Inc., General Address: 520 Ordway Avenue, Bowling Green, OH 43402-2756.

Philosophical Psychology

Philosophical Psychology is an international journal that explores the links between philosophy and psychology in both pure and applied settings. It specializes in articles that deal with the application of philosophical psychology to the cognitive and brain sciences and to areas of applied psychology. The journal places particular emphasis on articles concerned with discourse analysis, connectionism, and knowledge systems. The journal is published quarterly by the Carfax Publishing Limited, c/o Sue Dommett, P.O. Box 25, Abingdon, Oxford OX14 3UE, United Kingdom.

Professional Psychology

Professional Psychology publishes original articles on theoretical and practical issues, including articles on applications of research, standards of psychological practice, relations among professions, delivery of services, and innovative approaches to training. The journal is published bimonthly by the American Psychological Association, 750 First Street, NE, Washington, DC 20002-4242.

Psychological Bulletin

Psychological Bulletin contains evaluative reviews and interpretations of substantive and methodological issues in psychology. Original research is published only when it illustrates a methodological problem or issue. The journal is published bimonthly by the American Psychological Association, 750 First Street, NE, Washington, DC 20002-4242.

Psychological Record: Quarterly Journal in Theoretical and Experimental Psychology

Psychological Record contains theoretical and experimental articles and commentary on current developments in psychology. The journal is published quarterly by Psychological Record, Kenyon College, Gambier, OH 43022-9623.

Psychological Reports

Psychological Reports publishes experimental, theoretical, and speculative articles, comments, special reviews, and listings of new books. The orientation of the journal is toward general psychology rather than toward any one specialty. The journal is published bimonthly by Dr. C. H. Ammons, Editor and Publisher, P.O. Box 9229, Missoula, MT 59807.

Psychological Research

Psychological Research contains original reports of experimental investigations in perception, learning, communication, and related areas. Preference is given to papers emphasizing theoretical implications of the research reported. The journal is published semi-annually by Springer-Verlag, Tiergartenstr 17, Heidelberg 69121 Germany.

Psychological Review

Psychological Review publishes articles that make a theoretical contribution to any area of scientific psychology. Empirical reports, literature reviews, and methodological papers are generally not appropriate. The journal is published quarterly by the American Psychological Association, 750 First Street, NE, Washington, DC 20002-4242.

Psychological Science

Psychological Science publishes papers that cover not only psychology in the traditional sense but also topics in related fields – including cognitive science, neuroscience, linguistics, and social science – that are relevant to psychological research. The journal is published bimonthly for the American Psychological Society by Blackwell Publishers Ltd., 108 Cowley Road, P.O. Box 805, Oxford OX4 1FH, United Kingdom.

The Psychologist: The Bulletin of the British Psychological Society

The Psychologist: The Bulletin of the British Psychological Society is, as the name implies, the official journal of the BPS. The journal contains feature articles and theoretical, empirical, and practical articles of interest to a broad spectrum of psychologists. It also contains archival documents related to business of the BPS. It is published monthly by the British Psychological Society, St. Andrews House, 48 Princess Road East, Leicester LEI 7DR, United Kingdom.

Psychology and Aging

Psychology and Aging publishes original articles on adult development and aging, including reports of research, which may be applied, biobehavioral, clinical, educational, experimental (laboratory, field, or naturalistic studies), methodological, or psychosocial. It is published quarterly by the American Psychological Association, 750 First Street, NE, Washington, DC 20002-4242.

Psychology and Psychotherapy

Psychology and Psychotherapy publishes original contributions to knowledge in those aspects of psychology applicable to medicine and related clinical disciplines. Formerly titled the *British Journal of Medical Psychology*, it is published quarterly by the British Psychological Society, St. Andrews House, 48 Princess Road East, Leicester LEI 7DR, United Kingdom.

Psychology in the Schools

Psychology in the Schools contains articles reporting research, opinion, practice, theory, and problems of the school psychologist. Articles are intended to emphasize implications for practitioners working in school settings. It is published quarterly by John Wiley & Sons, Inc., Journals, 111 River Street, Hoboken, NJ 07030.

Psychology of Women Quarterly

Psychology of Women Quarterly is a feminist journal that aims to develop and encourage the psychology of women. It publishes empirical research, critical reviews, theoretical articles, and invited book reviews. It is published quarterly for the American Psychological Association by Blackwell Publishers Ltd., 108 Cowley Road, P.O. Box 805, Oxford OX4 1FH, United Kingdom.

Psychometrika

Psychometrika contains theoretical, methodological, review, and experimental articles dealing with the application of quantitative techniques to social, behavioral, and biological research. The journal is devoted to the "development of psychology as a quantitative rational science." It is published quarterly by the Psychometric Society, c/o Ontario Institute for Studies in Education, 252 Bloor Street W, Toronto, ON M5S 1V6 Canada.

Psychonomic Bulletin and Review

Psychonomic Bulletin and Review covers all areas of experimental psychology with theory articles and reviews. Brief reports of experimental work (less than 4,000 words) may be submitted, as well as more lengthy articles on experimental psychology. The journal is published quarterly by the Psychonomic Society, 1710 Fortview Road, Austin, TX 78704.

Quarterly Journal of Experimental Psychology

Section A. Human Experimental Psychology: Section A of *Quarterly Journal of Experimental Psychology* publishes original papers on experimental work in all branches of human psychology. Reviews and theoretical papers will also be considered. The section is published quarterly for the Experimental Psychology Society by Psychology Press, 27 Church Road, Hove, E Sussex BN3 2FA, United Kingdom.

Section B. Comparative and Physiological Psychology: Section B publishes original papers on experimental work in all branches of comparative and physiological psychology. Reviews and theoretical papers will also be considered. The section is published quarterly for the Experimental Psychology Society by Psychology Press, 27 Church Rd, Hove, E Sussex BN3 2FA, United Kingdom.

Social Cognition: A Journal of Social, Personality, and Developmental Psychology

Social Cognition publishes reports of empirical research, conceptual analyses, and critical reviews on the role of cognitive processes in the study of personality, development, and social behavior. The journal is published bimonthly by Guilford Publications, Inc., 72 Spring Street, New York, NY 10012.

Chapter Ten

Standards for Evaluating
the Psychology Paper

I n this chapter, I will enumerate some of the standards I believe
my colleagues and I use in evaluating the contribution to knowledge made by psychology papers. Little has been written about how
psychologists evaluate a paper's contribution. Nor have psychologists
passed down from one generation to another a clearly explicated
spoken tradition of evaluative standards. It is therefore remarkable
that psychologists find a high level of agreement in their evaluations
of each others' papers. In an *Annual Review of Psychology* chapter reviewing the literature on memory and verbal learning, Tulving and
Madigan (1970) noted their own remarkable agreement in evaluations
of papers, and at the same time offered some keenly perceptive tongue-
in-cheek comments regarding the state of the literature:

> In the course of preparation for this chapter, we selected a sample of 540 pub-
> lications – slightly less than one half of all relevant publications that appeared
> during the main time-period under review here – and independently rated each
> paper in terms of its "contribution to knowledge." We agreed to a remarkable
> extent in classifying all papers into three categories. The first, containing ap-
> proximately two thirds of all papers, could be labeled "utterly inconsequential."
> The primary function these papers serve is giving something to do to people
> who count papers instead of reading them. Future research and understand-
> ing of verbal learning and memory would not be affected at all if none of the
> papers in this category had seen the light of day.
>   The second category, containing approximately one quarter of all the pa-
> pers in our test sample, fell into the "run-of-the-mill" category. These represent
> technically competent variations on well-known themes. Their main purpose
> lies in providing redundancy and assurance to those readers whose faith in the

orderliness of nature with respect to ecphoric [learning and memory] processes needs strengthening. Like the papers in the first category, these articles also do not add anything really new to knowledge, and they, too, will have fallen into oblivion 10 years from now.

Many papers in the first two categories simply demonstrate again something that is already well known. Many others offer one or more of the following conclusions: (a) variable X has an effect on variable Y; (b) the findings do not appear to be entirely inconsistent with the ABC theory; (c) the findings suggest a need for revising the ABC theory (although no inkling is provided as to how); (d) processes under study are extremely complex and cannot be readily understood; (e) the experiment clearly demonstrates the need for further research on this problem; (f) the experiment shows that the method used is useful for doing experiments of this type; (g) the results do not support the hypothesis, but the experiment now appears to be an inadequate test of it. Apart from providing dull reading, papers with such conclusions share another feature: They contain an implicit promise of more along the same lines in the future. They make one wish that at least some writers, faced with the decision of whether to publish or perish, should have seriously considered the latter alternative.

The third category of papers in our sample, comprising less than 10 percent of the total, was classified as "worthwhile," including a small group of real gems. The papers in this category carry the burden of continuous progress in our field, by clarifying existing problems, opening up new areas of investigation, and providing titillating glimpses into the unknown. In most cases, the contribution that each particular paper makes is of necessity most modest. Nevertheless, the papers in this category unmistakably stand out from the large mass of other publications.[1]

Most psychologists would view the literature on memory and learning (circa 1970) less dismally than did Tulving and Madigan. The difference in opinion, however, would more likely reflect lesser severity in applying standards than disagreement over what standards to apply. In the next section of this chapter, I will present synopses of three real papers and one imaginary paper. The three real papers are considered by many psychologists to be classics in the field of psychology. As you read the synopses, try to pinpoint the characteristics of these papers that make them classics. The imaginary paper is a prime contender for Tulving and Madigan's first category of "utterly inconsequential" papers. This paper should lack the characteristics you observed in the first three papers. In the third section of the chapter, I will present eight standards that I believe separate truly important

papers from other papers, and will discuss how these standards apply
to the four papers synopsized below.

SYNOPSES OF FOUR PSYCHOLOGY PAPERS

A Classic Literature Review: Miller (1956)

George Miller's (1956) "The Magical Number Seven, Plus or Minus
Two: Some Limits on our Capacity for Processing Information" is undoubtedly one of the most influential and often cited literature reviews
ever published in a psychological journal. Miller opens the paper with
a confession:

> My problem is that I have been persecuted by an integer. For seven years this
> number has followed me around, has intruded in my most private data, and
> has assaulted me from the pages of our most public journals. This number as-
> sumes a variety of disguises, being sometimes a little larger and sometimes a
> little smaller than usual, but never changing so much as to be unrecognizable.
> The persistence with which this number plagues me is far more than a random
> accident. There is, to quote a famous senator, a design behind it, some pattern
> governing its appearances. Either there really is something unusual about the
> number or else I am suffering from delusions of persecution. (p. 81)

The remainder of the paper is devoted to a case history of the per-
secution. This case history is summarized in the following pages.

   Span of Absolute Judgments. In experiments on absolute judgment, subjects are asked to assign a number to represent the amount
of some attribute or attributes possessed by a stimulus. Consider some
examples of such experiments.

   Pollack (1952) had subjects assign numbers to tones of different
pitch. The pitches ranged in frequency from 100 to 8,000 cycles per second, and were equally spaced along a logarithmic scale of frequencies.
The experimenter varied the number of tones among which subjects
had to distinguish. The number of alternative tones ranged from 2 to 14.
As you would expect, subjects had little difficulty distinguishing between two tones, and a lot of difficulty distinguishing among 14 tones.
The main result of interest, however, was that subjects' discrimination
failed to increase beyond six different pitches. Whereas subjects were
able to discriminate six different pitches with virtually no errors, they
were unable consistently to discriminate more than six different pitches.

This result replicated when the range of pitches was changed by a factor of about 20 and when the spacing of tones was varied.

Garner (1953) studied absolute judgments of loudness. He spaced his tones over the intensity range from 15 to 110 decibels, and used conditions with 4, 5, 6, 7, 10, and 20 different intensities. He found that the maximum number of stimulus intensities subjects are able to judge without error is about five.

Beebe-Center, Rogers, and O'Connell (1955) studied taste intensities in a similar fashion. The stimuli in their experiment were varying concentrations of salt solution. They found that subjects were able to distinguish among about four different concentrations.

Hake and Garner (1951) had subjects judge the position of a pointer in an interval along a line. Subjects were thus required to divide up the line into subjective intervals. The experimenters presented stimuli at either 5, 10, 20, or 50 different positions along the line. In one condition, subjects were told to use the numbers from 0 to 100 in making their absolute judgments. In a second condition, subjects were told to use the same number of responses as there were different stimuli (5, 10, 20, or 50). Regardless of the rating scale, subjects were found able to distinguish about 10 different positions along the line.

In other experiments, subjects have been found to distinguish about five different categories for hue and six categories for brightness. When vibrators are placed along a subject's chest, the subject is able to distinguish about four different intensities of vibration, five different durations, and seven different locations.

Miller presents further data corroborating the basic pattern of findings described above: As measured by absolute judgments of unidimensional stimuli, subjects' limitations on processing of information (often called *channel capacity)* range over a remarkably small interval. This interval seems to be about seven plus or minus two categories, regardless of (a) sensory modality, (b) type of stimuli within modality, or (c) range of stimuli within modality.

Span of Attention. Suppose a random pattern of dots is flashed on a screen for a very brief amount of time. How many dots can a subject report without making errors? Kaufman, Lord, Reese, and Volkmann (1949) did this experiment, flashing from 1 to 200 dots on a screen for a period of 0.2 s. The subject was required to report the number of dots appearing on the screen. The authors found that subjects made practically no mistakes in reporting patterns containing as many as 5 or 6 dots. Beyond this number of dots, however, subjects made frequent errors. The span of attention for random dot patterns, therefore, also seems to fall into the seven plus or minus two range.

Span of Immediate Memory. Suppose you are presented with a sequence of random numbers, which you are asked to recall immediately upon completion of presentation. Most people are able to recall about seven digits without error. The same limit applies to random sequences of letters or words.

Limitations on Seven Plus or Minus Two. The spans of absolute judgment, attention, and memory all seem to be about seven plus or minus two. Yet we know from everyday experience that we are able to distinguish among more than seven faces, words, numbers, letters, etc. Hence, our limitation to seven categories would itself seem to be limited. How do we increase our ability to distinguish among stimuli? There seem to be three important ways.

First, we can make relative rather than absolute judgments. For example, suppose that we were presented with successive pairs of tone frequencies and were asked to judge which tone in each pair was higher in pitch. We easily would be able to distinguish more than seven distinct tone frequencies. Or suppose that subjects were asked to judge which of two markers on a line was further to the right. We then could distinguish even all 50 different placements of markers in Hake and Garner's experiment. By making relative judgments, we can distinguish far more than seven categories.

Second, we can increase the number of dimensions along which the stimuli differ. In the experiments described above on spans of absolute judgment, attention, and immediate memory, all the stimuli varied along only a single dimension. In everyday life, however, most stimuli vary along multiple dimensions. For example, discrimination among tones can be increased if pitch and loudness are varied simultaneously. If two perpendicular lines were used rather than just a single one, we could distinguish more than 10 different positions in the plane formed by the two lines. If the random dot patterns of Kaufman et al. (1949) were replaced with dots systematically arranged into a 5 × 5 square, we would have no trouble counting 25 dots. In each case, multidimensionality increases our capacity to make differentiations among stimuli.

Third, we can arrange the task so that subjects are required to make several absolute judgments in a row. Instead of presenting a single stimulus to the subjects and asking them to make an absolute judgment, we present several stimuli in rapid succession, and then ask the subjects to make an absolute judgment. For example, we might present several markers in rapid succession on a line, and then ask the subjects to give an absolute judgment for any one of them. They are now presented with a context for the absolute judgment that was missing in the Hake and Garner (1951) experiment.

Recording. Under what circumstances are we limited to seven plus or minus two categories, and under what circumstances are we not so limited? Consideration of the following situations may help elucidate the limiting circumstances:

1. People usually can repeat back only about 9 binary digits (0 or 1) presented in a sequence for memorization. Thus, they will probably be able to recall 001011010 after some practice in memorizing such sequences, but they probably won't be able to repeat back 0010110100010110. Under a special set of circumstances, however, a person can repeat back as many as 40 binary digits. This set of circumstances involves recoding binary digits into larger chains. In an octal (8-digit) recoding scheme, the subject thoroughly learns the following conversion table:

   000 = 0   010 = 2   100 = 4   110 = 6
   001 = 1   011 = 3   101 = 5   111 = 7

   Note that a string of 3 binary digits now has been recoded into a single octal digit. The subject masters this scheme and is then presented with a long string of binary digits. Every time he hears a consecutive triplet of digits, he converts it into a single octal digit. In reciting back the digits, he decodes the recalled octal digit back into a string of three binary digits. If the subject previously could have remembered 10 binary digits, he now can remember about 30 such digits, because he has recoded them into groups of 3.

2. When a telegraph operator first learns Morse Code, she perceives each *dit* and *dah* as a separate chunk, treating it in the same way that the naive subject treats a binary digit. As the telegraph operator learns to group *dits* and *dahs* into letters, however, her recall improves dramatically, reaching about the same level as for letters.

3. When you are asked to recall an English sentence, you have no trouble recalling more than seven plus or minus two letters. You probably also

can recall with little difficulty more than seven syllables or even words. Suppose, however, that you are asked to recall a sentence presented in a foreign language with which you are unfamiliar. You may be able to recall more than seven plus or minus two letters, but perhaps not more than seven plus or minus two syllables or words.

The above examples make clear the importance of the unit of encoding in assessing how much is judged, attended to, or remembered. By recoding stimuli into hierarchically organized higher-order units, we can process large amounts of stimulus information. The processing limit of seven plus or minus two applies not to any unit but only to the highest order unit used to encode a stimulus. Given that restriction, the processing limit is general to a wide variety of task domains, as Miller (1956) has amply shown.

And finally, what about the magical number seven? What about the seven wonders of the world, the seven seas, the seven deadly sins, the seven daughters of Atlas in the Pleiades, the seven ages of man, the seven levels of hell, the seven primary colors, the seven notes of the musical scale, and the seven days of the week? What about the seven-point rating scale, the seven categories for absolute judgment, the seven objects in the span of attention, and the seven digits in the span of immediate memory? For the present I propose to withhold judgment. Perhaps there is something deep and profound behind all these sevens, something just calling out for us to discover it. But I suspect that it is only a pernicious, Pythagorean coincidence. (p. 96)

An Experimental Investigation of Forced Compliance: Festinger and Carlsmith (1959)

One of the most influential papers ever published in the field of social psychology was Festinger and Carlsmith's (1959) "Cognitive Consequences of Forced Compliance." The paper investigates what happens when someone is forced to do or say something contrary to his own privately held opinions. Two theoretical positions had been advanced, each proposing a different outcome.

According to Janis and King (1954), opinion change will increase as a function of mental rehearsal of the previously disputed opinion. The best way to induce opinion change in a subject is to force him to think up and rehearse new arguments supporting the disputed opinion. Janis and King's research seemed to support this position. Subjects forced to improvise a speech supporting an opinion contrary to their own showed more change in favor of this opinion than (a) subjects merely hearing a speech advocating the disputed opinion and (b) subjects delivering a speech prepared by someone else and advocating the disputed opinion.

A different prediction was made by the theory of Festinger (1957). According to Festinger's theory, opinion change will be maximized if the pressure used to produce opinion change is just sufficient to produce the change. As the amount of pressure increases over the just sufficient amount, the amount of change toward the new opinion will decrease.

Festinger and Carlsmith's experiment was designed to distinguish between the two theories presented above. The basic idea was simple (although the execution of the experiment, described below, was rather involved). Three groups of subjects participated in an excruciatingly boring experiment. Each subject in one group was paid $1 to convince a naive subject that the experiment, in which the naive subject was about to participate, was interesting and enjoyable. Each subject in a second group was paid $20 to tell the same lie. After they had made the persuasion attempt, subjects in each of the two groups were asked to report on how interesting and enjoyable they had found the experiment. Subjects in the third (control) group were asked only to report on the experiment, not to persuade anyone that the experiment was interesting and enjoyable. According to Janis and King's theory, reports from subjects paid $20 to lie about the experiment should have been more favorable to the experiment than reports from subjects paid $1, if one assumes that the $20-subjects felt more rewarded for doing the task and therefore rehearsed more favorable thoughts about it. According to Festinger's theory, reports from subjects paid $1 to lie about the experiment should have been more favorable, since $1 provided only a minimally adequate incentive to lie. Both theories predict more favorable reports from subjects in these experimental groups than from subjects in the control group. Let us now see how the experiment was executed and how it turned out.

Method. Seventy-one male students in the introductory psychology course at Stanford University participated in an experiment on "Measures of Performance." The subjects were presented with two tasks chosen to be as boring and monotonous as possible. In the first task, each subject was told to put 12 spools onto a tray, then to empty the tray, then to refill the tray with the 12 spools, and so on. He continued in this task for one-half hour. In the second task, each subject was presented with a board containing 48 pegs. The subject's task was to turn each peg a quarter turn clockwise, then to turn each peg again a quarter turn clockwise, and so on. Again, the task lasted one-half hour. In both tasks, the subject was told to use just one hand and to work at his own speed. While the subject engaged in the task, the experimenter appeared to be taking notes on the subject's performance.

After the subject had completed the second task, the experimenter presented him with a spurious debriefing: He told each subject that there were two groups in the experiment. In one group, the subject's own, subjects simply came into the room and performed the tasks. In the other group, subjects were told before the experiment by a confederate of the experimenter that the tasks they were about to perform were fun, enjoyable, interesting, intriguing, and exciting.

At this point in the experiment, treatments for the control and experimental groups diverged. Subjects in the control group were asked to rate, among other things, how interesting and enjoyable the experiment had been. Subjects in the experimental ($1 and $20) groups were given further spurious information about the experiment. These subjects were told that, unfortunately, the confederate was unable to appear that day because of another important commitment. This left the experimenter in the predicament of having a subject in the "second group" waiting outside, but no one to tell him how enjoyable the experiment was. The experimenter then hit upon an idea that could relieve him of his predicament. Perhaps, he suggested, the subject would be willing to volunteer to be the confederate who would tell the new subject about the experiment. If the subject would be willing to do this, the experimenter would pay him for his services, and also for possible future services as the confederate. The subject was then told either that he would be paid $1 or $20, depending upon which experimental group he was in. After agreeing to tell the lie, the subject was introduced to the new, "naive" subject, who was in fact a confederate of the experimenter who had no intention of participating in the boring experiment. Her only job was to pretend to be a new, naive subject. After lying to this confederate about the experiment, the subject was taken to another room, and was asked to rate how interesting and enjoyable the experiment had been.

The rating of the experiment by the subject completed the experiment for all subjects, regardless of group membership. After making this rating (and some others as well), the subject was given a true debriefing about the purpose and execution of the experiment.

Results. The results of the experiment supported Festinger's theory. Ratings of the enjoyableness of the experimental tasks were expressed on a –5 to +5 scale. The mean rating was –.45 in the control group, +1.35 in the $1-group, and –.05 in the $20-group. The mean rating for the $1-group differed significantly from the mean ratings for both of the other groups: These subjects found the experiment more enjoyable than did subjects in either of the other groups. The mean rating for the $20-group did not differ significantly from the mean rating for the control group, although the difference was of course in the predicted direction. Festinger and Carlsmith (1959) drew two major conclusions from these results:

1. "If a person is induced to do or say something which is contrary to his private opinion, there will be a tendency for him to change his opinion so as to bring it into correspondence with what he has done or said."
2. "The larger the pressure used to elicit the overt behavior (beyond the minimum needed to elicit it) the weaker will be the abovementioned tendency." (pp. 209–210)

An Experimental Investigation of Organization in Memory: Tulving (1966)

Suppose that an experimenter reads to you the following list of words: *dog, carriage, license, clock, light, notion, apple, sojourn, branch, lecture, aluminum, happiness.* After completing the list, the experimenter asks you to recite back to her in any order the list of words. Suppose, though, that after you have recited back the words, the experimenter reads you the list again, with the words in a different order. She then asks you to recall the list again, reciting back as many words as you can in any order. The chances are excellent that you will recall more words on this second trial than you did on the first.

It is a well-known fact of learning theory that rehearsal of words in a list improves recall of those words over successive trials in a free-recall experiment. Learning theorists disagree, however, over as simple a matter as why recall improves over trials.

For many years, the predominant viewpoint was that of *frequency theory.* According to this theory, each time a person hears a word, the memory trace for that word is strengthened. The stronger the memory trace, the more likely a word is to be recalled. Hence, repetitions of a word will increase recall of that word as a function of the frequency with which the word is repeated.

An alternative point of view is based upon Miller's (1956) notions of recoding and unitization. This viewpoint is called *organization theory.* According to this theory, subjects hearing words in a list recode the words into higher-order subjective memory units. As subjects receive more trials on a list of words, the size of the subjective units increases. In recalling a list of words, subjects never remember more than about seven plus or minus two subjective units. Because the size of these units increases with rehearsal, however, the number of words recalled over trials increases. According to this theory, then, higher-order subjective organization rather than frequency of repetition determines increases in level of recall. Tulving's (1966) experiment was designed to distinguish between conflicting predictions of these two theories. In particular, Tulving's experiment was intended to show that greater frequency of repetition can actually reduce recall of words if the repetition somehow disrupts subjects' organization of higher order units.

Method. All subjects in Tulving's experiment were presented with an initial list of 18 words. They were given eight trials of free-recall learning in which to learn as much of the list as possible. Subjects then received one of two treatments. Subjects in a control group received a second list composed of 36 new words, none of which had appeared on the first list. Subjects in an experimental group received a second list composed of 18 old words (all of them from the original list) plus 18 new words (none of them from the original list). Subjects in both groups received eight trials in which to learn as much of the second list as possible.

The design of the experiment can be summarized in the following way:

	First list	Second list
Control group	A	BC
Experimental group	A	AB

All subjects received the same list, A, as the first list. Subjects received different second lists, however. Subjects in the control group received a second list composed of two new sublists, B and C. Subjects in the experimental group received a second list composed of one old sublist, A, and one new sublist, B. Subjects were not told about the structure of the lists or the way in which they were related.

Frequency and organization theories make different predictions regarding performance on the second list. According to frequency theory, performance on the second list should be superior if one has had prior exposure to part of the list's contents. Hence, experimental group subjects should learn the list faster than control group subjects and should show higher recall after the eight trials are completed. According to organization theory, however, learning of the second list by experimental subjects should be retarded, and final performance in the experimental group should be inferior to that in the control group. The reason for this prediction is that according to organization theory, the higher-order units formed during first-list learning may have been appropriate for that list, but they will probably be inappropriate for second-list learning. These units for the first list will thus interfere with the formation of new units for the second list. The overlap in words, and hence in subjective units, will thus hinder rather than facilitate second-list recall.

Results. The results of the experiment supported the prediction of organization theory. Subjects in the experimental group (receiving overlapping lists) showed slower learning and poorer final recall than did subjects in the control group (receiving nonoverlapping lists). The identical result was obtained when Tulving replicated the experiment with different subjects and with lists half as long as those used in this experiment. These data supplied a strong disconfirmation of a basic tenet of frequency theory – that recall increases with increased frequency of repetition.

An Imaginary Experiment on Person Perception

Dymond (1949, 1950) developed a scale measuring empathic ability, that is, the ability to make accurate judgments about others. She found that the scale was successful in predicting which persons were more accurate in their interpersonal assessments. She also found that higher empathy scores were associated with higher performance IQs on the Wechsler-Bellevue Adult Intelligence Scale. It is this result that forms the basis for the imaginary experiment described below.

Mcdumbo, an obscure and deservedly unknown researcher, observed that the relation between Wechsler-Bellevue Performance IQ and empathy scores might be due to either of two factors. On the one hand, it might represent a genuine relation between Performance IQ and empathy. On the other hand, it might be an artifact attributable to the greater dexterity required to receive higher scores on the Wechsler-Bellevue test. According to this latter hypothesis, the true relation is between manual dexterity and empathy, not between intelligence and empathy. The results are certainly consistent with either hypothesis.

In order to investigate this hypothesis, McDumbo administered the empathy test to two groups of subjects. Subjects in one group received the Wechsler-Bellevue Performance Scale in addition to the empathy test. Subjects in the other group received homemade pencil-and-paper tests closely resembling the Wechsler-Bellevue Performance Scale but requiring no physical manipulation of objects. If intelligence is responsible for the previously discovered relation between Wechsler-Bellevue and empathy scores, then the association should appear in scores for both groups. If, on the other hand, manual dexterity is responsible, only the Wechsler-Bellevue group should show a significant association between the ability and empathy tests.

The results of the experiment were ambiguous. Both the pencil-and-paper tests and the Wechsler-Bellevue Performance Scale showed significant associations with the empathy scale, but the degree of association for the pencil-and-paper tests was significantly less than that for the Wechsler-Bellevue. McDumbo therefore concluded that both intelligence and manual dexterity are important components of empathy.

EIGHT STANDARDS FOR EVALUATING
THE CONTRIBUTION TO KNOWLEDGE
OF PSYCHOLOGY PAPERS

Standard 1. The paper contains one or more surprising results that nevertheless make sense in some theoretical context (see Sternberg, 2002a, 2002b). The papers of Miller, Festinger and Carlsmith, and Tulving all contain surprising, counterintuitive results that make sense when viewed in a new theoretical context. The surprise in Miller's paper is the omnipresence of the number seven (plus or minus two) in a wide variety of tasks measuring human information-processing capacity. This result suggests some inherent limit on our capacity to process information of any kind.

In Festinger and Carlsmith's experiment, it is surprising to find that subjects paid $1 to lie about a boring experiment later feel more positively toward the experiment than do subjects paid $20. Common sense and reinforcement theory both would predict the opposite result. But the result makes sense in terms of Festinger's *dissonance theory*. Subjects who were paid $20 can justify their lie to themselves with little difficulty: They lied for the money. Subjects paid $1, though, can scarcely justify their lie on the basis of the money received. Hence, they convince themselves that they said the experiment was interesting because it *was* interesting.

In Tulving's experiment, the surprising result is that subjects who have already memorized half the words on a list they are about to learn actually learn the new list more slowly than do subjects who have memorized none of the words on the new list. Common sense and frequency theory would predict the opposite result. The result makes sense, however, when viewed in the context of organization theory: The old organization is nonoptimal for the new list, and decreases rate of learning by impeding the formation of new organizational units.

McDumbo's experiment contains no surprises. Because it had been shown previously that the Wechsler-Bellevue Performance Scale correlates with the empathy measure, the replication merely confirms this result. Because the pencil-and-paper tests measure about the same thing as the Wechsler-Bellevue, it also is unsurprising that these tests correlate significantly with the empathy scale. And because these homemade pencil-and-paper tests probably are inferior to the Wechsler-Bellevue as measuring instruments, it is not surprising that they show lower correlations with other variables, including the empathy scale.

Standard 2. The results presented in the paper are of major theoretical or practical significance. The first three papers all contain results of major theoretical and practical significance. Miller's results suggest that humans actually have a very small capacity for processing isolated bits of information. They also show, however, that this capacity can be increased manyfold by recoding lower-order information into higher-order units. In Miller's terminology, the number of chunks of information that can be processed remains constant (at about seven), but the amount of information per chunk increases. Thus, although we can recall only about seven isolated letters, we can recall far more letters if they are chunked into words or sentences.

Festinger and Carlsmith's findings are of theoretical significance because they suggest the superiority of dissonance theory over reinforcement theory in accounting for effects of forced compliance on private opinions. The practical significance of these results is obvious. In order to persuade someone to adopt your point of view privately, you should not give him the greatest possible reward. Rather, you should give him the minimum possible reward that will entice him to adopt your viewpoint publicly.

Tulving's findings are of theoretical importance because they suggest that simple frequency principles are inadequate to explain the effect of repetition in learning. Organizational principles seem to be needed as well as or instead of frequency principles. The findings are of practical importance because they show the importance of organizing in an effective way the material to be learned. Mere rote drill is a poor way to learn material, and an ineffective organization of material can actually impede learning.

McDumbo's experiment contains no results of major theoretical or practical importance. McDumbo presents no theory as to why empathy and performance IQ should be associated, although presumably a post hoc theory could be invented. The association is of some practical interest but seems unlikely to be applied to real-world settings: People are not likely to judge empathic ability on the basis of intelligence test scores.

Standard 3. *The ideas in the paper are new and exciting, perhaps presenting a new way of looking at an old problem.* The first three papers all deal with old problems. Miller's paper reviews the literatures on absolute judgment, attention span, and memory span. The Festinger and Carlsmith study forced compliance, a standard topic of investigation in social psychology. Tulving's paper investigates the effects of repetition on learning, probably the oldest and most basic problem in the field of learning. Each paper brings to an old problem a new perspective that seems to provide a better account of basic psychological phenomena than do old perspectives. McDumbo's paper contains no new or exciting ideas – indeed, it contains scarcely any ideas at all. It reports some empirical phenomena and provides an unconvincing explanation of these phenomena.

Standard 4. *The interpretation of results is unambiguous.* Lack of ambiguity is a standard that can be approached but not attained. When each of the first three papers was published, its impact was heightened by the seeming unambiguity in interpretation permitted by the results: The results seemed to demand the interpretation given to them. Nevertheless, the concept of a "crucial experiment" – an experiment that decides conclusively between two or more competing theories – is a myth. The experiments reviewed or reported in these papers proved to be no exceptions. Information theory, upon which Miller's article is based, has all but faded from the psychological scene. Bem (1967) has shown that Festinger and Carlsmith's result can be explained by self-perception theory as well as by dissonance theory. Sternberg and Bower (1974) have demonstrated that Tulving's result and others that followed it are more compatible with list-discrimination theory than with organization theory.

The level of ambiguity in the first three papers can be contrasted with the level of ambiguity in the fourth paper. Many years passed before these first three papers were shown amenable to persuasive alternative explanations, and in each case, the alternative explanation is nontrivial. In the case of McDumbo's paper, however, several alternative explanations are immediately apparent, most of them more convincing than McDumbo's explanation. The most plausible explanation is also the most trivial. McDumbo, you will recall, concluded that both performance IQ and manual dexterity are components of empathy. A more likely interpretation of the data is that manual dexterity is unrelated to empathy. The Wechsler-Bellevue correlated higher with the empathy scale than did the pencil-and-paper tests not because of the added manual dexterity component, but because it is a more reliable and valid measure of performance IQ.

Standard 5. *The paper integrates into a new, simpler framework data that had previously required a complex, possibly unwieldy framework.* Miller's paper best exemplifies this characteristic. Prior to publication of the paper, absolute judgment, attention, and memory generally had been viewed as separate phenomena, and had been studied more or less independently. Miller's paper suggested a way in which diverse capacities could be understood (at least to some extent) within a single, unified framework. Miller did not claim that these three capacities were a single capacity. Rather, he claimed that they were subject to the same information-processing limitations – limitations imposed by our ability to handle at one time only seven plus or minus two chunks of information.

Standard 6. *The paper contains a major debunking of previously held ideas.* Certain ideas become so deeply ingrained in our ways of thinking that we are scarcely aware that we hold these ideas. The ideas serve as unquestioned presuppositions. Festinger and Carlsmith's major finding flagrantly violated one of these unquestioned presuppositions – that a larger reinforcement for some behavior will work at least as well as a smaller one. Tulving's major finding also flagrantly violated a generally unquestioned presupposition – that repetition of elements in a to-be-learned list will result in at least as much learning as nonrepetition of those elements.

Timing is of the utmost importance in debunking a theory. Suppose that the theory to be debunked is Theory X, and the replacement theory is Theory Y. If everyone already believes in the validity of Theory Y, a paper debunking Theory X will have little impact. Such a paper will be seen as beating a dead horse. But if most people are deeply committed to Theory X, and new results are obtained that cannot be reconciled with Theory X but that are compatible with Theory Y, then the paper debunking Theory X can have a great deal of impact.

Standard 7. *The paper presents an experiment with a particularly clever paradigm or experimental manipulation.* Psychologists admire clever experimental paradigms, even if they are not theoretically motivated. That the paradigms of Festinger and Carlsmith and of Tulving were both clever and theoretically motivated made them all the more appealing. Paradigms have lives of their own, and their life span sometimes extends well beyond that of the theory that motivated them. Variants of Tulving's part–whole paradigm have continued to appear in the memory literature, even though organization theory now attracts little research.

Standard 8. *The findings or theory presented in the paper are general ones.* Miller's theory of chunking and higher-order unitization aroused widespread interest among psychologists in part because of its unusual generality: The theory seemed applicable to a wide variety of cognitive performances. Festinger's dissonance theory also attracted interest because of its generality: It seemed capable of explaining people's rationalizations in a wide variety of everyday situations. Tulving's organization theory also seemed quite general and was applied to memory for many different kinds of material. McDumbo, on the other hand, has no theory, and the result appears to have little generality: It merely expresses a relation between two specific variables.

A paper that meets all or even some of the standards described above is likely to fall into Tulving and Madigan's "third category." The student of psychology should be aware of these standards in evaluating the papers he reads, although the reader can expect to meet only a small number of them – and those modestly – in his own writing. Whereas the standards for good writing presented earlier in this book are ones that any student can and should meet, the standards presented in this chapter are ones to be strived for. The papers that meet these standards are the ones that are remembered when most other papers are long forgotten.

NOTE

1. Reproduced, with permission, from "Memory and Verbal Learning" by E. Tulving and S. A. Madigan, *Annual Review of Psychology*, Volume 21. Copyright © 1970 by Annual Reviews, Inc. All rights reserved.

Chapter Eleven

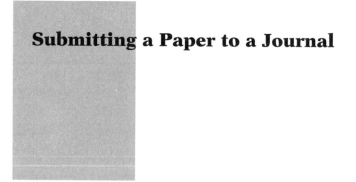

Submitting a Paper to a Journal

I f you write a paper that you believe makes a substantial contri-bution to psychological knowledge, you may want to consider submitting the paper for publication. Your academic adviser or course instructor can give you advice regarding the publishability of your paper, and an appropriate choice of a journal to which to submit the paper.

DECIDING UPON A JOURNAL

If you decide to submit a paper for publication, the first step you must take is to decide upon a journal to which you want to submit the paper. Seven considerations should enter your decision:

1. *Quality.* Journals vary widely in quality. Some journals publish papers that do little more than fill up journal space; other journals publish only outstanding contributions to the literature. Better journals gen-erally have higher rejection rates for submitted papers, so that the probability of a paper being accepted in such journals is lower. Your adviser or course instructor can help you match the quality of your paper to an appropriate journal.

2. *Content.* All journals limit by content the kinds of papers they accept. Journal editors use either or both of two criteria in deciding upon the appropriateness of a paper's content. The first criterion is substantive focus. What is the topic of research? The journal may accept, for ex-

ample, only developmental, or cognitive, or applied papers. The second criterion is methodological focus. How was the research done? The journal may accept, for example, only experimental, or theoretical, or review papers. Chapter 9 describes the content restrictions of many psychological journals.

3. *Readership.* Journals vary in (a) who reads them and in (b) how many people read them. Readership depends in turn upon the quality and content of each journal and, to a lesser extent, upon the cost of the journal. Journals publish annual statements of their circulation, so that the extent of the readership can be determined by looking through recent back issues of a journal for the annual statement. The composition of the readership can be inferred by assessing quality and content, and by examining the kinds of papers in which articles from the journal are cited.

4. *Length restrictions.* Most journals have implicit restrictions on length of submitted papers, and some journals have explicit restrictions. If the journal's editorial statement (carried in every issue of most journals) does not make any statement about length, an examination of several recent issues of the journal will indicate the range in length acceptable to the journal editor.

5. *Publication lag.* The length of time between acceptance of an article and publication of the article is the publication lag. Journals vary in publication lags from as little as 1 month to as much as 18 months or more. In submitting an article, the author should decide how long he is willing to wait for the article to be published, keeping in mind that there will be an additional lag from the time the paper is submitted to the time the paper is either accepted or rejected.

6. *Cost of submission.* Most journals do not charge authors for publication. Some journals do charge, however, so that publication of even a short article can cost an author several hundred dollars. The journal's editorial statement will indicate what costs, if any, are involved. The author must decide before submitting an article to such a journal whether she is willing and able to meet the costs of publication.

7. *Authorship restrictions.* A small number of journals restrict in some way their potential contributors. Submission may be by invitation only, or it may be limited to individuals belonging to or sponsored by members of some organization. The journal's editorial statement will indicate whether any such restrictions apply.

SUBMITTING THE PAPER

Once you have decided upon a journal, you should make certain that your paper meets the editorial requirements of the journal. In most cases, this means that the paper conforms to the APA guidelines outlined in Chapter 7. If your paper conforms to these (or other) guidelines, you are ready to send it out. Most journals require at least two copies of the paper (including the original), and you should of course keep at least one copy for yourself. Check the journal's editorial statement for the number of copies you are required to submit. Psychology papers may be submitted to only one journal at a time. You may not submit what is essentially the same paper to two different journals, even if the papers differ in minor respects. You should therefore send the paper initially to your first-choice journal, keeping in mind a second and possibly a third choice in case your paper is rejected. When you send the manuscript, include a cover letter indicating (a) your intention to submit the manuscript, (b) the title of the manuscript, (c) the length of and number of tables and figures in the manuscript, (d) requests for masked review (i.e., review that does not identify you to reviewers), if you wish it, (e) information regarding any previous presentations of the data (such as in scientific talks), (f) information regarding any closely related manuscripts, such as ones that report portions of the data, (g) notice of any possible conflicts of interest, and (h) verification that human or animal subjects have been treated in accordance with APA guidelines. Enclose any permissions that may be needed for reproduction of copyrighted material. Some journals permit elecronic submission, others do not. You must check the guidelines of each journal for submission requirements.

THE EDITORIAL DECISION

Most journal editors send out the articles they receive to reviewers. Some journals have a policy of "blind reviewing." All identifying information is removed from the manuscript, and the reviewer is not informed of the author's identity. Almost all journals keep the identity of the reviewer(s) a secret from the author. Once the journal editor has received the review(s), he may make any one of five decisions:

1. *Acceptance without revision.* The article is accepted as is and is immediately placed into the publication queue.
2. *Acceptance with revision.* The article is accepted contingent upon revisions, usually minor ones. The editor sends back the article and review(s), informing the author of the changes that need to be made.
3. *Rejection with suggestions for revisions.* The article is rejected, but the editor suggests ways in which the article might be made suitable for publication in the journal. Because the article is rejected, however, the editor does not commit himself to publication of the article, even if the specified changes are made. This decision is sometimes called "rejection without prejudice."
4. *Rejection.* The article is rejected outright. The editor makes clear in his letter to the author that the paper is not suitable for the journal.
5. *No decision.* The editor decides not to decide upon the article. He indicates to the author that he is withholding a decision pending either additional information or the incorporation of suggestions for revision.

What are the major reasons that editors reject articles? I asked this question of Professor Allan Wagner, former editor of *The Journal of Experimental Psychology: Animal Behavior Processes.* He indicated that by far the most common reason for rejection of papers is lack of substance: The paper represents too little work; the findings do not present a sufficient advance over what is already known; the findings are insufficient to establish a real, reproducible phenomenon. Other reasons for rejection include omission of necessary experimental procedures and controls, inappropriate or inadequate data analyses, shoddy scholarship, and a failure to place the work in a proper perspective. But Dr. Wagner indicated that the primary consideration in his decisions is the substance of the work. If the work represents a genuine contribution, then he (and other editors) will often bend over backward to help the author make the paper acceptable for publication.

THE AFTERMATH

If an article is rejected, the author can either give up on the article or else restart the editorial process by submitting the article elsewhere. If the article is accepted, the article goes into press. The author may be asked to sign over the copyright to the publisher of the journal. She may also be sent back a copyedited version of the article. This version has on it instructions to the printer, and may also have queries to the author. The copy editor may want to know, for example, whether a certain symbol is meant to be a particular Greek letter, or whether an editorial revision is acceptable to the author. Authors almost always receive proofs of their articles. Proofs are the printed version of the article as it will appear in the journal. The author checks the proofs for typographical and other errors. If an author makes changes in the article at this point, the author is usually charged for the cost of the changes to the printer. Finally, the article is published. Most journals are willing to supply reprints to the author. Some journals charge for any reprints the author orders; others supply a certain number of free reprints, and charge for additional ones.

If, as a student, you publish an article, you are to be congratulated. You have made an original contribution to psychological knowledge and, in the spirit of scientific enterprise, you have shared it with others.

Chapter Twelve

How to Win Acceptances from Psychology Journals: Twenty-Nine Tips for Better Writing

The price you pay for an ill-conceived or ineptly written article submitted to a psychological journal is:

a. express-mail receipt of a one-way ticket to the Bermuda Triangle.
b. an invitation to Hannibal (the Cannibal) Lecter's dinner table.
c. eternal damnation in the fires of hell.
d. rejection or, worse, benign neglect of the article if it is published.

The keyed answer to this problem is (d), although options (a) through (c) may come to pass in individual cases. You can have million-dollar ideas (although, as a psychologist, you'll probably never see the money), but if you do not express those ideas well, the impact of your work will be severely reduced or even nullified. The scientific process does not end with the completion of research. It continues through writing, publication, and the reactions of peers and public.

What can you do to write successfully? I will divide my discussion of what you can do into four parts: what you say, how you say it, what to do with what you say, and what to do with what others say.

Material in this chapter was previously published in the *APS Observer* and in Sternberg, R. J. (2001). Writing for your referees. In R. J. Sternberg (Ed.), *Guide to publishing in psychology journals* (pp. 161–168). New York: Cambridge University Press. Reprinted with permission of the American Psychological Society and of Cambridge University Press, respectively.

WHAT YOU SAY

1. *State clearly the problem you are addressing and then organize the article around the problem.* Sometimes it is hard to figure out exactly what problem the author of an article thought he or she was trying to solve. This phenomenon can occur because the author does not know what problem the article is supposed to solve, or because the nature of this problem was not clearly communicated. It is the author's responsibility to make clear early in the article what problem or problems the article tackles.

Once you have stated the problem, organize the article around it. Show why the problem is important – why it should matter to anyone beside you. If you do not know, why should a referee? In the literature review, use relevance to the problem tackled as the major basis for deciding what to cite. In the methods section, tell the story of how the successive analyses help solve the problem that was originally posed. And then, in the discussion section, summarize what you did and discuss its implications.

A clearly focused, tightly organized article has a great advantage in the review process. You are helping the referee understand what your goals are and how you are trying to reach them. If you leave it to the referees to figure theses things out, there is a good chance that the conclusions they come to will differ from your own.

2. *Start strong.* "Smith and Jones (1986) found that 83% of readers never got beyond the first paragraph of the majority of articles they began to read." This opening is an example of how to be boring, as are these: "Past research shows . . .," or "It is interesting to note that . . ." (says who?). A stronger start asks a question or states a problem pertinent to the theme of your article: "Why are so many psychology articles safe and cheap substitutes for sleeping pills?" for example, or "Dullness blunts the impact of many potentially interesting articles." Tell readers what the article is about in a provocative way that catches their attention.

3. *Make clear up front what the new and valuable contribution of your article is, and make sure you are right.* My conversations with journal editors suggest that the No. 1 reason for rejection of journal articles is lack of substance – there just is not enough new in the article to justify its publication in their journal. Reviewers, too, are on the lookout for articles that have little or nothing new to say.

It therefore behooves you to ask yourself what the new and valuable contribution of your article is, and to make clear near the beginning of the article what it is. Do not expect reviewers to figure it out for themselves. If you cannot figure it out, you cannot expect them to. If you cannot find such a contribution, either do more research or do more thinking before you submit the article.

4. *Tell readers why they should be interested.* "These findings are interesting and important. Therefore, you should support my promotion to tenure." Don't expect readers to know why you find a topic interesting or why they should find it interesting. Show them! Keep your audience in mind: The more you can relate your topic to concerns of your reader, the more interest you will generate. If you are writing for perceptual psychologists, make contact with the theoretical issues that concern people in this field. If you are writing for teachers, show how your findings can be used to improve teaching.

5. *Make sure that the article does what it says it will do.* "In this article, I will characterize the meaning of life, solve the problem of world hunger, and reveal at long last Richard Nixon's secret plan to end the Vietnam War." Many articles are declined by journals because they do not deliver what they promise. They claim much but deliver little. For example, experiments should follow from the theory you present. Make sure that you frame your article in terms of what you have really accomplished, not in terms of what you wished you had accomplished.

6. *Make sure that the literature review is focused, reasonably complete, and balanced.* "Thus, both studies showed that high levels of reasoning performance require people to wear propeller beanies on their heads. Other studies, showing that high levels of reasoning performance require pocket protectors, are irrelevant." Reviewers are infuriated by literature reviews that are biased in favor of a single point of view, especially if it's not their own (and chances are good that at least some of the reviewers will have views different from your own). Reviewers are even more upset when their own work is clearly relevant but not cited (can you say, "Sayonara to acceptance"?). And reviewers do not want to read about every marginally relevant study ever done. Make your review complete and current, but also keep it focused and concise so that it encompasses but does not overwhelm what you are studying.

7. *Make clear how your work builds on that of others.* No one likes a credit hog – someone that makes a contribution and then acts as though no one else has ever had any idea of value in the area of work. Sharing

credit goes beyond citing potential reviewers. It involves showing how your work builds on their work and the work of many others. Scholarship always requires drawing connections between what is new and what is old.

It also is important in citing references that you are up-to-date. Referees generally are not happy to see reference lists that would have been up-to-date a decade earlier. So check recent literature in the area in which you are working. In this way, you also are less likely to repeat what someone already has done.

Some authors may feel that, in setting out in a bold new direction, they really owe almost nothing to anybody else. But it is important to realize that, even when you oppose old ideas, you still are using those ideas as a base from which to map your campaign of opposition. And even when you move away from what others have done, had they not done what they had done, you would not have had their work to move away from. Thus it is important to show how you build on, not just how you go beyond, past work.

8. *Check your data analyses and interpretations.* If your article makes a substantial contribution, there is a good chance that someone will ask for your data, which you are obliged to provide to him or her. This "someone" may be a referee, or someone who later reads the article. One of the more embarrassing events in the life of an academic is to have one's data analyses demolished. It is therefore important to check that you have used the correct forms of analysis and to ensure that you have transcribed the statistics correctly.

Also make sure that your interpretations are correct. For example, more stringent levels of significance do not indicate stronger effects, but rather, lessen likelihoods that a given result would have been obtained under the null hypothesis.

9. *Always explain what your results mean – don't force the reader to decipher them.* "Finally, we obtained a 7-way interaction among the independent variables, clearly showing that the variables need to be considered in terms of their interactive as well as their additive effects." Interpret your results. With enough time, readers could figure out the meaning for themselves, but who has time? Don't leave the interpretation for the Discussion. Speculation and ideas that relate your work to that of others should go in the Discussion. Basic interpretations should accompany the results – while people still remember what they are.

10. *Make sure that your conclusions follow from your data.* High up on the list of annoyances to referees is the author whose claims go well beyond his or her data. Such authors are all too common. They may have a modest finding and then write about that finding as though they have changed the face of the earth. If your conclusions go beyond your data, chances are that referees will notice this fact and lash out at the conclusion and at you.

There is a place in most articles for speculation that goes beyond the boundaries of the data. This place is in the Discussion section of the article. But when you go beyond the boundaries of the data, make clear that you are speculating. Do not assume that referees or other readers will know that you are in a speculative state of mind.

11. *Make clear what the limitations of your work are.* Any good Discussion section includes at least some frank acknowledgment of the limitations of the study. Did you use just a single methodology, or type of stimulus material? Did you use a restricted range of types of participants? Did you look at behavior only in one kind of situation, perhaps an artificially contrived one? Referees and all readers appreciate honesty. Most important, referees are less likely to mention limitations in review that you already have mentioned, unless the referees see them as fatal flaws.

Many authors nurse the hope that the referees will not notice the flaws. Such a hope is likely to be wishful thinking. Moreover, it is a misguided wish. Worse even than getting a paper rejected before publication is having to retract it after publication or having to resist an onslaught of published criticism for flaws that you should have noticed. Save yourself the trouble by acknowledging the flaws yourself.

12. *Be sure to consider alternative interpretations of the data.* "Thus, the data overwhelmingly support the XYZ theory, and if you can't see it, you need to have your head examined." No data set is unequivocal. Sooner or later, someone will see one or more alternative interpretations. You are much better off recognizing and trying to discount the alternatives yourself than leaving the task to the reviewers or to your potential readers. Even if you cannot discount every alternative, readers will appreciate your honesty in recognizing that other explanations could exist. If the results are too inconclusive, your article may be turned down. But even published articles are not fully definitive, and readers expect you to admit as much.

13. *End strongly and state a clear take-home message.* "In sum, there is a need for further research to clarify the issues." What a snooze! There's always room for further research; readers don't have to be told that. Readers want a punch line. They want to go away from a paper with a clear conclusion, preferably a snappy one (which may or may not be in the last sentence). When the reader later tries to remember your article, this conclusion will probably be the mental access route. Leave readers with what you most want them to remember.

HOW YOU SAY IT

14. *Write sentences that are readable, clear, and concise.* Sure, you already know this, but some people go on and on and on, repeating themselves and pointing out the same thing over and over again, using dangling constructions, getting off the point, and obfuscating their points to the point where the reader loses sight of what the point is anyway – to the extent that there is one, or, as the case may be, more than one.

15. *Emphasize logical flow and organization.* Don't expect readers to understand the logical sequence of your ideas. It is important that the prose flow and that the organization emerge clearly. Write your ideas down in a sensible sequence. Readers should concentrate on what you say, not on how you say it. Logical organization can mean the difference between confusion and clarity.

16. *Explain what you're going to say, say it, and then restate what you've said.* In this way, you provide an advance organization for the reader, explicate the main content, and emphasize to readers what you want them to remember.

17. *Be creative, and give concrete examples.* Some academic writers harbor the illusion that the more abstract and high-sounding their writing is, the more readers will be impressed. On the contrary, most readers need concrete examples or analogies in order to understand other people's ideas. The more abstract the points, the more readers need examples. Readers are busy: Don't expect them to generate the examples. It's your responsibility. You have all read papers that left you drowning in abstractions. I'll leave it to you to think of specific examples.

18. *Don't assume that people will "know what you mean" or be familiar with abbreviations or jargon.* Sometimes when I'm writing an article, I notice a sentence or paragraph that isn't clear. Occasionally, I'm too lazy to change the offending text and hope no one will notice. I'm particularly likely to hope that people will know what I mean when I'm not sure what I mean myself, so that perhaps later they can tell me. Almost without fail, however, readers *don't* understand what I've said any better than I do. Reviewers complain about what they don't understand – and that includes abbreviations or jargon. QED.

19. *Write to be interesting.* An article tells a story. Like a story, it should capture readers' interest. You know what it's like to read (or worse, to have to read) someone else's boring articles. Well, guess what? That's what it's like for other people to read your boring writing. Write for your reader, not for yourself. Readers appreciate the effort to keep their interest. Ultimately, what matters is whether people read your articles, and if reviewers don't enjoy reading your work, they won't recommend it for publication. This in turn will make it difficult for others to read your articles, and it's hard to have an impact on the field if no one reads what you write. And don't tell people how "interesting" your results or your papers are. If your article is worthwhile, believe me, people will know it. An interesting point, don't you think?

20. *Write for a somewhat broader and technically less skilled audience than you expect to read the article.* Writers tend to overestimate the knowledge and technical sophistication of their readers, as well as the extent to which readers share their exact interests. You should therefore write for a slightly broader and less knowledgeable audience than you expect will read the article, keeping in mind that you don't want to insult your audience, either. Somewhere between "Visualize Maculation decamp" and "See Spot run" lies both your audience and the Land of Acceptance Letters.

21. *Avoid autobiography.* In some schools, you are expected to tell the story of your life when you write a paper, especially a dissertation. This story includes all your false starts, blind alleys, and tales of woe. You may even be expected to explain all the reasons your manipulation didn't work out the way it was supposed to. Journal space is precious, however, and there just isn't room for these autobiographical details. Therefore, journal articles are usually written in a manner that bears little resemblance to the way the research was actually conducted. This difference is not dishonesty: Professionals simply know how the system works. I first learned this fact when I was in graduate school. It was a dark and stormy night. I'd just received an editor's

letter. (For further details, see my *Complete Life and Works*, Vol. 21, published by Narcismo Press.)

WHAT TO DO WITH WHAT YOU SAY

22. *Proofread.* As the editor of *Psychological Bulletin*, I found that the single most annoying flaw in a submitted article is a slew of typographical errors. Why? Because they're the easiest thing for the author to correct. It's neither the editor's nor the reviewers' job to do your proofreading for you. Always proofread. It's the one thing you can most easily do to improve the impression you make. If you don't proofread, some reviewers and editors will simply tell you to do it. But others won't be so congenial, and you may have problems changing that first impression. No matter hwat, you loose. "Spell-check" features associated with word processors help, but they are no substitute for proofreading, as shown in the preceding sentence. A spellchecker would pick up the first spelling error (*hwat*) because it is not an English word, but it would not detect the other spelling error (*loose*), which is an English word.

23. *Check for fit to journal guidelines and subject matter.* One of the single most common causes of outright rejection is the submission of articles that even a casual review would reveal to be inappropriate for that journal. For example, people sent me, as editor, empirical studies of substantive psychological phenomena, despite the fact that *Psychological Bulletin* never accepts articles of this type. They wasted their own time and mine. We also returned articles that departed substantially from APA writing guidelines (e.g., are single spaced or use notes in place of references). You can save yourself and others a major headache by checking the submission guidelines, usually printed in each issue of the journal, to make sure that your article fits its intended home. (You've probably guessed by now that this very article was rejected from *Physical Sciences.*)

24. *Read your paper at least once while imagining yourself to be a critical reviewer or, even better, ask a colleague to do the same.* We tend to be enamored of our own work. We often don't see the flaws that would be obvious if the same paper had someone else's name on it. So try reading your paper with the same devastating analytical acuity you would use if you wished to demolish the work of your most loathsome enemy. Ask a colleague to do the same. In this way, you will be able to anticipate and perhaps eliminate some reviewer criticisms – use of faulty logic, for example. If your logic is faulty, your paper suffers; of course, this also means that if your logic is perfect, so is your paper.

25. *Cite likely referees (who conceivably merit citation).* Suppose I consider myself one of the world's greatest experts on the effects of high-fat, sugary foods on amorous behavior. I view myself as one of the few people who really knows what happens subsequently when romatically involved couples go out on a date and share a large piece of cheesecake. I get an article to review on the topic and look forward to reading it. First, of course, I check the references to see which of my superlative articles on this topic have been cited. I discover that none of them are cited. I cannot believe it. How could anyone write about this topic without citing my work? I now start reading the article, but I already know it is a pretty poor piece with awful scholarship. All I need to do is find some reason to reject it, and I most likely will.

It is impossible to anticipte everyone who might referee an article. Nor can one cite every potential reviewer. But it is important to cite likely referees who have made a serious contribution to work in the field that the article covers. And if the editor has sent the article to a particular reviewer, the editor, at least, considers the individual to be one of the more active contributors to the field the article covers. Thus, this suggestion is not a cynical one: The likely referees are the same people who are likely to be the major contributors to the field.

26. *Write for your likely referees and readers.* Expert article writers do not just write articles. They write for an audience. They decide on likely journals before they put pen to paper (or fingers to computer keys).

You can get a good idea of the types of articles a given journal publishes simply by reading the journal's mission statement (usually near the front or back of the journal) and by looking at recent past issues. But there is a more informal kind of knowledge you need to acquire either through you own experience or by profiting from the experience of others.

Many characteristics of journals go beyond mission statements. Some journals seem to emphasize methodological rigor above all else. One reads them and has the feeling that the study could be infinitely trivial but nevertheless published as long as it was methodologically sound. Other journals seem to emphasize articles that are interesting but flakey: The ideas are provocative but the evidence for them is slim. Still other journals seem more concerned about length than about anything else. These journals will not publish relatively longer articles, no matter how good those articles may be. One journal to which I have submitted seems to care more that the article is in standard APA journal-article format than about what is said in this or any other format. These kinds of characteristics tend to come and go as the editorships of journals change, but oftentimes, the "culture" of a given journal endures beyond any single editorial board.

It thus behooves you to find out as much as you can about the kinds of issues that are important to the editor and referees of a given journal. You can save yourself a lot of lost time by seeking journals that publish the kind of article you have written and by avoiding journals that do not publish this kind of article.

WHAT TO DO WITH WHAT OTHERS SAY

27. *Take journal reviews seriously, but remember that reviewers are not gods (a fact that has escaped some reviewers).* Many, but not all, criticisms by reviewers are credible. Sometimes, individual comments are downright asinine. But points gain force when they are repeated across reviews, or by the editor in his or her letter. You don't have to make every change suggested in every review. But should you be given the opportunity to revise, you are expected to write a letter accompanying your revision. This letter should explain to the editor how you dealt with each point of criticism, or why you did not respond to selected points. You should realize that although you usually don't have to address every point in every review, the comments made by the editor should not be ignored. Reviewers and editors do not expect perfection; they do expect, however, to be taken seriously. They put the time and effort into reviewing the article and want to see something for it.

One final note about reviewers. People often whine and moan about how nasty reviewers are. Some of them are. But remember: We have met the enemy, and we are it. Reviewers are drawn roughly from the same pool of people as those who write articles. If we all do our part, there will be fewer nasty reviews. And if you don't agree with me, you must be stupid and utterly worthless!

28. *Don't take reviewers' comments personally.* Reviewers criticize work, not people (unless they do their job incorrectly). I have written fairly strong critiques of the work of some of my closest friends in the field, and they have done the same of my work. We know better than to take professional differences personally. If you do so, you will find yourself holding grudges against an awful lot of people. Send me a self-addressed stamped envelope (using $10.00 worth of postage) if you'd like a copy of my own 300-page list of personal enemies!

29. *Perseverance pays, to a point.* During my editorship, no article submitted to the *Psychological Bulletin* was accepted outright with no changes. In other journals, the rate of outright acceptance may be slightly higher, but not by much. It can easily take two, three, or even more revisions before an article receives final acceptance. Journal editors differ in terms of how many rounds are typical. Moreover, even if one journal flatly rejects your article, another may love it. I'm not alone in having been brutally rejected by one journal, only to be welcomed with open arms by another. But if your article is being rejected across the board, you need at least to consider the possibility that you don't need to go to the supermarket for your next turkey.

Finally, remember that the journal reviewing process and science as a whole are basically conservative. Articles are often rejected because they're just not very good, but I do believe that some of the best work in psychology and in other sciences is rejected because people are not yet ready to hear the message (see Sternberg & Lubart, 1992). I'm not personally impressed by people who tell me they've never had an article turned down.

To do creative work, you must take risks, and to take risks, you must occasionally fail. Much more important than whether you fail (and everyone does sometimes) is how you handle the failure and learn from your mistakes. Should you ever reach the point where you never fail to get your articles accepted, and where no one ever disagrees with you, beware: You are probably not doing your best and most creative work. And if you really want to avoid rejections, then don't take chances. Never submit. You'll be completely safe from criticism, and from making a scientific contribution as well.

Chapter Thirteen

Writing a Grant or Contract Proposal

My first grant proposal was a horror story: It was long, verbose, and poorly organized. Fortunately for me, in 1975 one could write a grant proposal that had all of these flaws, plus others, and still get funded. I did. But in the 1990s, I probably wouldn't have had a prayer and would have had to rewrite the whole thing. In 1975, the competition for grants was stiff; in the 1990s, it was close to ridiculous. Only the very best proposals even have a chance of success, and many that meet all of the scientific criteria for funding are not funded, simply for a lack of money. Therefore, it is important to know how to write a grant proposal in order to maximize your chances of getting funded. In this chapter, I will describe some basics of proposals, some keys to writing good proposals, and some things that agencies look for in making funding decisions.

Different funding organizations have different guidelines for writing proposals. There would be no sense in consuming space in this book describing the requirements of various organizations; there are too many organizations and requirements, and the requirements are constantly changing. Rather, I will describe 18 keys to writing a good proposal. Paying attention to these keys does not ensure that you will be funded, but they will surely help!

SOME BASIC CONCEPTS
ABOUT GRANTS AND CONTRACTS

Before describing the keys, I will briefly summarize some basic concepts, beginning with a *proposal*. A proposal is a description of what will be done – usually research – if funding is given. The proposal may request money for salaries, equipment, supplies, travel, reproduction, communication costs, experimental subjects, or whatever. Some proposals request funding for educational programs rather than for research. Typically, a proposal contains a statement of what is being requested, a description of why the research or program is important, a review of relevant literature, pilot data showing that your hypotheses are plausible, a description of just what will be done with the money, a budget, human-subjects approval from the review board of your institution (if necessary), and the proposer's curriculum vitae. A proposal can be for a *grant* or a *contract*.

When you receive a *grant*, you receive support to accomplish some end, usually research, and almost always research that you have described in the grant proposal. Although grants can be given for other things, I will concentrate in this chapter on research grants. The agencies that give out grants almost always do some monitoring of how their money is spent, but the monitoring is generally flexible. If you want to add some experiments that were not in the original proposal, or modify ones that were in the proposal in order to capitalize on what you have already discovered, there will usually be no problem if your money was given to you in the form of a grant. Major changes in the research or budget generally require approval, however. In other words, if you request funds for paying personnel, and you want to switch some of those funds to travel, you probably will have to ask permission of the granting organization for the switch. However, if you want to switch funds from one category of personnel to another category of personnel (e.g., graduate to postdoctoral students), you are less likely to need to request permission for the switch. Organizations differ widely in their flexibility with respect to reallocation of funds. If you are not sure about a switch, always ask permission.

Contracts generally allow less flexibility than grants. All but the most minor deviations from the original plan generally require permission. Moreover, with contracts, usually you must generate specific producibles at agreed-upon times. These producibles can take various forms, such as progress reports, budget statements, technical reports, products, and the like. With a contract, you are generally held fairly strictly to the deadlines that are given for these producibles. The fundamental difference between a contract and a grant is that in a contract you are being contracted to produce specific pieces of work, whereas in a grant you are being given money to do more or less what you described in your proposal. Some funding organizations give only grants, others give only contracts, and still others give both. Should you be awarded a grant or a contract, it is essential that you be clear on the reporting requirements before you begin, as failure to render required financial or progress reports could result in termination of the funding.

Should you receive funding, it is also imperative that you make sure that you or a financial officer of your institution keeps careful track of spending and how money is allocated. Virtually all organizations require regular and fairly detailed reports of expenses. These reports are carefully scrutinized. If you are not keeping careful records, you may find yourself in some very hot water.

You should also realize that unless the grant is made directly to you personally – an unusual arrangement – the institution for which you work will most likely take out overhead on most or all expenses, as well as benefits on personnel expenses. *Overhead* refers to an amount charged by your institution for administering a grant. It goes to pay for the people who keep records, the space you use for doing the research, library facilities, custodial services, heating, air conditioning, and all other expenses the institution believes might conceivably be charged against your funding. Overhead rates are negotiated between your institution and the source of funding. Overhead ranges from zero (some foundations will not allow any overhead to be taken out of the grants they give) to roughly 70% in private universities. In non-university organizations, the overhead may be even higher. The percentage figure refers to the amount of money the institution takes out for every $1 you spend on research. For example, if you spend $1 on research at Yale University, the university will take out from the grant or contract another 64¢ as overhead. You can see that the charging of overhead results in your not having available to you for research all of the money that the granting institution provides. Different funding organizations have different arrangements both for requesting and for paying out overhead. In general, private universities charge more in overhead than do public ones, although there are many exceptions to this generalization.

Benefits refers to amounts of money taken out by the institution to pay for extra expenses that are associated with the hiring and maintenance of personnel. For example, if a research assistant is hired on a grant, the university will generally contribute some percentage of his or her salary toward retirement pension, health benefits, insurance benefits, Social Security, and the like. These charges are figured into benefits costs. Benefits have generally been going up, and can reach as high as 40% of personnel costs. In other words, for every $1 you pay an employee on a grant, the university may take out as much as 40¢ for benefits that the employee receives. When you combine overhead and benefits, you begin to realize just how limited is the amount of a grant that you will be able to use for research or other intended purposes.

There is one general exception to the taking out of overhead and benefits, and that is a grant received directly from a university or other institution for which you work. In other words, if you receive a direct grant from your university or other institution to do research, it will almost certainly not take out overhead and benefits on the money that it directly provides you. Rather, these costs will have already been figured in when the organization provided the money.

It is hard to overestimate the benefits of having a grant or contract. Most institutions have little or no money available for research, and almost all institutions smile on their faculty and students who receive outside support. If you are a faculty member, having a grant almost inevitably helps you when it comes to promotion or tenure time and also enables you to do the research that will get you the promotion or tenure. Moreover, even if you are able to do research without a grant, you will often find that you are better able to do the research you really want to do with more funds available. You can use the grant to pay for summer salary, among other things. Summer salary is money that you pay yourself over the summer in order to work on research related to the grant. You can pay yourself summer salary off a grant only if the salary your institution pays you is for less than 12 months. Many institutions pay on a 9-, 10-, or 11-month schedule, and so summer salary is an issue. In no case can you pay yourself for more than 12 months, and some institutions have rules that enable you to pay yourself only up to 11 or fewer months. A typical situation is that someone receives 9 months of salary from the institution and pays him- or herself 2 months of summer support off a grant if money in the grant is available to afford it. Remember that overhead and benefits will be taken out of your own salary, just as they would be taken out of salary paid to others.

In general, you need to be careful about payments to yourself or to anyone else, as it is common these days for grants to be audited at some time during their duration. Questionable expenses may be disallowed, and auditors who see any such expenses are likely to start digging further. Therefore, it is to your advantage to make sure that you spend money carefully and that you monitor your expenses.

EIGHTEEN TIPS FOR WRITING PROPOSALS

Having reviewed the major concepts behind proposals, we will now consider 18 tips for writing proposals.

1. *Clearly state the "big question" you hope to address.* You should state right up front what the big question is that you hope to address in your grant proposal. Do not leave it as a puzzle for your readers to figure out. If you are not sure of what the big question is, do not expect your readers somehow to be able to fill in what you are unable to supply.

   Evaluators generally prefer proposals that address some larger question and that address it in a fairly deep way. They look less favorably on proposals that are scattered and that seem to address a lot of smaller questions superficially, none of them very well. Therefore, you should be able to describe in a sentence or two the issue that you are dealing with and how you hope to address it.

2. *Show why the big question is important.* After stating clearly what the big question is that you hope to address, you need to say why it is important, and for whom. Again, do not assume that just because you think the question is important, anyone in his or her right mind will as well. You need to build a case for why the granting or contracting agency should fund research on this question in preference to other questions that other investigators might address. Even if the compe-

tition is restricted to proposals that all address the same issue, you need to say how you are framing the issue, and why it makes sense to frame it that way. For example, all proposals may be on memory, but why is your approach to memory a significant one? In sum, justify up front why the work you propose is important.

3. *State how your work both builds on and departs from work that has been done before.* Virtually all grant proposals contain some amount of literature review. The amount will depend in part upon the requirements of the agency that is providing the funds, and in part upon how much relevant past work there is. In your review, concentrate on past work that is clearly relevant; do not try to show that you know all literature that is remotely related to what you are going to study. But be sure that you cite work that is directly relevant. Many proposals are seen by outside reviewers, and these individuals tend not to be favorably impressed if their own work is not cited. Reviewers are likely to perceive their own work as highly relevant, even if you do not. It is therefore important in the literature review to show both how your work builds on what others have done, and how it is different from past work. If you do not show how your work builds on that of others, you are likely to be perceived as grandiose – as someone who does not appreciate the value to your own endeavors of what others have done. But if you do not make clear how your work goes beyond past work, you may be perceived as uncreative and as not having anything new to propose.

4. *State your theory and how it relates to the theories of others.* Funding agencies tend to look more favorably on work that has some motivating theory. The theory does not necessarily have to be your own. The important thing is that there be a set of ideas that motivates the work you propose. Merely proposing experiments or reviewing literature, or producing a product without any rationale or framework for what you are going to do, is usually considered unsatisfactory. Of course, agencies differ greatly in what counts as "theory." The important thing is that you show a coherent set of ideas motivating the work you propose and your awareness of how the set of ideas is similar to and different from that of others.

5. *Show why your theory is better than its competitors.* Show why you chose or formulated the theory you did and why you chose it in comparison with other competing theories. Usually, there are a number of different accounts of the same phenomena. For example, there are

a number of different theories of perceptual, learning, or attribution phenomena. In choosing one theoretical framework you are automatically excluding others. Justify your choice.

6. *Present pilot data.* With funds so tight these days, agencies have become more and more concerned that the work they fund has a good chance of being successful. Probably the single best way to convince an agency that the work is likely to be successful is to present pilot (preliminary) or informal data showing that the paradigms you suggest or that the results you expect are plausible. In other words, build the case for the new research by showing that there now exists at least a preliminary demonstration of the phenomenon you hope to uncover. In some cases, investigators have already done more than they let on. It is unethical to request funding for work already completed. But it is not only ethical but sensible to request funds for work that you have shown to a first approximation is likely to be successful. The pilot data need not have tremendous numbers of cases or even necessarily have been published. But they should be relevant to the phenomena you wish to study and successful in showing the likely success of your approach to these phenomena.

7. *Make sure that the research you propose fits the amount of time for which you are requesting funding.* Grants may be funded for anywhere from one year (or even less) to five years. Funding for more than five years is unusual. With most agencies, typical funding is for three years. Agencies and reviewers check to make sure that the work you are proposing is reasonable, given the time frame you are suggesting. If you propose only one year of work, an agency is not likely to want to fund you for three years. But conversely, it will wonder about your sense of reality if you propose five years of work to be done in three years. The work should match the time frame.

8. *Clearly state the proposed research, leaving no holes.* Reviewers are overburdened, and agencies have many more proposals than they can handle. Reviewers do not have time to figure out what you meant to say, or what you might have said had you remembered to say it. You need to write crystal clearly so that the reader can easily grasp your points, and so that there are no holes in the descriptions. Do not expect readers to fill in what you have not provided, because they will probably assume that what is missing you do not know.

9. *Be concise.* Many agencies have a page limit. Such page limits are strictly enforced. Some agencies will even return proposals that exceed

the specified page limit. Therefore, it is to your advantage to write not only clearly but also concisely. Often, you can go through a proposal after you have written it and have someone else do it as well, in order to cut excess verbiage. Remember also that readers of grants are often volunteering their time, so they want to read the maximum possible in as little time as possible. Therefore, reviewers as well as the agencies themselves appreciate concisely written proposals.

10. *Be super-organized.* Good organization is always important in writing, but there are times when it matters more and other times when it matters less. In grant proposals, it matters more. Often, agencies specify the organization for the proposal, and you are expected to use their guidelines. But even if they do so specify, organization within sections is important. You want to make the proposal as easy to read and as logical as possible. Readers almost never appreciate having to figure out where they are, or where they are going, in the proposal. Therefore, you should give some kind of advance organizer in the front of the proposal, as well as in each section. This advance organizer specifies what will come when. A sentence or two of summary at the end of each section also helps. It is often useful to construct an outline before you write the proposal in order to make sure that you are maintaining a tight and logical organization. If you have not done an outline in advance, consider doing one at the end in order to check whether the proposal is tightly organized. Again, with such a premium on funds, every little edge you can get will help you in the competition, and a well-organized proposal is a definite edge.

11. *If your proposal involves empirical research, make sure that you clearly describe how you will analyze the data.* In addition to describing clearly the proposed research, you are expected to show that you know how you will analyze the data. Where the data analysis is fairly straightforward, as with a simple two-way analysis of variance or even a set of *t* tests, the description of data analysis may be a very short paragraph. If more complex forms of data analysis are involved, however, make sure you specify clearly what you are going to do and why you are going to do it. If the form of analysis is nonstandard (e.g., some nonparametric statistical tests), it is in your best interest to specify a reference that justifies your use of the chosen technique. Make sure that you are explicit in your description and that the form of analysis does indeed fit the form of data you will collect.

12. *State clearly what the producibles of the work will be, especially for*

contracts. What will come out of the proposed research? Grant and contract monitors want to know. Do you expect to write articles, books, or particular chapters? Will there be any curriculum, or other kind of product? Be as clear as possible in stating what you intend to produce. Also, you should clarify in advance whose property the producibles will be. Such clarification is especially important for contracts, where typically the producibles become the property of the funding agency. You also want to know what credit (e.g., authorship, acknowledgment, etc.), if any, you will receive in the case of such producibles, and whether your name will even be identified with them.

13. *Make clear what kinds of results you might expect, and why they will be interesting.* Funding agencies are generally not interested in proposals that look like "fishing expeditions." They want you to show that you know what the plausible alternative outcomes might be and, especially, what these outcomes might mean. It especially helps to show that the results will be interesting, almost without regard to how they come out. Agencies know as well as you do that many experiments do not come out in the way the experimenter intends, and hence they would like to see that even if the results do not come out in the intended way, the funding will still produce something of interest. The more clearly you can specify the alternative outcomes, their meanings, and their value, the more confidence the agency will have that it is getting something for the money you want it to provide.

14. *State your qualifications for doing the proposed research.* When you submit a grant proposal, you virtually always submit along with it a curriculum vitae, which contains the record of your accomplishments. The curriculum vitae, at minimum, includes (a) your name, (b) your address, (c) your phone number, (d) your government identification (e.g., Social Security) number, (e) your educational history (degrees, starting with a college degree, or institutions attended), (f) your employment history (including all jobs, full-time or part-time, that are potentially relevant to the grant, but not those, such as being a waiter during the summer or a camp counselor, that have no relevance), (g) your special honors and achievements (such as Phi Beta Kappa, cum laude, honors, or any prizes you may have received), (h) your publications, if any, (i) past and current grant support, (j) committee service, offices held, or special assignments, (k) any consulting or other work you have done that might be potentially relevant to the grant, and (l) anything else you can think of that helps build a case for your receiving the grant. Granting agencies also typically ask if you are submitting the same proposal to any other agencies and for the percentage of your time that you plan to spend on the proposed grant. You may also include a brief statement outlining your main credentials in prose format. Again, the important thing is to emphasize that you have the needed background in order successfully to do the proposed work.

Obviously, a new investigator will have a thinner curriculum vitae than will a more established investigator, but granting agencies take this fact into account. Often, they give a slight edge to younger investigators, realizing how difficult it is for them to get started. Whether an agency does so or not depends on the particular agency. Although you should be sure to include all relevant qualifications, avoid including things that are obviously irrelevant and may make a statement about you. Including irrelevant things (such as your summer experience as a waiter) makes it look as though you are padding the curriculum vitae and that you have so few worthwhile things to say that you have been forced to say things that are worthless.

15. *Request all the funds you need to do the proposed work, but no more.* You need to think very carefully about how much money you need to do the proposed work. It is usually very difficult to obtain supplementary funds later on. At the same time, agencies have "mental radar" for detecting padded budgets. If you ask for considerably more money than you need, your budget request is likely to be cut, and you may even be turned down because the research is deemed not worthy of the funds being requested.

16. *Show that you have the facilities that you need to do the research.* It does not make sense to propose to do research that requires a supercomputer if you do not have such a computer available, or that requires you to have extensive knowledge of French if you do not know French. Therefore, you should state the facilities that you have available to get the research done. If there are facilities you will need that you do not have (such as microcomputers or work stations), you can request these in the budget line for equipment. Remember, though, that equipment funds tend to be rather modest in most agencies, and you might even want to talk with someone in the agency in advance in order to determine whether your equipment request will be considered

reasonable. You can also request funds for consultants, if they are a "human facility" you will need to get the work done (e.g., translators in cross-cultural work).

17. *Write a clear and compelling abstract.* Although the abstract is placed at the beginning of the grant proposal, people almost always write their abstract after they write their proposal. It is much easier to state the main points of your proposal after you have written it than before. The abstract should state the big question, name and briefly describe the theory, summarize the proposed research, and summarize the kinds of conclusions you hope to draw (although not, necessarily, the specific results, which you do not yet know). Some reviewers of grant proposals decide from the abstract how interesting the proposal is likely to be, so it is to your advantage to take care in writing the abstract, again remembering that there may be a length requirement that you may not exceed.

18. *Make sure that you have observed all formal requirements in writing the proposal.* As I noted earlier, agencies sometimes return proposals that do not strictly adhere to their guidelines. Government bureaucracies such as the National Institutes of Health have people whose job it is to check that proposals conform to guidelines. To you and me, this job may seem like the most boring one in the world; to others, it is a living. And they want to justify their living. So be scrupulous in checking adherence to length, margins, type size, format, and all other requirements. Such detail might seem like a Mickey Mouse exercise, and for you, perhaps it is. But formal requirements are taken seriously.

WHAT DO AGENCIES LOOK FOR?

Different agencies look for different things in grant proposals. Foundations and some government agencies pay very close attention to whether the proposed research fits into their list of priorities. Therefore, you want to make sure that the proposal matches the priorities of the funding organization. If it does not, it may be turned down, no matter how good the proposed research is. They also look for whether the proposal deals with important questions, whether the work has the potential to make a real contribution to science or society, whether the work is interesting, and whether the investigator will be able to accomplish the proposed work. Readers also evaluate whether the experiments fit the theory that is supposed to underlie them, whether there are any errors in experimental designs or other aspects of methodology, whether the data analyses are correct and fit the proposed form of data to be collected, and whether the resources are there to do the proposed work. Having been on a granting panel for several years myself, I think that the most important single criterion is the potential contribution of the work to science. Methodological errors can be remedied, budgets can be pared down, and mistaken judgments about details (such as in the number of subjects that will be required) can all be corrected. But work without the potential to make a contribution is viewed as nonfundable. Therefore, more than anything else, you want to show that the work is worthwhile. If you can do that, the agency is more likely to be forgiving of other defects of the proposal.

Remember that a grant or contract proposal is not just expository writing, it is *persuasive writing*. You need to persuade an agency that your proposed work is so valuable that the agency simply must fund it. Ideas generally don't sell themselves. You need to sell them.

Getting funded these days requires a measure of good luck. Although you can never guarantee good luck, you can help make your own good luck by following the keys to writing proposals that are outlined in this chapter.

Chapter Fourteen

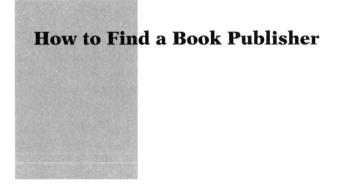

How to Find a Book Publisher

Although good books differ from one another in a multitude of ways, good book proposals are surprisingly similar. All of them have a set of standard features. In this chapter, I will describe what these features are.

CHOOSING A PUBLISHER

One thing you should realize right away is that whereas a scientific article generally may be submitted to only one scientific journal at a time, a book proposal typically may be submitted to several publishers simultaneously. It is to your advantage to submit the proposal to multiple publishers, because what greatly interests one publisher may be of limited or no interest to another. Each publisher has its own set of priorities and standards for judging proposals. Before sending a book proposal to a given publisher, look at some of that publisher's recent books in order to determine if your book would be a good match. Or you may even want to write the publisher a letter of inquiry, briefly describing what you would like to do and asking whether the house would be interested in seeing a full-length proposal. In this way, you can save yourself and the publisher the bother of a submission if the proposal does not fit into its publishing program. Publishers vary in the level of prestige, the quality of the books they produce, the amount of royalties they pay, and in many other respects. You may therefore want to talk to publishers' representatives (called acquisitions editors) as well as to other people who have worked with various publishers to get advice as to which houses are worth pursuing. Looking at a house's publication list, however, is usually the best way of evaluating both the range and quality of the books it produces.

In my own career, I have worked with a large number of different publishers and have found that they vary greatly in almost every respect imaginable. Some are completely honest, others less so. Some always pay royalties on time; others get around to it sooner or later, but often later. Some spare no expense to produce the finest-quality books; others produce books that start to come loose from the binding as soon as they are opened. Working with a publisher is like forming a close relationship. It is to your advantage to make sure that you carefully investigate the publisher with which you will enter into the relationship.

Three fundamental kinds of proposals are frequently found in psychology. Two of these are relatively infrequent, and I will not discuss them here: textbook proposals and trade-book proposals. Textbook proposals are, as their name implies, for texts, and they require certain special techniques that are beyond the scope of this book. Trade-book proposals are for books that will sell primarily in general bookstores. These proposals are even more specialized and difficult to write, and they often are submitted to publishers through literary agents. Again, they are beyond the scope of this book. In this chapter, I will concentrate on the features of scholarly-book proposals, the kind that psychologists most often write.

THE PROPOSAL

A book proposal opens with the words "Book Prospectus" or "Book Proposal" at the top, and below it, the proposed title and author or authors of the book. You then start the main body of the proposal by describing what the book is about. What story do you want to tell? Why is it a story that bears telling, and what makes it interesting? Book publishers have to sell books, and so no matter what the scholarly value of the contribution, they have to care whether you have interesting things to say. If you do not, they would likely lose money if they published the book. Even university presses, which are willing to take more risks on scholarly work that has scholarly value even if it does not have great sales potential, still need their books to sell in order to remain financially solvent.

Next, you need to specify the intended audience or audiences for your book. What kinds of people are likely to read it? Will it be written in a language that can be understood only by people in the field, or by graduate students as well, or by undergraduates, or even by educated laypersons? Publishers are interested not only in the level of the book but also in the breadth of audience to which it will appeal. Is your book written only for developmental psychologists, or will it be of interest to a broader range of psychologists? The broader the range of people who may be interested in the book, the better the potential sales, and therefore the greater the potential interest of the publisher. On the other hand, if the appeal is very broad, then the publisher will check to make sure that the book makes a real contribution and is not written at such a general level that it has nothing new or interesting to say. Audiences can range across as well as within fields. For example, you might write your book to appeal to people in education as well as to those in psychology, or to people in sociology or anthropology as well as psychology. Perhaps certain computer scientists or philosophers would also have an interest. Specify as completely as you can who might be interested and why.

After specifying what the book is about, why it is important, and who the potential audience is, provide a general outline of the book. This outline should cover the chapters of the book and, if there are parts into which the chapters are organized, a description of what they will be. It should give the chapter names and a summary of what will go into each chapter. The book should show a logical organization and a sensible progression of ideas from beginning to end. Try to make the summaries as readable as possible, illustrating abstract points with concrete examples whenever such examples will help clarify the points you want to make. You need not cover every detail in every chapter, but you need to convey a sense of the flavor of the book. You also need to show in the sequencing how you developed the main idea of the book that you stated at the beginning. Even scholarly books must tell a story, and you cannot expect readers to figure out what the story is. The proposal should make clear what the story will be.

Occasionally, people submit prospectuses for edited books. Such books consist of a sequence of chapters by different authors, all revolving around some general theme. In the case of edited books, it is particularly important to show how the chapters tie together. There are any number of edited books that seem to be a motley collection of unrelated essays, and such books generally do not sell well. With edited books it is especially important to have an introductory chapter that sets the framework for the chapters to follow, and a concluding chapter that integrates the various contributions of the authors.

After describing the main contents of the book, you need to describe the competition. This section is particularly important, because book publishers want to know what they are up against. When there are potential competitors for a new volume, the potential audience for that new volume is reduced, so it is particularly important that the publisher be assured that your book will make some kind of unique contribution that the other books do not make. Therefore, it is important to state not only what the competition is but also why your book is better, or more nearly complete, or more up to date, or more wide ranging, or more representative of the field, or whatever. The same principle holds for both written and edited books. Pay a lot of attention to this section, because unless it is well done, your book may be rejected not because it is perceived as inadequate but because the competition is perceived as insurmountable.

Typically, the next thing you will specify is nitty-gritty detail. What is the proposed length of your book in double-spaced, single-sided manuscript pages? How many tables, roughly, do you expect there to be? How many figures? Generally, you are expected to provide figures, but not tables, in camera-ready form, meaning that the figures can be photographically reproduced and used as is. If you need special kinds of reproduction, such as that required for color plates, you need to specify as much. Most important, you need to specify the expected completion date for the book. It is generally better to pick a date that is somewhat later but more realistic than one that is somewhat earlier but that you cannot meet. Publishers of scholarly books are usually willing to give reasonable extensions on due dates if it appears that you cannot meet the deadline that you set for yourself. (Publishers of textbooks and trade books tend to be less forgiving because such books often involve substantial advances, and the publisher is losing money each day that the advance on royalties is not recovered. Moreover, the publisher may have made specific sales commitments for such books, commitments it will be unable to meet if books are delivered late.)

You need also to specify your qualifications for doing the book. It is common to include a curriculum vitae and possibly a written summary of accomplishments. Publishers want to make sure that you are qualified to write the book. Moreover, with books, as with practically anything else, name recognition counts. It is generally easier for a well-established author to get a book proposal accepted than for a new author. However, publishers are always looking for new, potentially successful authors, and so if you can convince them that you have a product of quality that will sell, they may be quite interested in your book, even if you are new to the field or have not previously published widely or at all.

Some publishers require that you submit a sample chapter or several sample chapters of the book, especially if you are not a well-known author. Practices differ widely among publishers, and indeed, some publishers may agree to publish the book only if they have the complete item in front of them to evaluate. If you can write one or more sample chapters, it is to your advantage to send them, because publishers will then have a better idea of what the book will actually consist of. If you do send a sample chapter, or several such chapters, it is important to make sure that the chapters represent the best effort you can make.

At the end, you will want to summarize the main points of your proposal. Here, and possibly at the beginning, it does not hurt to pay attention to special features. What sets your book apart? What particular features does the book have that would make it particularly salable? For example, do you take a new approach to a problem that you think is bound to catch the eye of the reader? Do you have access to special information that no one else has reviewed? Do you have recent data that are likely to shed a new perspective on the field? Publishers are always interested in knowing special angles that may increase sales.

CONTRACT OFFERS

Up to now, I have discussed what you need to do to convince a house that it should contract your book. But if several publishers are interested, you will then be in a position of asking them what it is that makes *them* special. Why should you publish with their press as opposed to another that is interested in your book? There are a number of different things to look for in choosing among alternative publishers, or even deciding whether you should pursue more alternatives.

1. *Royalties.* Royalties are sums of money paid to the author, based on a percentage of sales. Royalties can be paid either on "gross receipts" or on "net receipts." These two quantities are quite different, and it is important to know on which quantity the publisher bases its royalties. Relatively few book contracts grant royalties paid on gross receipts. "Gross receipts" refer to the selling price of the book. For example, if your book costs $40, and your royalty rate is 10% of gross, you will receive $4 per book sold.

   By far the more common way of writing contracts is in terms of net receipts. Net receipts are the publisher's actual receipts for the books it sells. For example, suppose that the publisher sells to a bookstore. Although the book may sell for $40, the publisher will receive considerably less than $40 from the bookstore, because bookstores receive a discount in buying books from a publisher so that they can make a profit when they sell the books to their customers. Your royalty would be based on the amount the publisher received from the bookstore (perhaps $30), rather than on the ultimate selling price of the book. If there are sales to book clubs, net receipts may be proportionately even less than they are for bookstores. Publishers frequently give away sample copies for promotional purposes, and no royalties are paid on these sample copies. Moreover, royalties tend to be lower on foreign sales and on paperback sales (in case there is a paperback). Royalties are usually lower in foreign sales because of the added costs entailed in such sales, especially when they are done through a distributor, or a "middle man" who takes a portion of the receipts. Paperback books receive lower royalties because they generally have to be priced lower than hardcovers, and so publishers receive less profit per book.

   In comparing royalties among publishers, make sure that you are comparing "apples with apples." In other words, make sure that the royalties are on the same basis (for example, net receipts), and that they involve the same exclusions (for example, for sample copies that are given away free by publishers for promotional purposes).

It is sometimes possible to work out a sliding-royalty arrangement with a publisher. Such an arrangement more fairly shares risk between author and publisher. Publishers are often reluctant to give higher royalties because they want to make sure that they recover their own costs of producing and marketing the book. A sliding-scale arrangement results in a higher proportion of royalties being paid as more books are sold. For example, you might receive a royalty of 10% of net on the first 2,500 copies sold, 12% of net on the next 2,500 sold, and 15% of net on all copies sold thereafter. Sliding-scale royalties are usually negotiable (both in terms of thresholds for increases in royalties and for amounts of increase), especially if competing publishers are in the picture. However, not all publishers are willing to offer a sliding-scale arrangement.

What level of royalty can you expect on a scholarly book? Typically, it seems to the author, surprisingly little. Commonly, royalties are between 10% and 12% of net receipts. A high royalty rate is 15%, and rates above that are relatively rare. Although this level might not seem like much to you, you need to remember that most of the expenses are being borne by the publishing house, which is eager to not only recover those expenses but to make a profit as well. The more competitive offers you have, and the stronger they are, the higher a rate of royalty you may be able to negotiate for yourself.

2. *Advance on royalties.* An advance is money paid up front by a publisher in anticipation of future royalties. Once the book is published and begins selling, royalty payments to the author will be withheld until the publisher has recouped the advance. In the event that the book does not sell enough copies to earn back the advance given to the author, the publisher forfeits the money – the author does not have to pay back the advance. Usually, the only circumstances under which authors must pay back an unearned advance are those in which they don't finish the book or if they complete it but the publisher deems the manuscript unacceptable and declines to publish it. These eventualities are usually spelled out in the contract.

Some publishers are willing to give small advances on royalties, although advances for scholarly books are relatively rare and, when they are given, relatively small. At most, they will be a few thousand dollars, and such levels would be high for scholarly books. In general, unless you are a well-known author or have multiple competitive offers, you should not expect an advance on royalties.

3. *Payment of royalties.* Check when royalties are paid. Most publishers pay once a year. However, it is to your advantage if the royalties are paid twice a year, because you receive them more quickly after books are sold. The month or months in which royalties are paid varies, although a typical schedule would be that royalties are paid once a year in May for sales of the preceding calendar year. Publishers are generally not flexible on royalty payment schedules, as they tend to do all their accounting for all their books at the same time.

4. *Publication lag.* Publication lag is the time between the submission of the final draft of your book and the publication of that book. Publishers vary widely in how long it takes them to produce a book. Typically, the publication lag should be no longer than 1 year. At this writing, I am working with a publisher that has taken close to 2 years to publish a book, and for certain this will be the last time I work with that publisher. You can ask the publisher to write into the contract a "reasonable" amount of time, although the publisher will usually write the language to exclude delays due to unforeseen causes. Remember, to minimize publication lag, you should submit the book in a form that maximizes efficiency for the publisher. For example, having camera-ready figures that can be readily reproduced helps cut the time to publication. Submitting manuscripts electronically (on computer disk) also can help.

5. *Marketing and promotional efforts.* Publishers will rarely write into a contract the specific marketing and promotions efforts that they will do for your book, but you may be able to get them to write a separate letter. Such a letter generally will have no legal force, and thus it will represent a "moral" rather than a legal commitment. In publishing, as in most endeavors, oral agreements mean little, if anything: If you do not have it in writing, you do not have it. You should get a clear sense of what the publisher plans to do in order to promote the book. Will the book appear at professional conventions? Will it be advertised in journals? Will there be direct-mail promotions? If so, to whom will the mail be sent? Books do not sell themselves. They need efforts not only on your part in writing but also on the publisher's part in marketing, and you should find out as much about the intended marketing as possible.

6. *Physical appearance of the book.* As I mentioned before, publishers differ widely in how attractive the books they produce are. Publishers also differ widely in the quality of their books' materials. The best indication

of the quality of the production of your book is the quality of production of other books published by the same house. Therefore, review copies of other books that the publisher has produced and check the quality of the binding, the paper, the printing, and the like. Are the publisher's books attractive? A book should last for many years, and so it pays for you to know how well produced the book will be.

7. *Out-of-print policy.* Some publishers keep almost all of their books in print for many, many years; others put them out of print if the book stops selling some minimum number of copies. For some publishers, this minimum may be quite high. Therefore, it is to your advantage to inquire of the publisher as to its out-of-print policy, because it can have a major effect on the life of your book. And it is something that authors often forget to consider in choosing a publisher. Some houses will put a book out of print after only a couple of years, and you will want to know in advance if that is a possibility for your book. If it is, make sure that your book contract states that the rights to the book will revert to you in case the book does go out of print.

8. *In-house assistance.* You need to make clear in negotiating a contract exactly who is going to do what. Sometimes publishers will compile indexes; other times they expect authors to do them. Many scholarly books separate author indexes from subject indexes, and some houses will do one (e.g., the author index) but not the other. Usually authors are expected to obtain permissions for long quotations or figures taken from other volumes, but some publishers will take on this responsibility. Some publishers have in-house copy editors; others send their manuscripts to freelance copy editors. Moreover, publishers differ in the care with which they copy edit the manuscripts they receive. Copy editing is important because it involves the correction of various errors, as well as the clarification of the text. Therefore, having a good copy editor is important.

9. *Communication.* I have found that the quality and quantity of communication with publishers differ widely across publishers, and they depend on more than just how chatty I happen to feel about a particular book. Some publishers' representatives (acquisitions editors) seem to disappear the moment you sign the contract; others are there to support you throughout the entire book-writing process. Obviously, it is to your advantage to work with the kind of editor who is willing to communicate more rather than less. Having a good editor to work with can make the entire publishing process remarkably smooth,

whereas having no one to work with or having someone who is un-helpful or unpleasant can turn a simple process into a nightmare. Therefore, you ought to know in advance with whom you are going to work and convince yourself that it is someone with whom you are going to enjoy working and from whom you will be able to profit.

10. *Hidden aspects of the contract.* Although I do not take my contracts for scholarly books to a contracts lawyer, I do take those for textbooks and trade books to such a lawyer. And it probably is not a bad idea to show even a contract for a scholarly book to a lawyer. There are often hidden features of the contract that you will not be able to see, but that a lawyer will see. Every contract that I have brought to a lawyer has contained passages that are unduly unfavorable to the author that I never would have recognized as such. Therefore, you should read the contract carefully; do not just assume that the contract will be written in a way that is favorable to you. On the contrary, it is gener-ally written to be maximally favorable to the publisher. Business be-ing business, publishers look out for themselves. Therefore, check your contract very carefully, and if you have any doubts about it, take it to a lawyer. I recommend that you consult a lawyer who specializes in contracts, because such attorneys, in my experience, are much more knowledgeable than general practitioners, who may have handled very few contracts.

11. *Reputation of the publisher.* The most important consideration of all I have saved for last, and that is the reputation of the publisher. Pub-lishers, like organizations of any kind, differ widely in quality. Some of them are completely reputable, others less so. Some of them are world renowned, others fly-by-night organizations that may disappear before your book is ever published. Investigate the reputation of the publisher with which you are considering signing by checking with others who have published with that house and by asking for a cata-logue of its published titles. One of the best signs of a good publisher is the stable of authors who have published with it and who continue to do so. If possible, speak with authors who have worked with the press. Do not assume that a publisher must be good because you have heard of it or because it writes on impressive stationery or has fancy headquarters.

I especially warn readers about so-called subsidy publishers or vanity presses. These "publishers" require that you pay a large amount of money up front in order to have your book published. They will

publish almost anything, provided that you are willing to pay the publication costs. Their royalties are much higher than those of other
houses, but don't be seduced by this fact; these publishers can afford
to pay higher royalties because they take essentially no risk. In my
opinion, such publishers are houses of last resort, because authors
rarely receive back in royalties what they have paid to have the books
published. Moreover, the vanity presses know this fact and may even
state it in their literature. Such presses make little effort to promote
the books, because their real receipts are in the payments made by
authors to get their books published. Even worse, publishing with
such a press probably will not enhance your professional credentials.
Psychologists and others know who these publishers are and may devalue rather than value a book published by one of these houses.

Let me make one last observation in closing. I have written or edited more than 50 books, and the writing and editing of books has been
one of the most enjoyable experiences I have had as a psychologist. My
experiences with publishers have ranged from excellent to poor, but I
have learned from my mistakes, as will you. Going through the steps
of publishing a book can be one of the most rewarding experiences of
a career as a psychologist, and after all is said and done, many of the
greatest contributions that have been made in psychology have been
made through books. Therefore, although you may experience anxieties, enjoy yourself. If you write a book, you are in for an experience
that is always challenging, often rewarding, and many times great fun.

Chapter Fifteen

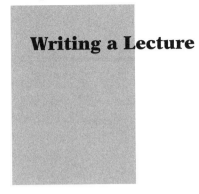

Writing a Lecture

Lecturing is one of the most important parts of being a psychologist. All of us have attended countless lectures and know what a difference it makes to listen to someone exciting versus someone dull. Sometimes, you may not have any choice in terms of the material you present. But there are 15 keys that everyone can follow to write better lectures. Here they are.

1. *Do not read.* Listening to a lecture that is read directly from the text is one of the more boring experiences known to humankind. Written language does not sound like oral language. If you ever read a transcription of a good talk, you will find it hard to comprehend. It should be! People just do not talk the way they read. When you hear a talk that is read word for word, the talk sounds unnatural. It is also boring to hear. Therefore, when you write a lecture, you are best off doing it in outline form, or in some other form that will enable you to talk the lecture rather than read it.

2. *Start off exciting.* Listeners often decide in the first minute or two whether they are going to continue to listen to a lecture or whether they are going to tune out. Starting with an exciting opening can therefore make the difference between capturing an audience and losing it from the start. I try to start off with an anecdote, a joke that is relevant to the lecture, a concrete example of something I'll be talking about, or some other topic that catches the interest of my listeners. Jokes can be good in an opening, but only if they are related to the rest of the talk. In fact, many people find it annoying to hear a joke that is obviously canned and that is used by either the same person or

255

others as an opening for almost any speech they give. A creative opening can make the difference, but you have to be willing to put in the
effort to make sure that it is creative and not canned.

3. *Organize and emphasize.* A person who is knowledgeable about a field
may be able to follow a poorly organized lecture, but someone who is
new to a field is much less likely to be able to do so. Therefore, organize your lecture clearly and tightly. A logical sequence of points
will help the listeners understand. Moreover, organize hierarchically.
Emphasize main points and deemphasize subordinate ones. Listeners
who are new to an area cannot be expected to know what your main
points are. You need to tell them, and to give them a sense of what is
more important to remember and what is less so.

4. *Say what you are going to say, say it, and say what you have said.* In
giving a lecture, even more than in writing, it is important to start by
foreshadowing your main points in the organization of your talk, then
to give the main body of the talk, and finally to summarize the main
points of what you have said. Such an organization helps listeners both
to be prepared for the main body of the lecture and to understand what
they have learned after the lecture is done. This organization may seem
redundant, but some redundancy helps listeners better understand
the content. Obviously, you do not want to say the same things again
and again, but you do want to emphasize and reemphasize your main
points in order to be sure that your listeners understand them.

5. *Use concrete examples.* In speaking, as in writing, concrete examples
help listeners understand fairly abstract points or points that may be
slightly beyond their initial comprehension. A talk that never leaves
an abstract plane is likely to be incomprehensible to many listeners.
Whether people are willing to admit it or not, they learn best from
general points that are illustrated by examples. Do not expect the members of the audience to be able to fill in their own examples – you provide them.

6. *Do not cram.* Don't you just hate it when someone tries to give 2 hours
of material in 40 minutes? So do the people who are going to listen to
you. Some lecturers try to show how erudite they are or how quickly
they can think by cramming in too much material for the time that
they are given to lecture. Most people in the audience will be unim-
pressed and, to the contrary, will come to the conclusion that you do
not know how to lecture. The idea is not to present as much material
as possible, but to make the material you present as clear and as

comprehensible as possible. Therefore, make sure that the amount of material fits the time you have to present it. It is better to present less and clearly convey main points than it is to overpresent and have your audience understand next to nothing.

7. *Be enthusiastic.* Do not expect your audience to be enthusiastic if you are not. If you are enthusiastic, you may or may not transmit your enthusiasm to your audience. But if you are unenthusiastic, you certainly will not transmit any enthusiasm at all. Enthusiasm is contagious, and by showing yours, you may win converts to your way of seeing things that you otherwise would not win. You have always hated to hear people who are bored with what they present; so will your audience.

8. *Make it relevant.* One of the best things you can do to increase comprehension of a lecture is to make the lecture relevant to the people to whom you present it. Obviously, some lectures lend themselves to relevance better than do others. But the more you can adjust your lecture to the interests and prior knowledge of your audience, and the more you can make it relevant to their own concerns, the more likely the audience will be to listen and comprehend. You probably find yourself listening more if you feel that you are learning something useful in a class. Your audience will do the same. Moreover, even if you cannot make the lecture completely relevant to your audience, show why it may be interesting anyway. Do not expect them to know. The more you can show why your audience should find something interesting, the more likely they are to respond to what you have to say.

9. *Know your audience.* A corollary of making your talk relevant to your audience is knowing who your audience is in the first place. When I give a talk or a lecture, I always try to find out as much as I can about the people to whom I am talking. How much knowledge do they have about the topic? What are their interests? What are they looking for in my talk? The more you know your audience, and the more you can adjust your remarks to fit your audience, the better you are likely to be received.

10. *Vary your pace and the kinds of content you present during the course of the lecture.* Varying pace and kinds of content helps maintain audience interest. Too much of anything can become too much of a good thing. Therefore, it helps to vary level of abstractions with concrete examples, generalities with specifics, and lighter topics with heavier ones. Variety is the spice of life, and it is also the spice of a good talk.

11. *Pace yourself.* Many people have a tendency to talk too fast. I am one of them. For the listener, the result is often that he or she is lost before even beginning to understand what the lecture is about. Therefore, you do not want to talk too fast, or to labor so slowly over your words that people lose track of where they are. The best procedure is to vary your pace somewhat but to stay within a range of speed that enables you to remain comprehensible.

12. *Do not be condescending.* No one likes to hear a condescending lecturer, or one who obviously has no respect for the audience. If people are turned off to you, they are likely to be turned off to your material as well. Being condescending or arrogant, or treating people as though they lacked even the most basic mental abilities, is a great way to turn people off completely to everything you have to say. It is generally better to err on the side of modesty than on the side of being a know-it-all, if only because your talk should speak for itself. If you give a good talk, people will respect you for doing it, without your acting as if you are the world's greatest expert on the topic of your talk.

13. *Do not be defensive.* Accept questions, comments, and even criticisms openly. If you want people to learn, then it helps to give them a chance to interact with you. If you react defensively to what they say, the chances are that they will not want to say anything. Therefore, belittling the contributions of your audience, or immediately defending yourself against anything you perceive to be an attack, hurts the audience's ability to learn from you, and yours to learn from the audience. Accept comments openly and profit from them.

14. *Do not wing it.* People quickly recognize if you have come into a lecture unprepared. You have always recognized it in others, and people recognize it in you. Therefore, be prepared.

15. *Be confident.* Perhaps most important, be confident and self-assured. No one is expected to be perfect, and no one is expected to know everything. If you have prepared for your lecture, and you have a reasonable command of your material, give it your best shot and have the confidence in yourself to do well. And then go and enjoy yourself. If you do, your audience probably will as well.

Chapter Sixteen

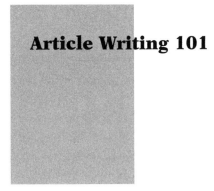

Article Writing 101

This final chapter summarizes 50 tips from experts on writing articles.

GENERAL TIPS

1. *Ask yourself whether your ideas are interesting to you, and why they would be interesting to other people (Tesser, 2000):* All of us read articles that leave us gasping for breath: How could anyone find the work interesting other than the author? You are more likely to avoid the embarrassment of proposing boring ideas if you ask yourself why others and not just you should be interested in the ideas you have to offer.

2. *Realize that new ideas are often difficult to get accepted (Sternberg, 2000b; Tesser, 2000):* The more your ideas depart from mainstream ways of thinking, the harder it probably will be to get your ideas accepted. Thus, the more the ideas depart from the mainstream, the more effort you have to devote in your article to convincing people that what you have to say is worth listening to.

3. *Write the article that emerges from your research rather than the article you planned to write (Bem, 2000):* It is rare that the research you do leads you to the particular outcomes you expected. Write up the article that

This chapter is reprinted from R. J. Sternberg (2000). Article Writing 101: A Crib Sheet of 50 Tips for the Final Exam. In R. J. Sternberg (Ed.), *Guide to publishing in psychology journals* (pp. 199–206). New York: Cambridge University Press. Reprinted with permission.

259

best takes into account what you found rather than the one that takes into account what you had hoped to find but never did.

4. *Explore the data to find out what they have to say and not just what you expected them to say (Bem, 2000; Grigorenko, 2000):* Data often are perverse: They come out a way you did not expect or perhaps never even considered. You should analyze your data to find out what they really tell you rather than only analyzing them for what you thought they might tell you.

5. *A good article tells a story (Eisenberg, 2000; Salovey, 2000):* You may view story writing as different from professional writing in psychology. In fact, in many ways they are the same. A good psychological article has a story to tell, and develops that story from the beginning to the end, or at least the end as the author knows it.

6. *Write the story the data tell rather than the story of your discovery of the data's story (Bem, 2000):* Readers do not want an autobiographical account of how you got to where you are. They just want to know where you are and why.

7. *Write for the student in Psychology 101 (Bem, 2000):* Many writers grossly overestimate the background knowledge of their readers. Write an article that any bright introductory-psychology student could understand. Be accurate, clear, well-organized, and direct. Write linearly. Stick to material that elaborates your main story and avoid subplots. Avoid jargon where possible, but if you need it, be sure to define it.

8. *Make clear what is new in your article (Sternberg, 2000b):* It often is not clear what is new in an article. Make sure you state it directly rather than hoping readers will see it.

9. *Write with your referees in mind (Sternberg, 2000b):* Think of people likely to review your article and the kinds of objections they are likely to raise. They represent many other readers who may see things differently from you and who need to be convinced of the validity of what you say.

10. *Write in the manner of an hourglass, starting broadly, becoming more specific, and then ending broadly (Bem, 2000):* You should start your article dealing with the broad questions you will address. Then you should get specific in terms of what you did. Finally, you should discuss broadly the implications of your work.

11. *Make clear how your study tests your hypotheses (Kendall et al., 2000):* Sometimes a set of hypotheses is presented and research is presented,

but it is not at all obvious how the research actually tests the hypotheses. Make clear how it does.

12. *Polish and proofread (Bem, 2000; Eisenberg, 2000; Sternberg, 2000b):* Do not expect referees or editors to do your rewriting for you or to tolerate loose, sloppy, or error-laden writing. Polishing and proofreading are *your* responsibilities.

13. *Do not use synonyms, especially for technical terms, just for the avoiding redundancy (Bem, 2000):* Readers may believe you are varying the words you use because you are referring to different concepts.

14. *Make length proportional to contribution (Kendall et al., 2000):* Journals have limited space. Longer articles therefore consume a valuable resource. Hence you need to be confident that the longer your article, the greater its contribution.

15. *Use a title that clearly expresses what the article is about and that also, if possible, captures attention (Sternberg, 2000b):* An irrelevant title tricks people into scanning (but rarely reading) something they do not want to read. A boring title may lead them to avoid reading the article altogether.

16. *Write an abstract that contains the information a reader most would want to know (Sternberg, 2000b):* Some people never will see anything more than the abstract. The better the abstract captures the key ideas and findings of your article, the better disseminated your work will be.

17. *Accept feedback nondefensively but critically (Wagner, 2000; Warren, 2000):* Most of the comments you get from referees will help you to produce a better article. Some will not. In revising an article, make the changes that will improve the article. Consider making the changes that, at least, will not hurt the article. But do not make the changes that *will* hurt it. In your letter to the editor, you can explain why you did not make certain changes. The editor, of course, is free to accept or not accept your explanation, as he or she wishes.

18. *A good literature review (whether as a general article or as part of an article) defines and clarifies a problem; summarizes previous research in order to inform the reader of present research; identifies relations, contradictions, gaps, and inconsistencies; and suggests next steps (Eisenberg, 2000):* The literature review thus informs readers of where things have been, where they are, and where they need to go.

19. *A good author writes with his or her readers in mind (Eisenberg, 2000; Reis, 2000):* Write with your readers in mind. Ask yourself how well they will be able to understand what you write. For example, readers

often get confused by pronouns without clear antecedents and imprecise language.

20. *A good article has a take-home message (Eisenberg, 2000):* Often readers finish an article without any clear idea of what the main point of the article was suppose to be. A good article has a clear take-home message so that the reader briefly can summarize what the article was about.

21. *Write for a class of journals (Eisenberg, 2000):* You should have a journal or class of journals in mind when you write an article. The article then can be targeted to the readership and requirements of that journal or class of journals.

22. *Choose carefully the journal to which you submit your article (Warren, 2000):* You can save yourself a lot of time by choosing a journal that is appropriate in terms of what it publishes and that is likely to accept an article of the quality yours is.

23. *Do not take reviews personally (Warren, 2000):* Reviews are of work, not of you. Some reviewers get personal. Ignore such remarks. Read the reviews in the spirit of using them to improve your article.

24. *When you resubmit an article, be clear as to how you handled each of the points made in the reviews:* Reviewers and editors get annoyed when they are ignored. You should follow most of their suggestions and indicate how you did so in a resubmission letter. Those suggestions you cannot accept should be highlighted in the letter and you should explain why you did not follow them.

25. *Relate what you are writing about to people's everyday experiences (Kendall et al., 2000):* You capture people's attention and interest when you draw the people in by relating what you are studying to experiences they have faced or expect to face in their lives.

26. *Use interesting rhetorical questions (Kendall et al., 2000):* People often find themselves wanting to answer rhetorical questions, thus drawing themselves into the article they are reading.

27. *Say clearly why what you are studying should matter to your readers (Kendall et al., 2000):* Do not expect readers to see on their own the importance of your work. Make clear why the work should matter to them.

28. *Review relevant literature in a way that relates it to the argument you want to make (Kendall et al., 2000):* No one likes to read an unfocused, rambling literature review. Organize your literature review around the ideas that you wish to communicate in your article.

29. *Use direct quotes only when necessary (Kendall et al., 2000):* Use direct quotes only if they are needed to convey the flavor or exact message of an original text. Otherwise, they just clutter up and often obscure your message.

30. *State your research question(s) clearly (Kendall et al., 2000; Sternberg, 2000b):* You need to be very clear just what questions will be addressed in your article. Often you also need to make clear what questions the reader may expect to be addressed that are not, in fact, addressed.

31. *Treat differences of opinion with respect (Kendall et al., 2000):* Treat others the way you would want them to treat you – with respect – even if you disagree with what they say and are convinced that anyone in his or her right mind would see things as you do.

32. *Keep in perspective the importance of your own work (Kendall et al., 2000):* Readers tend to be turned off by authors who glorify the importance of their own work beyond reasonable bounds or who fail to make clear the ways in which their own work builds on the work of others.

33. *Be generous in your citations of others (Smith, 2000; Sternberg, 2000b; Tesser, 2000; Wagner, 2000):* No one likes to be ignored, especially referees of articles. It therefore is important to cite relevant past work, especially if someone is likely to be a referee of your article. It further is important to cite work that is not consistent with your point of view in addition to the work that is consistent.

34. *Be current in your citations of others (Smith, 2000):* No one likes to read an article whose author obviously stopped keeping up with the field a decade ago. Make sure your citations are current.

35. *Avoid secondary sources (Smith, 2000):* Extensive use of secondary sources suggests laziness on the part of author. Cite the primary sources. In this way, you not only show better scholarship skills, but increase greatly the likelihood that what you say people said will correspond to what they actually did say.

36. *Actively solicit feedback (Sternberg, 2000b; Wagner, 2000; Warren, 2000):* You can avoid a lot of headaches and heartaches if you anticipate the comments referees are likely to make before they get a chance to make them. Ask colleagues to read your work and comment on it before you submit the work to a journal.

37. *The main elements of design are type of design, how participants were assigned to groups, independent variables, and dependent variables (Reis, 2000):* Make sure your design section contains the necessary elements.

38. *Make clear why the design you chose is appropriate to the problem you have studied (Reis, 2000):* Do not expect readers to figure out why you designed your study as you did.

39. *Make clear what the strengths and limitations of your design are (Grigorenko, 2000; Reis, 2000):* Claim only what you can on the basis of the design you used, and show readers that you know what appropriate claims are.

40. *Provide top-down structure (Salovey, 2000):* It often is difficult for readers to follow the line of argument in an article. By providing top-down structure and making transparent how you will organize, you facilitate your readers' understanding of what you have to say.

41. *Let the story of your data guide your writing of Results, rather than an arbitrary order based on statistical tests (Salovey, 2000):* Do not write your Results section merely to conform to the order of output in a bundle of computer outputs. Write in the order that best conveys the message you wish to convey.

42. *Justify your choices of statistical tests (Grigorenko, 2000; Salovey, 2000):* Do not assume readers will know why you did the tests you did. Explain why you did them.

43. *Be thorough in your reporting of results without being overwhelming (Grigorenko, 2000; Salovey, 2000; Sternberg, 2000b):* Often referees will ask for just those data analyses you chose to omit, so include the full set of data analyses you need to tell your story completely. But omit analyses that are irrelevant to the story you have to tell.

44. *If you cleaned up your data, be clear as to how you did it (Grigorenko, 2000):* Say how you handled missing data, outliers, or any other peculiarities in the data, such as non-normality.

45. *Be sure your conclusions follow from your data (Grigorenko, 2000; Sternberg, 2000b):* It is often tempting for an author to go beyond the data in establishing conclusions, saying what he or she wants to conclude rather than what the data allow him or her to conclude. Draw only the proper conclusions, and properly label anything else as speculation.

46. *The Discussion should make clear what you have contributed, how your study helped resolve the original problem, and what conclusions and theoretical implications can be drawn from your study (Calfee, 2000):* A good Discussion goes well beyond summarizing the results: It relates your results back to why you originally did the study, and makes clear the meaning of what you found out.

47. *The Discussion should be viewed as argumentation, not just as explanation (Calfee, 2000):* Good writing in articles is not merely expository, but persuasive. You are trying to convince readers of the validity of your position, and often, of the lack of validity of alternative positions. However, be realistic in terms of what alternative positions you can rule out.

48. *Decide what is worth emphasizing in your Discussion and what is not (Calfee, 2000):* Good writing is hierarchical: It makes clear what the important points are, and which are merely the supporting points.

49. *Use the Discussion to make clear the limitations of your work (Sternberg, 2000b):* Reviewers will notice them. You take some of the wind out of their sails when you anticipate what they are likely to say in objection to your work.

50. *Never end an article with an expression like "Further research is needed" (Sternberg, 2000b):* What a bore! Of course further research is needed.

You now are ready to write better articles. The tools are right in this book. You need only use them.

References

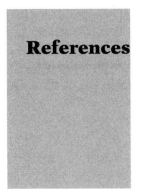

Alexander, J. E., & Tate, M. A. (1999). *Web wisdom: How to evaluate and create information quality on the web.* Mahwah, NJ: Erlbaum.

American Psychological Association. (2001). *Publication manual of the American Psychological Association* (5th ed.). Washington: American Psychological Association.

American Psychological Association. (2002). *Posting articles on the Internet.* Retrieved September 17, 2002, from http://www.apa.org/journals/posting.html.

Beebe-Center, J. G., Rogers, M. S., & O'Connell, D. N. (1955). Transmission of information about sucrose and saline solutions through the sense of taste. *Journal of Psychology, 39,* 157–160.

Bem, D. J. (1967). Self-perception: an alternative interpretation of cognitive dissonance phenomena. *Psychological Review, 74,* 183–200.

Bem, D. J. (2000). Writing an empirical article. In R. J. Sternberg, (Ed.), *Guide to publishing in psychology journals* (pp. 3–16). New York: Cambridge University Press.

Calfee, R. (2000). What does it all mean? The discussion. In R. J. Sternberg (Ed.), *Guide to publishing in psychology journals.* New York: Cambridge University Press.

Cameron, L. (1984). Maternal feelings for the newborn. Unpublished M.Sc. thesis, University of Newcastle upon Tyne.

Clark, H. H. (1974). Semantics and comprehension. In T. A. Sebeok (Ed.), *Current trends in linguistics* (Vol. 12): *Linguistics and adjacent arts and sciences* (pp. 1291–1428). The Hague: Mouton.

Clark, H. H., & Chase, W. (1972). On the process of comparing sentences against pictures. *Cognitive Psychology, 3,* 472–517.

Cleveland, W. S. (1985). *The elements of graphing data.* Monterey, CA: Wadsworth.

Cooley, W. W., & Lohnes, P. R. (1971). *Multivariate data analysis.* New York: Wiley.

David, S. S. J., Chapman, A. J., Foot, H. C., & Sheey, N. P. (1986). Peripheral vision and child pedestrian accidents. *British Journal of Psychology, 77,* 433–450.

Dietz-Uhler, B. (2002). *The effectiveness of an exercise to critically examine information on the World Wide Web.* Unpublished manuscript, Miami University.

Dymond, R. (1948). A scale for the measurement of empathic ability. *Journal of Consulting Psychology, 13,* 127–133.

Dymond, R. (1950). Personality and empathy. *Journal of Consulting Psychology, 14,* 343–350.

Ehrenberg, A. S. C. (1978). *Data reduction: Analyzing and interpreting statistical data.* New York: Wiley.

Ehrenberg, A. S. C. (1982). *A primer in data reduction: An introductory statistics textbook.* New York: Wiley.

Eisenberg, N. (2000). Writing a literature review. In R. J. Sternberg, (Ed.), *Guide to publishing psychology journals* (pp. 17–36). New York: Cambridge University Press.

Festinger, L. (1957). *A theory of cognitive dissonance.* Evanston, IL: Row, Peterson.

Festinger, L., & Carlsmith, J. M. (1959). Cognitive consequences of forced compliance. *Journal of Abnormal and Social Psychology, 58,* 203–211.

Fowler, H. W. (1965). *A dictionary of modern English usage* (2nd ed.). Revised by E. Gowers. New York: Oxford University Press.

Garner, W. R. (1953). An informational analysis of absolute judgments of loudness. *Journal of Experimental Psychology, 46,* 373–380.

Grigorenko, E. L. (2000). Doing data analyses and writing up their results: Selected tricks and artifices. In R. J. Sternberg, (Ed.), *Guide to publishing in psychology journals* (pp. 98–120). New York: Cambridge University Press.

Hake, H. W., & Garner, W. R. (1951). The effect of presenting various numbers of discrete steps on scale reading accuracy. *Journal of Experimental Psychology, 42,* 358–366.

Harris, J. S., & Blake, R. H. (1976). *Technical writing for social scientists.* Chicago: Nelson-Hall.

Hays, W. L. (1973). *Statistics for the social sciences* (2nd ed.). New York: Holt, Rinehart and Winston.

Janis, I. L., & King, B. T. (1954). The influence of role-playing on opinion change. *Journal of Abnormal and Social Psychology, 49,* 211–218.

Kaufman, E. L., Lord, M. W., Reese, R. W., & Volkmann, J. (1949). The discrimination of visual number. *American Journal of Psychology, 62,* 498–525.

Kendall, P. C., Silk, J. S., & Chu, B. C. (2000). Introducing your research report: Writing the introduction. In R. J. Sternberg, (Ed.), *Guide to publishing in psychology journals* (pp. 41–57). New York: Cambridge University Press.

Kratnz, J. H., & Dalal, R. (2000). Validity of web-based psychological research. In M. H. Birnbaum (Ed.), *Psychological experiments on the Internet* (pp. 35–60). San Diego, CA: Academic Press.

Lindsay, W. R., Gamsu, C. V., McLaughlin, E., Hood, E. M., & Espie, C. A. (1987). A controlled trial of treatments for generalized anxiety. *British Journal of Clinical Psychology, 26,* 3–15.

Lovie, P. (1986). Identifying outliers. In A. D. Lovie (Ed.), *New directions in statistics for psychology and the social sciences.* Leicester: The British Psychological Society, and London: Methuen.

Merriam Webster's collegiate dictionary (10th ed.) (1993). Springfield, MA: Merriam-Webster.

Miller, G. A. (1956). The magical number seven, plus or minus two: some limits on our capacity for processing information. *Psychological Review, 63,* 81–97.

Minium, E. W. (1978). *Statistical reasoning in psychology and education* (2nd ed.). New York: Wiley.

Morrison, D. F. (1976). *Multivariate statistical methods* (2nd ed.). New York: Mc-Graw-Hill.

NUA Surveys. (2002). *How many online?* Retrieved September 15, 2002, from http://www.nua.ie/surveys/how_many_online/index.html.

Piaget, J. (1952). *The origins of intelligence in children* (M. Cook, tr.). New York: International Universities Press.

Pollack, I. (1952). The information of elementary auditory displays. *Journal of the Acoustical Society of America, 24,* 745–749.

Poulton, E. C. (1985). Geometric illusions in reading graphs. *Perception and Psychophysics, 37,* 543–548.

Publication manual of the American Psychological Association (5th ed.) (2001). Washington, DC: American Psychological Association.

Reips, U.-D. (2000). The web experiment method: Advantages, disadvantages, and solutions. In M. H. Birnbaum (Ed.), *Psychological experiments on the Internet* (pp. 89–120). San Diego, CA: Academic Press.

Reis, H. T. (2000). Writing effectively about design. In R. J. Sternberg, (Ed.), *Guide to publishing in psychology journals* (pp. 81–97). New York: Cambridge University Press.

Runyon, R. P., & Haber, A. (1991). *Fundamentals of behavioral statistics* (7th ed.). New York: McGraw-Hill.

Salovey, P. (2000). Results that get results: Telling a good story. In R. J. Sternberg, (Ed.), *Guide to publishing in psychology journals* (pp. 121–132). New York: Cambridge University Press.

Seheult, A. (1986). Simple graphical methods for data analysis. In A. D. Lovie (Ed.), *New directions in statistics for psychology and the social sciences.* Leicester: The British Psychological Society, and London: Methuen.

Smith, R. A. (2000). Documenting your scholarship: Citations and references. In R. J. Sternberg, (Ed.), *Guide to publishing in psychology journals* (pp. 146–160). New York: Cambridge University Press.

Sternberg, R. J. (1988). *The psychologist's companion* (2nd ed.). New York: Cambridge University Press.

Sternberg, R. J. (Ed.) (2000a), *Guide to publishing in psychology journals.* New York: Cambridge University Press.

Sternberg, R. J. (Ed.) (2002a), *The anatomy of impact.* Washington, DC: American Psychological Association.

Sternberg, R. J. (Ed.) (2002b), *Psychologists defying the crowd.* Washington, DC: American Psychological Association.

Sternberg, R. J., & Bower, G. H. (1974). Transfer in part–whole and whole–part free recall: a comparative evaluation of theories. *Journal of Verbal Learning and Verbal Behavior, 13,* 1–26.

Sternberg, R. J., & Lubart, T. I. (1992). Buy low and sell high: An investment approach to creativity. *Current Directions in Psychological Science, 1*(1), 1–5.

Sternberg, R. J., & Tulving, E. (1977). The measurement of subjective organization in free recall. *Psychological Bulletin, 84,* 538–556.

Strunk, W., Jr., & White, E. B. (1979). *The elements of style* (3rd ed.). New York: Macmillan.

Tatsuoka, M. M. (1971). *Multivariate analysis: techniques for educational and psychological research.* New York: Wiley.

Tesser, A. (2000). Theories and hypotheses. In R. J. Sternberg, (Ed.), *Guide to publishing in psychology journals* (pp. 58–80). New York: Cambridge University Press.

Tufte, E. R. (1983). *The visual display of quantitative information*. Cheshire, CT: Graphics Press.

Tukey, J. W. (1977). *Exploratory data analysis*. Reading, MA: Addison-Wesley.

Tulving, E., & Madigan, S. A. (1970). Memory and verbal learning. In P. H. Mussen & M. R. Rosenzweig (Eds.), *Annual review of psychology* (Vol. 21, pp. 437–484). Palo Alto, CA: Annual Reviews, Inc.

U.S. Department of Commerce. (2002). *A nation online: How Americans are expanding their use of the Internet, February 2002*. Retrieved September 15, 2002, from http://www.ntia.doc.gov/ntiahome/dn/index.html.

Velleman, P. F., & Hoaglin, D. C. (1981). *Applications, basics, and computing of exploratory data analysis*. North Scituate, MA: Duxbury Press.

Wagner, R. K. (2000). Rewriting the psychology paper. In R. J. Sternberg, (Ed.), *Guide to publishing in psychology journals* (pp. 187–198). New York: Cambridge University Press.

Wainer, H. (1984). How to display data badly. *The American Statitician, 38,* 137–147.

Warren, M. G. (2000). Reading reviews, suffering rejection, and advocating for your paper. In R. J. Sternberg, (Ed.), *Guide to publishing in psychology journals* (pp. 189–186). New York: Cambridge University Press.

Webster's third new international dictionary of the English language, unabridged (1976). Springfield, MA: Merriam-Webster.

Winer, B. J. (1991). *Statistical principles in experimental design* (3rd ed.). New York: McGraw-Hill.

Zakon, R. (2002). *Hobbes' Internet Timeline v5.6.* Retrieved September 15, 2002, from http://www.zakon.org/robert/internet/timeline/.

Appendix A: Sample Psychology Paper

This appendix contains a sample student psychology paper. The paper was written a number of years ago by an undergraduate majoring in psychology: myself. The data presented in the paper are real but previously unpublished. The paper is presented (with minor modifications) as it was actually typed, rather than as it would appear in a journal. The purpose of including the paper in this volume is to illustrate the proper format for a paper typed according to APA guidelines. Remember, though, that your paper should be double-spaced throughout, rather than single-spaced, as here.

The Effects of Time-Limit Cues upon
Test Means, Variances, and Reliabilities
Robert J. Sternberg
Yale University

Effects of Time

2

Abstract

Two 3-min, 40-item multiple-choice synonyms tests were
administered consecutively to 411 juniors in a suburban high school.
Students were divided into three groups, labeled Groups 1, 2, and 3.
Each group received successively more information about time
limits. Directions for a given group were identical before each test.
Under the naive condition (first test), the test mean and variance
were significantly higher for Group 3 than for Group 1. Under the
sophisticated condition (second test), no significant differences were
observed. Alternate-form reliability was significantly higher for
Group 3 than for either Group 1 or Group 2. The results are
discussed in terms of psychometric properties of tests and fairness
of test instructions to students.

Effects of Time

3

The Effects of Time-Limit Cues upon
Test Means, Variances, and Reliabilities

Mental ability test directions have long followed a variety of
procedures regarding time limits. Directions for some tests, such as
those for the Ohio State University Psychological Test (Toops, 1941),
impose no time limit at all. Most test directions, however, do impose
a time limit.

Directions for tests that impose time limits differ in the amount
of information they convey to subjects about time limits. Some sets
of directions, such as those for Level 5 of the Lorge–Thorndike
Intelligence Tests (Lorge & Thorndike, 1957) and for the Terman–
McNemar Test of Mental Ability (Terman & McNemar, 1941), inform
subjects that they will be timed, but do not specify to them just how
much time they will have. Other sets of directions, such as those for
grades 9–12 of the Henmon–Nelson Tests of Mental Ability (Lamke
& Nelson, 1957) and for the Beta Test of the Otis Quick-Scoring
Mental Ability Tests (Otis, 1954), inform subjects both of the
existence of a time limit and of what the time limit is. The Otis
directions further provide for subjects to be visually reminded of
how much time they have left to work. Examiners are instructed to
write on a blackboard the time that the test began, and they are
urged to write below it the time that the test will end.

In all four of these speeded tests, subjects are informed that they
will be timed. The amounts of information they are given about time
limits differ, however. There seem to exist in these tests, and in
others like them, two basic procedures and a variation in one of
them regarding how much information subjects are given about
time limits. For convenience, the two procedures and variation will
be referred to as Procedures 1, 2, and 3, and subjects taking tests
under these procedures will be referred to as subjects in Group 1,
Group 2, and Group 3, respectively. Under Procedure 1, subjects are
not told how much time they will have to work and are also
reminded during the test of how much time they have left to work.

This experiment was designed to investigate the effects of subjects' differential exposure to time-limit cues upon means, variances, and reliabilities of tests administered under two conditions. The first (naive) condition was the administration of a first test under a particular procedure. The second (sophisticated) condition was the administration of a second form of that test under the same procedure immediately following the administration of the first test.

The motivation underlying this experiment is that supplying subjects with more information about time limits results in a test that is both fairer to subjects and psychometrically more sound. Subjects not given full information about time limits will not know how quickly they are expected to work, and hence will not be able to pace themselves to finish as many test items as they can. Subjects who might do quite well if they knew how much time they had may do quite poorly simply because they do not realize how quickly they need to work. These considerations led to five hypotheses regarding experimental outcomes:

1. The mean of a first test administered under Procedure 1 will be lower than that of the test administered under Procedure 2, and this mean in turn will be lower than that of the test administered under Procedure 3.

Subjects taking a first test under each of the successive procedures should be increasingly better able to employ what Millman, Bishop, and Ebel (1965) call time-using strategies. Such strategies are employed by test-wise examinees in order to obtain high scores. Millman et al. (1965) note that a "rule of thumb is to determine how far one should be when a specific proportion of the testing period has elapsed" (p. 714). Periodic checks on rate of progress facilitate the maintenance of proper speed (Cook, 1957; Millman et al., 1965).

2. The means of an alternate form of the first test, when the alternate form is administered to each group immediately after and under the same procedure as the first test, will not differ significantly from each other.

The signal to stop work on the first form of the test can itself serve as a time-limit cue. The less information subjects have when

Effects of Time

5

they take the first test, the more information this implicit cue can be expected to impart. Thus, subjects in each successive group will profit increasingly less from the cue, and test means will tend to converge.

3. The variance of a first test administered under Procedure 1 will be lower than that of the test administered under Procedure 2, and this variance in turn will be lower than that of the test administered under Procedure 3.

Subjects may differ greatly in the speeds at which they can solve test items, but the extent of the difference will be masked if subjects work at their typical rates rather than their maximum rates. Greater amounts of time-limit information enable potentially rapid test takers to show how rapidly they can work.

4. The variances of an alternate form of the first test, when the alternate form is administered to each group immediately after and under the same procedure as the first test, will not differ significantly from each other.

Because the signal to stop work on the first form of the test serves as a time limit cue telling subjects the tests are strictly timed, subjects in each group realize they must work at their maximum rate on the second test. Hence, the variances in the different groups should tend to converge.

5. If two alternate forms of a test are administered under the same procedure, one immediately following the other, the alternate form reliability of the test will be lower under Procedure 1 than under Procedure 2, and lower under Procedure 2 than under Procedure 3.

As an implicit time-limit cue, the signal to stop work on the first test imparts new time limit information to subjects. The greater the amount of new information transmitted, the greater will be the potential for new variance to enter into scores on the second test. The greater the amount of new variance that enters into scores on the second test, the lower will be the correlation (alternate form reliability) between forms of the test. In other words, increasing the amount of time-limit information explicitly given to subjects increases the extent to which two successive forms of the test measure the same thing.

Method

Subjects

Subjects were 411 juniors in a suburban New Jersey public high school. There were 140 students in Group 1, 148 students in Group 2, and 123 students in Group 3.

Materials

The stimulus materials were alternate forms of a 40-item multiple-choice synonyms test. Test items were ordered and forms equated according to the frequency of occurrence of the test words in the English language as reported by Thorndike and Lorge (1944).

Design

Dependent variables were the number of items correctly answered on each form of the synonyms test minus one-fourth the number of items incorrectly answered. Omissions were not counted as incorrect. Independent variables were time-limit instructional procedure (1, 2, or 3) and test form (1 and 2). Each subject was assigned to only one instructional procedure, but all subjects received both test forms under that procedure. Homerooms (where testing took place) were randomly assigned to groups. In the high school, students are assigned to homerooms at random.

Procedure

Students were tested by their homeroom teachers preceding their daily classes. The students were given no advance notice of the tests. Instructions for each of the three groups were identical except for time-limit and group-coding information. Students were instructed to answer as many items as they could, but to guess on items only if they had some idea of what the correct answer was,

Effects of Time

7

because a percentage of the number of wrong (but not omitted) answers would be subtracted from the number of correct answers.

Students in Group 1 were told that they would be timed, but they were not told how much time they would have. Students in Group 2 were told before the beginning of each of the two tests that they would have 3 min in which to work on the particular test. Students in Group 3 were also given this information, and were further informed that they would be told when they had 2 min, 1 min, and 30 s left to work.

After the initial instructions were completed, students in all groups received Form 1 of the synonyms test. After the test, the instructions were repeated, and then students received Form 2 of the synonyms test. Following administration of Form 2, the homeroom teacher collected the test booklets, ending the experimental session.

Results

Test means, variances, and alternate form reliabilities are presented in Table 1.

Insert Table 1 about here

Test 1 Means

The first hypothesis was partially confirmed by the results. The three group means for the first test fell into the rank order predicted, although only the difference between the first and third means was significant, $t(261) = 1,85, p < .05$.

Test 2 Means

The Test 2 means were consistent with the second hypothesis. None of the means differed significantly from each other.

Effects of Time

8

Test 1 Variances

The experimental data provided a partial confirmation of the third hypothesis. Test 1 variances fell into the rank order predicted, although again, only the difference between the Group 1 and Group 3 variances was significant, $F(122,139) = 1.67, p < .01$.

Test 2 Variances

The Test 2 variances were consistent with the fourth hypothesis. None of the variances differed significantly from each other.

Alternate-form Reliabilities

The rank order of the alternate-form reliabilities was that predicted by the fifth hypothesis. The difference between Groups 1 and 3 was significant, $z = 3.40, p < .01$, as was the difference between Groups 2 and 3, $z = 2.47, p < .01$.

Discussion

The data presented above suggest that authors of mental ability tests may have been too cavalier in determining how much time-limit information should be imparted to examinees. Reduced time-limit information has been shown in this experiment to result in lower test means and variances for an initial test, and to result in lower alternate form reliability. This last finding is of particular importance, because it suggests that withholding time-limit information from subjects may result in a psychometrically poorer test. Telling subjects the time limit of a test and reminding them during testing of how much time is left is fairer to the subjects, because it enables them to budget their time, and fairer to the tester, because it gives a better, more consistent view of each subject's maximal performance. Given the choice, subjects opt for the additional information.[1]

Effects of Time

9

It would be worthwhile to determine whether differences in test means, variances, and reliabilities hold up across different types of test content, and to determine whether differences extend to other test statistics, particularly predictive validity. An experiment investigating the generalizability of these findings is presently being prepared (Sternberg, 1971). If the findings are generalizable, then test authors should provide an explicit rationale for the type of time-limit instructions they select.

Effects of Time
10

References

Cook, D. L. (1957). A comparison of reading comprehension scores obtained before and after a time announcement. *Journal of Educational Psychology, 48*, 440–446.

Lamke, T. M., & Nelson, M. J. (1957). *The Henmon–Nelson Tests of Mental Ability,* Grades 9–12. Boston: Houghton Mifflin.

Lorge, I., & Thorndike, R. L. (1957). *The Lorge–Thorndike Intelligence Tests,* Level 5. Boston: Houghton Mifflin.

Millman, J., Bishop, H., & Ebel, R. (1965). An analysis of test-wiseness. *Educational and Psychological Measurement, 25*, 707–726.

Otis, A. S. (1954). *Otis Quick-Scoring Mental Ability Tests*, Beta Test. New York: Harcourt, Brace, & World.

Sternberg, R. J. (1971). *Effects of time-limit cues upon validity of verbal and mathematical ability test scores.* Manuscript in preparation.

Terman, L. M., & McNemar, Q. (1941). *Terman–McNemar Test of Mental Ability.* Yonkers, NY: World Book Company.

Thorndike, E. L., & Lorge, I. (1944). *The teacher's word book of 30,000 words.* New York: Teachers College, Columbia University.

Toops, H. A. (1941). *The Ohio State University Psychological Test.* Chicago: Science Research Associates.

Effects of Time
11

AUTHOR NOTES

An earlier version of this paper was submitted to Professor Leonard Doob in partial fulfillment of the 1969 requirements for Psychology 36a, Yale University. I am grateful to Dr. Doob for his comments on the paper. A version of this paper was presented at the 1972 annual meeting of the National Council on Measurement in Education, Chicago, Illinois.

If this paper appeared in a journal, requests for reprints would be sent to Robert J. Sternberg, PACE Center, Box 208358, Yale University, New Haven, Connecticut 06520.

FOOTNOTE

[1] An informal poll of 15 students who had participated in the experiment revealed unanimous agreement that providing greater amounts of time-limit information is better for students because it enables them to budget their time more efficiently.

Effects of Time
    13

Table 1
Means, Variances, and Alternate-Form Reliabilities

Group	Means		Variances		Reliabilities[a]
	Test 1	Test 2	Test 1	Test 2	
1	7.43	12.35	32.49	43.82	.74
2	8.10	11.64	41.47	59.75	.79
3	8.95	12.89	54.17	56.25	.88

[a]Reliabilities are of the alternate-form type.

Appendix B: Writing for British and European Journals

Guidelines for submitting papers to British Psychological Society journals are given in *Suggestions to Contributors*, obtainable from The British Psychological Society, St Andrews House, 48 Princess Road East, Leicester LE1 7DR, United Kingdom. BPS style differs only slightly from APA style, and BPS journals will accept papers prepared in accordance with APA guidelines. The most important style differences are:

1. Commas are not used before *and* and *or* for the last item in a series of three or more items.
    The subject, confederate and experimenter all entered the room together.
2. Capital letters are used for the first letters of major words in titles of books in *both* text *and* the references.
    Balderdash's classic work *Writing for Meaning* is widely cited.
    Balderdash, H. Q. (1969). *Writing for Meaning*. Los Angeles: Perfection Press.
3. Capital letters are *not* used for the first letters of major words in titles of articles in *either* the text *or* the references.
    The article reporting the experiment was to be entitled, "A factor analysis of pen-pushing power".
    Muddlehead, M. M. (1976). A factor analysis of pen-pushing power. *Journal of Junky Experiments*, **5**, 406–409.
4. There are some spelling differences. For example, *centred* rather than *centered*, *labelling* rather than *labeling*.

285

5. Degrees of freedom are reported differently.

$t = 2.93$, d.f. $= 68$, $P < 0.01$,

$F = 1.18$, d.f. $= 2,28$, $P > 0.05$.

6. Spaces rather than commas are used to separate numbers with five or more digits on either side of the decimal point.

1437; 25 125; 382.654 53.

7. For decimals, zeroes are *always* used before the decimal point.

The average score was a pitiful 0.73.

The proportion of subjects finishing the task was 0.86.

8. For citations to papers with multiple authors, the names of the authors are connected by "&", whether the citation is direct or indirect.

McLeod & O'Dowd (1963) found the artifact.

An artifact was discovered (McLeod & O'Dowd, 1963).

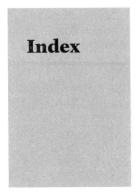

Index

abbreviations: and APA guidelines, 129–30; and journal articles, 226–7
ability/capacity, misuse of, 105
abstract: and experimental research papers, 55; and grant proposals, 242; and lectures, 256; and psychology papers, 65, 71, 273
accuracy, and evaluation of information on Internet, 84
acquisitions editors, 244
Acta Psychologia (journal), 174
active voice, and passive voice in psychology papers, 71–2
adapt/adopt, misuse of, 98
Adolescence (journal), 174
advances, on royalties, 250
advisers, and critical reading of psychology papers, 76
affect/effect, misuse of, 98–9
affirmative constructions, in psychology papers, 72
aggravate/irritate, misuse of, 99
Alexander, J. E., 85
algorithm/heuristic, misuse of, 105–6
allusion, misuse of, 99
ambiguity, and interpretation of results in psychology papers, 213

American Behavioral Scientist (journal), 174
American Journal of Community Psychology, 174–5
American Journal on Mental Retardation, 175
American Journal of Psychology, 175
American Psychological Association (APA): guidelines for psychology papers, 119–41, 218, 228; on publishing of articles on Internet, 93–4; submitting figures to journals of, 164; Web site of, 82–3. *See also American Psychologist*
American Psychological Society, 82, 83
American Psychologist (journal), 175
among, misuse of, 99
amount of/number of, misuse of, 99
and/or, misuse of, 99
anecdotes, and opening of lecture, 255–6
Animal Learning and Behavior (journal), 175
Annual Review of Psychology, 198–9
antecedents, and pronouns in psychology papers, 73–4
anxiety/fear, misuse of, 106

APA. *See* American Psychological Association
APA Monitor (newspaper), 175–6
apparatus, experimental research paper and description of, 57
appendix: and digressions in psychology papers, 68; and experimental research papers, 63
Applied Psychological Measurement (journal), 176
applied research/basic research, misuse of terms, 106
archival research, and Internet, 86–8
articles. *See* journals
artificial intelligence/simulation, misuse of terms, 106–7
audience: and book proposals, 246; for journal articles, 227; for lectures, 257; and organization of outline for library research paper, 32. *See also* readers
audits, of grants, 236
authority, and evaluation of information on Internet, 84
author cards, for library research papers, 22–3
author identification notes: and APA guidelines, 138–9; and example of student psychology paper, 282
author's name, and experimental research papers, 54–5
autobiographical information: and journal articles, 227–8; and picture of research presented by journal articles, 17–18
average: and presentation of data in tables, 145–6; as misused word, 107
avoidance learning/escape learning, misuse of terms, 107

basic research/applied research, misuse of terms, 106
because, misuse of, 104

background: of readers of journal articles, 260; and writers of psychology papers, 75
Beck, Susan, 85
Beebe-Center, J. G., 201
Behavioral and Brain Sciences (journal), 176–7
Behavioral Neuroscience (journal), 177
Behavioral Science (journal), 177
Behavior Research Methods, Instruments, and Computers (journal), 176
Behavior Therapy (journal), 176
benefits, and grants, 235
between/among, misuse of, 99
between-subject variables, and experimental research papers, 40–2
"blind reviewing," 218
boldface type, and APA guidelines, 128
books: and author cards for library research papers, 23; and book proposals, 245–8; choosing publisher for, 244–5; and contract offers, 248–54
box plots, 149–52
brackets, and rules of punctuation, 126
Brain and Cognition (journal), 177
Bright Planet software company, 80
bring/take, misuse of, 100
British Journal of Development Psychology, 177–8
British Journal of Educational Psychology, 178
British Journal of Mathematical and Statistical Psychology, 178
British Journal of Psychology, 178
British Journal of Social Psychology, 178
British Psychological Society (BPS), 119, 285
budgets, and grant proposals, 241

Cameron, L., 148, 153
Canadian Journal of Experimental Psychology, 179
Canadian Psychology/Psychologie Canadienne (journal), 179
capacity/ability, misuse of, 105
capitalization: and APA guidelines, 126–8; and British journals, 285
captions, of figures, 163–4
Carlsmith, J. M., 204–207, 210–15
certainly, misuse of, 100
Chapman, A. J., 154–5
"chartjunk," and data presentation, 142
Chat Groups, and Internet, 79
Child Development (journal), 179
citations: and APA guidelines for psychology papers, 136–8; and British journals, 286; of referees in psychology papers for submission to journals, 229, 263; of sources and findings in psychology papers, 75. *See also* references; sources
clarity, in writing of psychology papers, 66–7, 226
classical conditioning/operant conditioning, misuse of terms, 107–108
Cleveland, W., 142, 153–4, 155, 158, 160–2
Clinical Psychology Review (journal), 179
Cognition (journal), 179
Cognitive, Affective, and Behavioral Neuroscience (journal), 179–80
Cognitive Neuropsychology (journal), 180
Cognitive Psychology (journal), 180
Cognitive Therapy and Research (journal), 180
collaborators, communicating with via Internet, 94–5
colleagues, and critical reading of psychology papers, 76, 228–9, 263

colon, and rules of punctuation, 122
columns, of tables, 144–5
commas: and APA guidelines, 121; and British journals, 285
communication: between author and publisher, 252–3; and exposure of conceptual gaps, 6–7; and Internet, 94–5
compare to/compare with, misuse of, 100
competition, and book proposals, 247
completion date, and book proposal, 247–8
Comprehensive Dictionary of Psychological and Psycho-analytical Terms: A Guide to Usage (English & English, 1958), 165–6
comprise, misuse of, 100
compulsion/obsession, misuse of, 108
computers: programs as appendix in experimental research papers, 63; and scoring of data by direct entry, 47–8. *See also* Internet
Concise Encyclopedia of Psychology: Abridged (Corsini et al., 1998), 166
conclusions: and experimental research papers, 60–1; and journal articles, 225, 264; and presentation of facts, 9–10. *See also* results
concrete examples: in lectures, 256; in psychology papers, 71, 226
conferences, and Internet, 91
conflict of interest, and APA guidelines, 141
consent forms, 48–50
Contemporary Psychology (journal), 180
content footnotes, 139
continual/continuous, misuse of, 100

contract offers, from book publishers, 248–54
contracts, and research grants, 233–4
control group/experimental group, misuse of terms, 108–9
control issues, and research via Internet, 89
Cooley, W. W., 53
copy editors, 220, 252
copyrights, and permission to reproduce materials, 47, 125, 141, 252
corporate authors, and citations, 137
Corsini Encyclopedia of Psychology and Behavioral Science, 3rd. ed. (Craighead & Nemeroff, 2002), 166
costs, of research via Internet, 89
Counseling Psychologist, The (journal), 180
coverage, and evaluation of information on Internet, 85
Creativity Research Journal, 181
criticism: and indirect method of proof, 12–14; and reviews of journal articles, 230–1
"culture," of journals, 230
culture-fair test/culture-free test, misuse of terms, 109
currency: and evaluation of information on Internet, 84–5; of textbooks, 36
Current Directions in Psychological Science (journal), 181
curriculum vitae: and book proposals, 248; and grant proposals, 240–1

dangling constructions, avoidance of in psychology papers, 72–3
dash, and rules of punctuation, 123
data: guidelines for presentation of, 142–64; as misused word, 100

data analysis: and experimental research papers, 42, 53; and grant proposals, 239; and journal articles, 224
data collection, via Internet, 88–90
Data Reduction (Ehrenberg, 1978), 142
David, S. S. J., 154–5
debriefing sheet, 50, 51
deduction/induction, misuse of, 109
default, explanation by in scientific papers, 12–14
degrees of freedom, and British journals, 286
delusion, misuse of *hallucination*, *illusion*, and, 110
demographics, of Internet users, 79–80
dependent variables: misuse of term, 110; selection of for experimental research papers, 39–40
Department of Defense, and Internet, 78
descriptive statistics: and experimental research papers, 58; misuse of term, 110
Developmental Psychology (journal), 181
Developmental Review (journal), 181
deviation IQ/ratio IQ, misuse of terms, 110–11
Dictionary of Behavioral Science, 2nd ed. (Wolman, 1989), 166
Dictionary of Psychology (Chaplin, 1991), 166
Dictionary of Psychology, 3rd ed. (Reber & Reber, 2002), 166–7
Dietz-Uhler, B., 85
different from/different than, misuse of, 100
digressions, psychology papers and avoidance of, 68
directions, for experimental tasks, 47

direct quotes, in journal articles, 263
discover/invent, misuse of, 100
discussion: and experimental research paper, 60–2; and journal articles, 264–5; and student psychology paper, 279–80
discussion boards, on Internet, 87
disinformation, on Internet, 83
disinterested/uninterested, misuse of, 101
Dissertations and Theses from Start to Finish (Cone & Foster, 1993), 167
divided bar charts, 155–6
double quotation marks, 123–5
drawings, preparation of for publication, 162–3
drop-out rates, and research via Internet, 89
Dymond, R., 209–10

ecological validity, tradeoff between experimental control and, 39
edited books: and author cards for library research paper, 23; prospectuses for, 246–7
Educational and Psychological Measurement (journal), 181–2
effect/affect, misuse of, 98–9
Ehrenberg, A., 142, 147
electronic submission, of journal articles, 95
Elements of Graphing Data, The (Cleveland, 1985), 142
e-mail, 94–5
emphasis: and discussion section of journal articles, 265; and organization of lectures, 256
empirical research, and grant proposals, 239
empiricism/nativism, misuse of, 111
Encyclopedia of Human Behavior (Ramachandran, 1994), 167

Encyclopedia of Psychology (Kazdin, 2000), 167
Encyclopedic Dictionary of Psychology (Harre & Lamb, 1983), 167–8
enormity/enormousness, misuse of, 101
enthusiasm, and lectures, 257
equations, and APA guidelines, 132–3
erasures, and rules of legibility, 120–1
error bars, in graphs, 157–8, 161
escape learning/avoidance learning, misuse of terms, 107
Espie, C. A., 157
ethical issues, and research via Internet, 89
Ethical Principles of Psychologists and the Code of Conduct (American Psychological Association, 2002), 168
Ethics in Plain English: An Illustrative Casebook for Psychologists (Nagy, 1999), 168
Ethics for Psychologists: A Commentary on the APA Ethics Code (Canter, 1994), 168
ethnicity, of Internet users, 79–80
European Journal of Social Psychology, 182
evaluation, of contribution to knowledge of psychology papers, 210–15
exhaustive alternatives, 12–13
experimental control, tradeoff between ecological validity and, 39
experimental design: and introduction of experimental research papers, 56; and journal articles, 263–4; and methods section of experimental research papers, 58
experimental group/control group, misuse of terms, 108–9

experimental manipulation, and
    evaluation of psychology papers,
    214
experimental materials, and experi-
    mental research papers, 43–7, 57
experimental psychology, use of
    term, 111–12
experimental research papers: and
    data analysis, 53; and execution
    of experiments, 52–3; and plan-
    ning of research, 35–52; and
    reporting of results, 53–64. *See
    also* scientific writing
experimenter effects, on research
    results, 53, 88
*extrinsic motivation/intrinsic
    motivation*, misuse of, 112

facilities, and grant proposals,
    241–2
factor, misuse of, 112
factor analysis, 112
facts: as misused word, 101;
    presentation of and purpose of
    psychology papers, 9–10
faculty: and grading of student
    papers, 7–8; and ideas for
    experimental research papers,
    35–6; and research grants,
    235–6. *See also* universities
Family Process (journal), 182
farther/further, misuse of, 101
fear/anxiety, misuse of, 106
Fedworld (Web site), 82, 87
Festinger, L., 204–207, 210–15
fewer/less, misuse of, 101
figures: numbers expressed in,
    134–5; preparation of for pub-
    lication, 162–4; and presentation
    of data, 59, 147–64; relation
    between text and, 143
first-person singular, in psychology
    papers, 75
fixation/regression, misuse of,
    112–13
Foot, H. C., 154–5

footnotes: and APA guidelines,
    139–41; and student psychology
    paper, 283
formality, and audience for
    psychology paper, 66
format, and APA guidelines, 119–20
former/latter, misuse of, 101
fortuitous/fortunate, misuse of, 102
Forum for Behavioral Science in
    Family Medicine, 91
Fowler, H. W., 98
framework, and evaluation of
    psychology papers, 213–14
further/farther, misuse of, 101

Gamsu, C. V., 157
Garner, W. R., 201, 203
gender, of Internet users, 79
generalizability: of experimental
    materials, 44; and selection of
    subjects, 42
general references, for psychology
    papers, 165–73
*Genetic, Social and General
    Psychology Monographs*, 182
genotype/phenotype, misuse of, 113
Gifted Child Quarterly (journal),
    182
"Good, the Bad, and the Ugly, The"
    (Web site), 85
government databases, on Internet,
    82
grading, and quality of writing,
    7–8
Graduate Study in Psychology
    (American Psychological
    Association, annual), 168–9
grammar, and APA guidelines,
    121–30
grants: basic concepts about,
    233–6; definition of, 233; writing
    of proposals, 236–43
graphs, and presentation of data,
    153–62
Guide to Reference Books, 11th ed.
    (Balay, 1996), 169

Haber, A., 53
Hake, H. W., 201, 203
hallucination, misuse of *delusion*,
  illusion, and, 110
Hays, W. L., 53
headings, and APA guidelines,
  130–1
heuristic/algorithm, misuse of,
  105–106
Hoaglin, D. C., 149
home Web pages, of specific
  researchers, 82, 91
Hood, E. M., 157
hopefully, misuse of, 102
horizontal spacing, and APA
  guidelines, 120
hourglass, as metaphor for writing
  of journal articles, 260
Human Development (journal), 182
Human Performance (journal), 182
hypertext, and Internet, 78
hyphen, and rules of punctuation,
  122–3
hypothesis: experimental research
  paper and reformulation of, 60;
  and negative versus positive
  results, 14–16; and writing of
  journal articles, 260–1

identification/imitation, misuse of,
  113
illusion, misuse of *delusion*,
  hallucination, and, 110
imitation/identification, misuse of,
  113
implications, of arguments in
  library research papers, 25, 33
imply/infer, misuse of, 102
importance, of arguments or
  findings: and grant proposals,
  236–7; and journal articles, 262,
  263; and library research papers,
  25, 33–4
indefinite *this*, 74
independent variables: misuse of
  term, 110; selection of for

experimental research papers,
  38–9, 40–2
indexing, of books, 252
induction/deduction, misuse of, 109
infer/imply, misuse of, 102
inferential statistics: and
  experimental research papers,
  58; misuse of term, 110
*Information Sources in the Social
  Sciences* (Fisher, 2002), 169
informed consent, 48–50
in-house assistance, to authors, 252
Instant Messaging, and Internet, 79
institutional affiliation, and experimental research papers, 55
Instructor's Resource Guide
  (American Psychological
  Association, 2001), 170
Intelligence (journal), 183
intelligence quotient (IQ), and
  misuse of terms, 110–11
interesting, as misused word, 102
internal consistency, and library
  research papers, 24–5, 33
*International Encyclopedia of the
  Social & Behavioral Sciences*
  (Smelser & Baltes, 2001), 169
International Journal of Psychology,
  183
Internet: conducting research on,
  85–90; critical evaluation of
  information on, 83–5; definition
  of, 78–80; disadvantages of,
  77–8, 89–90, 92, 96–7; disseminating research findings on,
  90–4; publishing articles on,
  92–6; searching of, 80–3;
  usefulness of as research tool,
  77, 96
*intrinsic motivation/extrinsic
  motivation*, misuse of, 112
introduction: of experimental
  research papers, 55–6; of
  psychology papers, 65
invent/discover, misuse of, 100
irregardless, misuse of, 102

Is Psychology the Major for You?
(American Psychological
Association, 1987), 169
italics, and APA guidelines, 128–9
its/it's, misuse of, 102

Janis, I. L., 204–205
jargon, in journal articles, 226–7
jokes, and opening of lectures,
255–6
John Hopkins University, and
library Web site, 83, 84
Journal of Abnormal Psychology, 183
*Journal of Adolescent and Adult
Literacy*, 183
*Journal of Applied Behavior
Analysis*, 184
*Journal of Applied Developmental
Psychology*, 184
Journal of Applied Psychology, 184
Journal of Community Psychology,
184–5
Journal of Comparative Psychology,
185
*Journal of Consulting and Clinical
Psychology*, 185
Journal of Counseling Psychology,
185
*Journal of Cross-Cultural Psy-
chology*, 185–6
Journal of Educational Psychology,
186
*Journal of Experimental Analysis of
Behavior*, 186
*Journal of Experimental Child
Psychology*, 186
Journal of Experimental Psychology,
186–7
*Journal of Experimental Social
Psychology*, 187
Journal of General Psychology, 187
Journal of Genetic Psychology, 188
*Journal of the History of the
Behavioral Sciences*, 188
Journal of Humanistic Psychology,
188

Journal of Mathematical Psychology,
188
Journal of Memory and Language,
188
Journal of Nonverbal Behavior, 189
*Journal of Occupational and
Organizational Psychology*, 189
Journal of Parapsychology, 189
Journal of Personality, 189
*Journal of Personality and Social
Psychology*, 189–90
*Journal of Psycoeducational
Assessment*, 190
Journal of Psychology, 190
Journal of Research in Personality,
190
journals: and author cards for
library research papers, 22; and
figures, 164; and ideas for
experimental research papers,
36–7; and Internet, 82; picture
of research presented by, 16–18;
quality of writing and acceptance of articles by, 8, 221–31;
as references for psychology
papers, 174–97; submitting
psychology papers to, 216–20;
tips on writing of articles for,
259–65; Web pages of and information for contributors, 95;
writing for British and European, 285–6
*Journal of Social and Personal
Relationships*, 190
Journal of Social Psychology, 191
Journals in Psychology (American
Psychological Association,
1997), 170
*Journal Supplement Abstract Series
(JSAS)* and *JSAS Catalog of
Selected Documents in Psychology*, 169–70

Kaufman, E. L., 201–2
keyword outline, for library research paper, 27, 28, 29–30, 31–2

keywords, and titles of experimental research papers, 54
King, B. T., 204–205
knowledge: evaluation of psychology papers for contribution to,
210–15; experimental research
papers and frontiers of, 36–7;
and overestimation of reader
background by writers of journal
articles, 260

latent content/manifest content,
misuse of, 113–14
latter/former, misuse of, 101
lawyers, and book contracts, 253
lay/lie, misuse of, 102–3
layout, of tables, 146
learning/maturation/performance,
misuse of, 114
Learning and Motivation (journal),
191
lectures, writing of, 255–8
legends, of figures, 163
legibility, rules of, 120–1
length: and evaluation of student
papers, 8–9; of grant proposals,
238–9; and writing of journal
articles, 261
less/fewer, misuse of, 101
library research papers: deciding
on topic for, 19–22; and literature reviews, 22–6; and outline,
26–33; writing of, 33–4
*Library Research in Psychology:
Finding it Easily* (American
Psychological Association), 170
lie/lay, misuse of, 102–3
Lindsay, W. R., 157
LISTSERV(R), 79, 91
literally, misuse of, 103
literature review: and grant proposals, 237; and introduction of
experimental research papers,
56; and journal articles, 223,
261, 262; and library research
papers, 20–1, 22–6

logic: and misconceptions about
psychology papers, 16–18; and
organization of journal articles,
226; and persuasion in psychology papers, 65, 66
Lohnes, P. R., 53
Lord, M. W., 201–2
Lovie, P., 53, 152

Madigan, S. A., 198–9
magazines, and Internet, 82
mailing lists, and Internet, 79
manifest content/latent content,
misuse of, 113–14
margins, and APA guidelines,
119–20
marketing and promotion, of
books, 251
*Mastering APA Style: Student's
Workbook and Training Guide*
(American Psychological
Association, 2001), 171
maturation, misuse of *learning,
performance,* and, 114
McLaughlin, E., 157
mean/average, misuse of, 107, 114
measurement, units of and APA
guidelines, 131
median, misuse of, 114
*Membership Directory of the
American Psychological Association* (American Psychological
Association, 2001), 171
*Membership Register of the Ameri-
can Psychological Association*
(American Psychological
Association, annual), 171
Memory and Cognition (journal),
191
*Merriam-Webster's Collegiate
Dictionary,* 10th ed. (1993), 129
*Merrill-Palmer Quarterly: Journal
of Developmental Psychology,*
191
methods: and example of student
psychology paper, 277–8; and

methods (*cont.*): negative results,
15–16; overexplanation of in
psychology papers, 68–9; as
section of experimental research
papers, 56–8
Miller, G., 200–4, 208, 210–15
Minium, E. W., 53
misinformation, on Internet, 83
misused words: nontechnical
terms, 98–105; technical terms,
105–118
mode, misuse of, 114
Modern Language Association
(MLA), 3
Morrison, D. F., 53
Motivation and Emotion (journal),
191–2
multiple authors, and citations,
137, 286
Multi User Domains (MUDs), 79
Multivariate Behavioral Research
(journal), 192
*Multivariate Experimental Clinical
Research* (journal), 192
mutually exclusive alternatives,
12–13

National Institutes of Health (NIH),
48, 242
National Science Foundation
(NSF), 48
nativism/empiricism, misuse of,
111
nature-nurture, misuse of, 114
negative constructions, in
psychology papers, 72
negative results, 14–16
neurosis/psychosis, misuse of, 115
New Mexico State University, 84
newsgroups, and Internet, 78–9, 87
newspapers, and Internet, 82
nonthematic organization, 61–2
null hypothesis, misuse of, 115
numbering: of footnotes, 140; of
pages, 120; of tables, 147
number of/amount of, misuse of, 99

numbers: and APA guidelines,
133–5; and British journals, 286;
and figures, 163; rounding of in
tables, 146

objectivity, and evaluation of
information on Internet, 84
obsession/compulsion, misuse of,
108
O'Connell, D. N., 201
only, misuse of, 103
*operant conditioning/classical
conditioning*, misuse of terms,
107–108
ordering, of sections of experimental research papers, 63–4
organization: experimental
research papers and non-
thematic versus thematic, 61–2;
of grant proposals, 239; of
journal articles, 226; of lectures,
256; of outline for library
research papers, 28–32
outliers, in box plots, 152
outlines: and book proposals, 246;
for library research papers, 26–33
out-of-print policy, 252
overhead, and grants, 234–5
overstatements, avoidance of in
psychology papers, 69

paper, and APA guidelines, 119
paradigm, and evaluation of
psychology papers, 214
paragraphs, seriation of, 135–6
parameter/statistic, misuse of, 115
parentheses, and rules of punctuation, 125–6
participants: description of in
experimental research papers,
57–8; research via Internet and
interaction with, 90
participles, and referents in
psychology papers, 73
passive voice, and active voice in
psychology papers, 71–2

Perception (journal), 192
Perceptual and Motor Skills
  (journal), 192–3
performance, misuse of *learning,*
  maturation, and, 114
periods, in abbreviations, 130
permissions. *See* copyrights
personal experience: and journal
  articles, 262; as source of ideas
  for experimental research
  papers, 38
Personality and Individual Differ-
  ences (journal), 193
Personality and Social Psychology
  Bulletin, 193
personnel costs, and grants, 235
Personnel Psychology: A Journal of
  Applied Research, 193
perspective, evaluation of psychology papers for new, 212–13
persuasion: and grant proposals,
  243; and journal articles, 265;
  and logic in psychology papers,
  65, 66; understatement versus
  overstatement as means of, 12,
  14; as purpose of scientific
  writing, 10–12
phenomenon, as focus of scientific
  report, 18
phenotype/genotype, misuse of, 113
Philosophical Psychology (journal),
  193
photographs, preparation of for
  publication, 163
physical appearance, of book,
  251–2
Piaget, J., 111
pie charts, 156
pilot data, and grant proposals,
  238
pilot subjects, 50, 52
placement: of figures, 163–4; of
  footnotes, 141; of tables, 146–7
point of view, and presentation of
  facts, 9–10
Pollack, I., 200

populations: and data collection on
  Internet, 88; misuse of term,
  115–16; and selection of
  subjects, 42–3
possessive pronouns, and
  antecedents, 73–4
posting, of published material on
  Internet, 92–3
preparation, for lectures, 258
Preparing for Graduate Study in
  Psychology: 101 Questions and
  Answers (Buskist & Sherburne,
  1995), 171
presuppositions: and evaluation of
  psychology papers, 214; and
  library research papers, 25, 33
primacy/recency, misuse of, 116
Primer in Data Reduction, A
  (Ehrenberg, 1982), 142
principal/principle, misuse of, 103
printers, and computer, 120
producibles, and grant proposals,
  239–40
Professional Psychology (journal),
  193–4
profile, of researchers on Web sites,
  91
pronouns, without antecedents in
  psychology papers, 73–4
proof, indirect method of, 12–13
proofreading: of figures, 164; of
  journal articles, 261; of
  psychology papers, 75–6, 228
proofs, of journal articles, 220
propaganda, and information on
  Internet, 83
PsychINFO, 82, 172
Psychological Abstracts (American
  Psychological Association), 172
Psychological Bulletin, 194, 228,
  231
Psychological Reader's Guide, 172
Psychological Record (journal), 194
Psychological Reports (journal), 194
Psychological Research (journal),
  194

298

Psychological Review (journal), 194–5
Psychological Science (journal), 195
Psychologist, The: Bulletin of the British Psychological Society, 195
Psychology: A Guide to Reference and Information Sources (Baxter, 1993), 172
Psychology and Aging (journal), 195
psychology papers: APA guidelines for, 119–41, 218, 228; example of, 271–84; misconceptions about, 2, 6–18; references available for, 165–97; rules for writing, 65–76; standards for evaluation of, 198–215; submission of to journals, 216–20; writing of and acceptance by journals, 221–31. *See also* experimental research papers; library research papers; scientific writing
Psychology and Psychotherapy (journal), 195
Psychology in the Schools (journal), 196
Psychology of Women Quarterly (journal), 196
Psychometrika (journal), 196
Psychonomic Bulletin and Review, 196
psychosis/neurosis, misuse of, 115
PsycLIT, 82
publication lag, 251
Publication Manual of the American Psychological Association, 5th ed. (2001), 119, 172–3
publications and publishing, and Internet, 91, 92–6. *See also* books; journals
public records, and Internet, 87
publishers. *See* books; journals
punctuation, and APA guidelines, 121–6

qualifications: and book proposals, 248; and grant proposals, 240–1

qualifiers, psychology papers and avoidance of, 69–70
quantitative issues, and APA guidelines, 131–6
Quarterly Journal of Experimental Psychology, 196–7
quartile plots, 149–53
quotation marks, and rules of punctuation, 123–5

random sampling, 43
ratio IQ/deviation IQ, misuse of terms, 110–11
readers, writing of psychology papers for, 66, 229, 261–2. *See also* audience
reading: of lectures, 255–8; of psychology papers by advisers and colleagues, 76, 228–9, 263; and sources of ideas for experimental research papers, 36–8. *See also* reviews
recency/primacy, misuse of, 116
redundancy, elimination of in psychology papers, 67–8
Reese, R. W., 201–2
reference footnotes, 139
reference list, as section of psychology papers, 138
references: and APA guidelines for psychology papers, 136–8; and experimental research papers, 63; and journal articles, 224; and student psychology paper, 281. *See also* citations; sources
referents, and participles in psychology papers, 73
regression/fixation, misuse of, 112–13
rejection, of psychology papers submitted to journals, 219–20
relevant, misuse of, 104
reliability/validity, misuse of, 116
replication, of experimental results, 15

repression/suppression, misuse of, 116–17
reprints, of journal articles, 220
reputation, of book publishers, 253–4
resubmission, of journal articles, 262
results: combining of with discussion in experimental research papers, 61–2; and evaluation of psychology papers, 214–15; and example of student psychology paper, 278–9; overexplanation of in psychology papers, 69; as section of experimental research papers, 58–60. *See also* conclusions
reviews, of journal articles: and Internet, 95–6; by journal referees, 229, 230–1, 261, 262, 263; and writing with referees in mind, 260
revision, of journal articles, 231, 262
Rogers, M. S., 201
rows, of tables, 144–5
royalties, and publication of books, 249–50
ruling, of tables, 147
Runyon, R. P., 53

sample chapters, of books, 248
sample/population, misuse of terms, 115–16
sample size, 43
scale breaks, in bar charts, 156, 162
Science Citation Index, 173
scientific writing: and explanation by default, 12–14; and failure to report negative results, 14–16; persuading and informing as characteristics of successful, 10–12; phenomenon as focus of, 18. *See also* experimental research papers; psychology papers

scoring, experimental research papers and means of, 47–8
search engines, and Internet, 80–1
Seheult, A., 149
self-selection, and research via Internet, 89
semicolon, and rules of punctuation, 122
sentence outline, 28
sentences, use of simple versus complicated in psychology papers, 71
seriation, and APA guidelines, 135–6
sexist language, avoidance of in psychology papers, 76
Sheehy, N. P., 154–5
short sentences, 71
significance: and evaluation of psychology papers for contribution to knowledge, 211–12; as misused word, 117
simplicity, of sentences and words in psychology papers, 70–1
simulation/artificial intelligence, misuse of terms, 106–7
since, misuse of, 104
single quotation marks, 125
sliding-royalty arrangements, 250
Social Cognition (journal), 197
Social Psychology Network, 83, 91
Social Science Citation Index, 173
Society for Judgment and Decision Making, 91
Society for Personality and Social Psychology, 91
socioeconomic status, of Internet users, 79
sources, of information for psychology papers: general references, 165–73; journals as, 174–97; primary and secondary in journal articles, 263. *See also* citations; references
spellcheckers, 228

spellings: and APA guidelines, 129; and British journals, 285

split infinitives, 74

Standards for Educational and Psychological Testing (American Psychological Association, 1999), 173

state/trait, misuse of terms, 117

states, and Web sites, 87

statistic/parameter, misuse of, 115

statistical power, and research via Internet, 88

statistical significance: misuse of term, 117; and reporting of tests in experimental research papers, 59–60

statistical tests, and journal articles, 264

statistics, and APA guidelines for presentation of, 132

stem-and-leaf displays, 148–9, 152–3

stencil keys, 47

story writing, and articles for journals, 260

stratified samples, 43

Strunk, W., Jr., 98, 104

subconscious/unconscious, misuse of terms, 117

subject matter, of psychology papers submitted to journals, 228

subjects: experimental research papers and selection of, 42–3; experimental research papers and suitability of experimental materials for, 45; experimental research papers and testing of pilot, 50, 52; use of term, 57–8

subsidy publishers, 253–4

Suggestions to Contributors (British Psychological Society), 285

summary statements, in psychology papers, 74

suppression/repression, misuse of, 116–17

synonyms, in journal articles, 261

table footnotes, 139–40

tables: and presentation of data, 59, 143–7; relation between text and, 143; and student psychology paper, 284

take/bring, misuse of, 100

take-home message, of journal article, 262

Tate, M. A., 85

Tatsuoka, M. M., 53

technical variance, and research via Internet, 89–90

text: equations merged with, 133; relation between tables or figures and, 143

textbooks: and book proposals, 245; currency or obsolescence of, 36

that, misuse of, 104

thematic organization: of experimental research papers, 61, 62; for library research papers, 30–1

theory: and grant proposals, 237–8; and evaluation of psychology papers, 214–15

Thesaurus of Psychological Index Terms (American Psychological Association, 2001), 173

this, use of indefinite in psychology papers, 74

time: and lectures, 256–7; for research funded by grant proposal, 238

titles: of experimental research papers, 54; of psychology papers, 65; of tables, 147

top-down structure, of journal articles, 264

topic, selection of for library research papers, 19–22

topic cards, for library research papers, 23–6

topic outline, 27, 28

trade-book proposals, 245

training, of psychology students in writing, 1, 2

trait/state, misuse of terms, 117

transitions, in psychology papers, 74–5
try, misuse of, 104
Tufte, E. R., 142, 149, 153
Tukey, J., 148, 149, 151, 152
Tulving, E., 198–9, 207–10, 210–15
typeface, and APA guidelines, 120

unconscious/subconscious, misuse of, 117
uninterested/disinterested, misuse of, 101
unique, misuse of, 104
universities: and direct grants, 235; and overhead rates for grants, 234–5; and psychology department Web sites, 83. *See also* faculty
university presses, 245–6
USENET/NETNEWS, 78–9
utilize, misuse of, 104

validity: and library research papers, 24, 33; misuse of term, 116. *See also* ecological validity
vanity presses, 253–4
variability/variance, misuse of, 118
variables, and misuse of terms, 112. *See also* dependent variables; independent variables
variance/variability, misuse of, 118
Velleman, P. F., 149

vertical spacing, and APA guidelines, 120
Volkmann, J., 201–2
volunteer bias, and research via Internet, 88

Wagner, A., 219
Wainer, H., 142, 154
Webster's Third New International Dictionary (1976), 129
whereas, misuse of, 105
which, misuse of, 104
while, misuse of, 104–5
White, E. B., 98, 104
white noise, definition of, 118
whom, misuse of, 105
whose, misuse of, 105
Widener University, 84, 85
Winer, B. J., 53
within-subjects variables, and experimental research papers, 40–2
word-processing, and APA guidelines, 119–21
words: numbers expressed in, 134; use of precise in psychology papers, 70. *See also* misused words
World Wide Web (WWW). *See* Internet

Yale University, 35, 36, 234

DATE DUE
